Table of Contents

Visual Basic 4 Nuts & Bolts: For Experienced Programmers

Gary Cornell
and
Troy Strain

Osborne **McGraw-Hill**

Berkeley New York St. Louis San Francisco Auckland Bogotá Hamburg London Madrid Mexico City
Milan Montreal New Delhi Panama City Paris São Paulo Singapore Sydney Tokyo Toronto

Osborne **McGraw-Hill**
2600 Tenth Street
Berkeley, California 94710
U.S.A.

For information on translations or book distributors outside the U.S.A., or to arrange bulk purchase discounts for sales promotions, premiums, or fundraisers, please contact Osborne **McGraw-Hill** at the above address.

Visual Basic 4 Nuts & Bolts: For Experienced Programmers

234567890 DOC 99876

ISBN 0-07-882141-X

Publisher
Lawrence Levitsky

Acquisitions Editor
Cindy Brown

Technical Editor
Dave Jezak

Copy Editor
Gary Morris

Proofreader
Linda Medoff

Computer Designer
Richard Whitaker

Illustrator
Rhys Elliott

Quality Control Specialist
Joe Scuderi

Cover Design
Ted Mader Associates

Acknowledgments

One of the best parts of writing a book is when the authors get to thank those who have helped them, for rarely (and certainly not in this case) is a book truly the product of the authors' work alone. First and foremost, we have to thank the team at Osborne McGraw-Hill. Their patience, dedication, help, cheerfulness—you name it—went way beyond the call of duty. To Cindy Brown, Marcela Hancik, Richard Whitaker and Rhys Elliott: thanks! Dave Jezak went far beyond what authors can expect (or hope) to have from a tech reviewer. We are truly grateful.

Next, we have to thank those people at Microsoft (whose names we unfortunately don't know) who created the latest version of Visual Basic. It's a very useful upgrade and a truly interesting product. Tracy van Huff handles author liaison at Microsoft. Her patience with odd requests and her general all-around helpfulness also went way beyond the call of duty. Without the information she supplied, this book could never have been completed.

Gary Cornell would like to thank all his friends who put up with his strange ways and occasionally short temper for lo, so many months. In particular, thanks to Bruce, Caroline, and Kurt; without their special friendship and help, his part of the book would have been impossible to write.

Troy would like to thank his wife Tracy because—well, there are far too many reasons for him to list them all here, but he certainly wants to thank her for her understanding the many late nights needed to write that one last chapter. He also wants to thank his 23-month-old son Nathan, who recently discovered the Reset button on daddy's computer.

About the Authors ...

Gary Cornell is a computer programmer and professor of mathematics at the University of Connecticut. He has written or coauthored several acclaimed books on microcomputers, including the best-selling *Visual Basic 3 for Windows Handbook.*

Troy Strain is the former beta test manager for Visual Basic at Microsoft Corporation. He was a software test lead with Microsoft for seven years.

Introduction

When Visual Basic was released in 1991 it was the most exciting computer language product to hit the market in quite a while. The press had rarely been so excited by a product. So what was all the hype about? Exactly what is Visual Basic and what can it do for you? Well, it's an easy-to-use, yet extraordinarily powerful tool for developing Windows applications. The latest version of Visual Basic adds many new features, chief among them the ability to build 32-bit executables for both Windows 95 and Windows NT.

If this doesn't seem like enough to justify all the hoopla, remember that with Visual Basic, C and C++ expertise will, at most occasionally and perhaps not, be required. No longer will you have to be an expert C programmer and keep about 20 pounds worth of documentation around in order to develop lightning-fast Windows applications.

About This Book

This book is a short guide to Visual Basic for experienced programmers. We assume you have some programming experience (what language really doesn't matter), and that concepts like loops and decision structures are familiar to you. The idea we had in writing this book was to distill the essence of Visual Basic and present it to you clearly and concisely. We've tried hard to stress the new ways of thinking needed to master Visual Basic programming, so even experts in more traditional programming languages can benefit from this book. We've taken this approach because trying to force Visual Basic into the framework of older programming languages is ultimately self-defeating—you can't take advantage of its power if you continue to think within an older paradigm.

We assume that after you know what makes Visual Basic "tick," you can use the online help and the manuals supplied with Visual Basic as needed. We don't burden you with a lot of silly examples; we assume that you have written lots of code before. We feel that once you are well grounded in the ways of thinking in Visual Basic, you can look at the sample code supplied with it if you need more examples than we give in this book.

How This Book Is Organized

This book can be used in a variety of ways, depending on your background and needs. People familiar with Visual Basic might want to skim the early chapters and spend more time on the later chapters where we cover the underlying language in Visual Basic. People familiar with Pascal or C but not an event-driven language like Visual Basic might want to spend more time on the early chapters and skim the chapters that cover the underlying language. (In any case, we do suggest looking at all the chapters, because no matter what your language background, there is information specific to Visual Basic to be found in them all.) Here are brief descriptions of the 13 chapters:

- Chapter 1 gives you an introduction to Visual Basic.
- Chapter 2 shows you the Visual Basic environment.
- Chapter 3 starts you right off with the notion of a customizable window (called a form) that is the heart of every Microsoft Windows (and thus Visual Basic) application. You'll see how to add and manipulate basic Visual Basic objects.
- Chapters 4 and 5 survey the version of Basic used in Visual Basic.
- Chapter 6 is a brief introduction to objects in Visual Basic.
- Chapter 7 covers error handling.
- Chapter 8 discusses debugging techniques.
- Chapter 9 covers techniques for handling files.
- Chapter 10 introduces you to dynamic data exchange (DDE), object linking and embedding (OLE), and OLE automation.
- Chapter 11 introduces you to Visual Basic's powerful graphics.
- Chapter 12 covers more advanced user interface features.
- Chapter 13 is a brief introduction to Visual Basic's database features.

Note: This book does not cover how to use Visual Basic to develop client/server applications.

Conventions Used in This Book

Keys are set in small capital letters in the text. For example, keys such as CTRL and ALT appear as shown here. Arrow and other direction keys are spelled out and also appear in small capital letters. For example, if you need to press the right arrow key, you'll see, "Press RIGHT ARROW." When you need to use a combination of keys to activate a menu item, the keys will be separated by plus signs (+) and the entire key combination will appear in small capital letters. For example, "Press CTRL+ALT+DEL" is how we would indicate the "three-fingered salute" that (thankfully) is a lot less common in Windows 95. On the other hand, ALT F, P means press the "ALT" and "F" keys, and then the "P" key—you don't have to hold down the "ALT" key.

DOS commands, filenames, and file extensions appear in full capital letters: COPY .EXE, .TXT, and so on. Microsoft Windows 95 is referred to just as Windows most of the time. (Earlier versions are referred to as Windows 3.***x***.) We try to follow Visual Basic's own documentation conventions. Built-in functions and procedures appear with the first letter of each word capitalized, such as Font, DatabaseName, and so on. Menu choices are indicated with a bar between them, e.g., "Choose Run|Run." The syntax for a command in Visual Basic is most often set as regular text in an inline list. Items in the syntax that the programmer can change appear in italics. For example, the Rename command used to rename a file would appear as

Rename (*OldFileName, NewFileName*)

Finally, programs are set in a monospace font, as shown here:

```
Private Sub Form_Click()
 Print "Hello world!"
End Sub
```

We have numerous notes and tips that are indicated by various icons. For example, a general tip is something like the following:

Tip: Since this book is meant for experienced programmers, we don't supply that much code. The megabytes of code supplied as samples with Visual Basic are a good complement to the material presented here.

Tips of interest to Visual Basic 3 users are indicated as shown here:

Visual Basic 3 Tip: Any Visual Basic 3 program that uses binary file-handling techniques may need to be rewritten.

Chapter 1

Getting Started

This chapter gives you an overview of Microsoft's Visual Basic Version 4.0. For example, the two programs described later in this chapter introduce the event-driven, object-oriented model that makes Visual Basic so powerful. Note, however, that since we are assuming you are not a naive user, this chapter (and book) does not show you how to install Visual Basic, start it, manipulate windows within the Windows environment, and so on—we are assuming that you know these things. However, we are *not* assuming any expertise in Visual Basic or Windows programming—just a general level of programming sophistication that may have come from working in any environment.

Note: The Learning Microsoft Visual Basic tutorial available on the Help menu is a nice complement to the material presented in this chapter.

Why Windows and Why Visual Basic?

Microsoft Visual Basic Version 4.0. The full name is rather a mouthful: we will just say Visual Basic from now on. If we need to distinguish the current version of Visual Basic from earlier ones, we will give their version numbers.

Graphical user interfaces, or *GUIs* (pronounced "gooies"), have revolutionized the microcomputer industry. They demonstrate that the proverb "a picture is worth a thousand words" hasn't lost its truth. Instead of the cryptic C:> prompt that DOS users have long seen (and some have long feared), users are presented with a desktop filled with icons and with programs that use mice and menus. Perhaps even more important in the long run than the *look* of Microsoft Windows applications is the *feel* that applications developed for it have. Windows applications generally have a consistent user interface. This means that users can spend more time mastering the application and less time worrying about which keystrokes do what within menus and dialog boxes. (Of course, Windows 95 applications look a bit different than Windows 3.1 applications did: the consistency is *within* versions of Windows, not *between* versions of Windows.)

While programmers have long had mixed feelings about GUIs, beginning users seem to like them, and so Windows programs are expected to be based on the GUI model (and to have the right look and feel). Therefore, if you need to develop programs for any version of Windows, you'll want a tool to develop GUI-based applications efficiently.

For a long time there were no such tools. Before Visual Basic was introduced in 1991, developing Windows applications was much harder than developing DOS applications. Programmers had to worry about too much, such as what the mouse was doing, where the user was inside a menu, and whether he or she was clicking or double-clicking at a given place. Developing a Windows application required expert C programmers and hundreds of lines of code for the simplest task. Even the experts had trouble. (The Microsoft Windows Software Development Kit that was required in addition to a C compiler weighed in at nine and one-half pounds.) This is why when Visual Basic 1.0 was released, Bill Gates, chairman and CEO of Microsoft, described it as "awesome." Steve Gibson in *Infoworld* said Visual Basic is a "stunning new miracle" and will "dramatically change the way people feel about and use [Microsoft] Windows." Stewart Alsop was quoted in the *New York Times* as saying Visual Basic is "the perfect programming environment for the 1990s." As Charles Petzold, author of one of the standard books on Windows programming in C, put it in the *New York Times:* "For those of us who make our living explaining the complexities of

Windows programming to programmers, Visual Basic poses a real threat to our livelihood." The latest version of Visual Basic continues in this tradition: sophisticated Windows 95, Windows NT, and even Windows 3.1 applications can now be developed in a fraction of the time previously needed. Programming errors (bugs) don't happen as often as they did, and if they do, they're a lot easier to detect and fix. Simply put: *with Visual Basic, programming for Windows has become not only more efficient but it has become fun*—most of the time.

Some of Visual Basic 4.0's advantages over the first three versions of Visual Basic are

- Ability to generate 32-bit applications for both Windows 95 and Windows NT.
- With Visual Basic you can take advantage of Microsoft's OLE technology—including the ability to build OLE servers (see Chapter 10).
- You can build programs using some of the techniques of object-oriented programming (see Chapter 6).
- The ability to extend the Visual Basic programming environment. (You can create or use third-party tools that "add-in" seamlessly into the Visual Basic environment.)
- Conditional compilation to allow you to do multiplatform development more easily.

Note: Although the Enterprise version of Visual Basic is not covered in this book, it makes developing both client/server and group projects much easier as well.

How You Develop a Visual Basic Application

The first step in developing a Visual Basic application is to plan what the user will see—in other words, to design the screens. What menus do you want? How large a window should the application use? How many windows should there be? Should the user be able to resize the windows? Where will you place the *command buttons* that the user will click on to activate the applications? Will the applications have places (*text boxes)* in which to enter text?

In Visual Basic, the objects a programmer places on the windows he or she is designing are called *controls*. The number of controls you have at your disposal depends on the version of Visual basic you are using. The Standard edition has more than 20, the professional more than 50. (See Chapter 3 for a survey of the controls supplied with Visual Basic.) Moreover, since Visual Basic has inspired third-party vendors to create a large number of controls for specialized tasks, you can almost always find a custom control for a specialized task. (To create your own controls, you will most often use C or C++.)

Note: If you have some familiarity with object-oriented programming (OOP), then you should be aware that Visual Basic controls are not quite objects in the sense of OOP. (Please see Chapter 6 for more on object-oriented programming and how Visual Basic's controls fit in with the tenets of OOP.)

Visual Basic makes it easy to design the screen. You literally draw the user interface, almost as if you were using a paint program. In addition, when you have finished drawing the interface, the command buttons and other controls that you have placed in a blank window will automatically recognize user actions such as mouse movements and button clicks. Visual Basic also comes with a menu design feature that makes creating both ordinary and pop-up menus a snap.

Only after you design the interface does anything like traditional programming occur. Controls in Visual Basic will recognize events like mouse clicks; how the objects respond to them depends on the code you write. You will almost always need to write code in order to make controls respond to events. This makes Visual Basic programming fundamentally different from the kind of conventional procedural-oriented programming found in early versions of Basic, Pascal, or C.

Programs in conventional programming languages run from the top down. For older programming languages, execution starts from the first line and moves with the flow of the program to different parts as needed. A Visual Basic program usually works completely differently. The core of a Visual Basic program is a set of independent pieces of code that are *activated* by, and so *respond* to, only the events they have been told to recognize. This is a fundamental shift. Now, instead of a programmer designing a program to do what the programmer thinks should happen, the user is in control.

The programming code in Visual Basic that tells your program how to respond to events like mouse clicks begins inside what Visual Basic calls *event procedures*. An event procedure is a body of code that is only executed in response to an external event. In almost all cases, everything executable in a

Visual Basic program is either in an event procedure or is used by an event procedure to help the procedure carry out its job. In fact, to stress that Visual Basic is fundamentally different from ordinary programming languages, the documentation uses the term *project,* rather than *program,* to refer to the combination of programming code and user interface that goes into making a Visual Basic application possible.

Here is a summary of the steps you take to design a Visual Basic application:

1. Customize the windows that the user sees.
2. Decide what events the controls on the window should recognize.
3. Write the event procedures for those events (and the subsidiary procedures that make those event procedures work).

Here is what happens when the application is running:

1. Visual Basic monitors the windows and the controls in each window for all the events that each control can recognize (mouse movements, clicks, keystrokes, and so on).
2. When Visual Basic detects an event, if there isn't an internal built-in response to the event, Visual Basic examines the application to see if you've written an event procedure for that event.
3. If you have written an event procedure, Visual Basic executes the code that makes up that event procedure and goes back to step 1.
4. If you have not written an event procedure, Visual Basic waits for the next event and goes back to step 1.

These steps cycle continuously until the application ends. Usually, an event must happen before Visual Basic will do anything. Thus, event-driven programs are more *reactive* than *active*—and that makes them more user friendly.

What You Need to Run Visual Basic

Visual Basic is a sophisticated program. The standard edition requires Windows 95 or version 3.51 (or later) of Windows NT. (It is theoretically possible but rather unusual to use the 16-bit version of the professional edition under Windows 3.1.) So, at the very least, you'll need a machine powerful enough for these 32-bit operating systems. Realistically, you'll want

- A fast 486 or Pentium and at least 8MB of RAM—16 would be much better.
- A hard disk with at least 60MB free. (If you want to install both the 16- and 32-bit versions of Visual Basic, the amount of space needed increases to more than 70MB.)

Working with Visual Basic

In this section you'll see a step-by-step process that uses Visual Basic to build two programs. One is a modification of the traditional "Hello World" program; the other is a bitmap viewer. The viewer particularly shows off how efficient Visual Basic is at developing Windows applications—it uses only two lines of code! In C or C++ the same amount of functionality would take several hundred lines.

When you start up Visual Basic, if you are using Windows 95, your initial screen will look something like Figure 1-1. (There will be some minor changes under Windows NT.) You'll see a lot more about the Visual Basic environment in the next chapter, but for now it is probably easier if you just follow the steps without worrying too much about the environment.

Note the blank window, which has a grid of dots, in the center of the screen. This is the *form* that you will customize. You use the grid to align controls such as command buttons and list boxes on the screen (you'll learn more about this in Chapter 3). When you run your project (or compile it so that it can be run independently of the Visual Basic development environment), forms become the windows that users see.

At the top of the blank form is the title bar with its caption. (*Caption* is the Visual Basic term for what appears in the title bar of the form.) Currently, this form is titled Form1, which is the default caption that Visual Basic gives to a form when you start working on a new project.

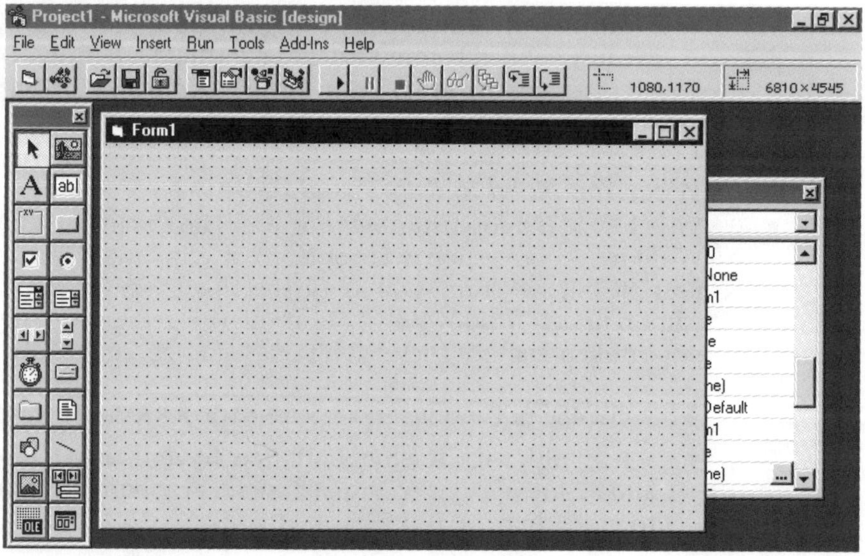

The initial Visual Basic screen under Windows 95
Figure 1-1.

To the left of the Form1 window is the Toolbox. (If you do not see it, press ALT V, X to reveal it. What you see in your toolbox will, of course, depend on which version of Visual Basic you have.) The Toolbox is where you find the controls you will place on the form. Partially obscured is the Properties window, which you use to customize the form and the various controls you'll place on it.

For now, concentrate on Form1. You should be completely comfortable with the methods for changing the size and location of this form before you move on. In many Visual Basic applications, the size and location of the form at the time you finish the design (usually called *design time*) is the size and shape that the user sees at *run time*. This is not to say that Visual Basic doesn't let you change the size and location of forms as a project runs (see Chapter 4); in fact, an essential property of Visual Basic is its ability to make dynamic changes in response to user events.

One way to resize a form that is common to all Microsoft Windows applications is to first click inside the form so that it is active. (You can always tell when a window is active because the title bar is highlighted.) Then move the mouse to any part of the border of the form. The mouse pointer changes to a double-headed arrow when you're at a hot spot. At this point, you can drag the form to change its size or shape. Similarly, to move the form, you can click anywhere in the title bar and then drag the form to a new location. The size and location of a form are examples of what Visual Basic calls *properties* of the form.

To start developing the first sample application, do the following:

1. Change the form's default size, shape, and location by manipulating it at some of the hot spots or by dragging it around the screen.
2. Run the project by choosing Start from the Run menu.

Notice that what you see is an ordinary-looking Windows window with the same size, shape, and location that you left the form in at design time. Next, notice that when you run this new project, the window that pops up has standard Windows features like resizable borders; a control box (in the upper-left corner); and maximum, minimum, and exit buttons (in the upper-right corner). This shows one of the most important features of Visual Basic: your forms become windows that already behave as they should under the version of Windows you are using, without your having to do anything.

Return to the development environment by pressing ALT+F4 or double-clicking on the control box. Notice that your application automatically responds to this "standard" way of closing a Windows application. This illustrates the important point that, in many cases, Visual Basic applications behave as Windows users expect, without requiring any special intervention by the user.

A "Hello World"-Type Program

Now we will show you how to write a project that displays "Hello new user" in the title bar of a blank window in response to a user clicking the mouse. We'll complicate it a little by making the title bar of this window start out with the words "Waiting for a click!"

Here are the necessary steps to do this.

1. Move to the Properties window and click on the item marked Caption, as shown here. The word "Caption" should be highlighted after the click.

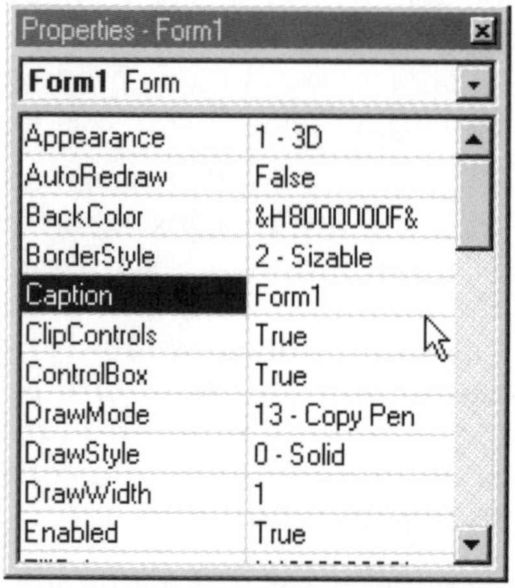

2. Click in the right-hand column and then type the sentence **Waiting for a click!**
3. What we have just done is called *setting a property of the form.* If you run the project (remember that's what Visual Basic calls an application in the development stage) by pressing F5 or choosing Run|Start, what you'll see will look like Figure 1-2.

A First Event Procedure

In order to illustrate using an event procedure, it's probably easier to start with a whole new project. To begin a new project, choose File|New Project and respond to the message box asking you if you want to save the changes to Form1 by clicking on the No to All button.

Once Visual Basic presents you with a new project, use F7 or choose View|Code to see the Code window. Click on the right-hand list box called "Proc," and then scroll through the list box and click on the item marked Click. Your screen should look like Figure 1-3. Notice in Figure 1-3 that the form is obscured but still visible. If you click on any part of the form, you'll

1

First step in the "Hello new user" project
Figure 1-2.

go back to the form and the Code window will be hidden. (You can use F7 or View|Code to bring it to the front at any time.)

Notice the *event procedure template* shown in Figure 1-3. (As with any template, an event procedure template gives you a framework in which to work—in this case, a framework in which to write your code.)

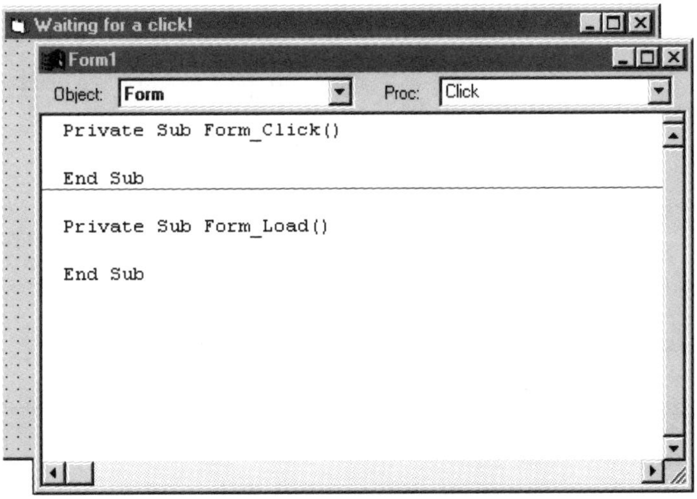

Initial screen for an event template
Figure 1-3.

```
Private Sub Form_Click()

End Sub
```

Although the syntax used for event procedures may seem obscure, don't worry about it now. It will be explained in Chapters 4 and 5. For now,

1. Make sure the cursor is between these two lines.
2. Type the following line of code: **Form1.Caption = "Hello new user"**

Your screen will look like Figure 1-4. Now run the project (by pressing F5) and click inside the form. Notice the caption of the form changes.

End the project and return to the design environment by using ALT+F4 or double-clicking on the Control box.

Adding a Control

So far our application uses no controls. Let's modify the project by introducing a command button that changes the caption after a click. Also, let's change the project so that if you click anywhere other than on the command button, a message box pops up, telling you to click on the button. To do this,

1. Go to the line of code that you typed and select it using ordinary Windows techniques (a mouse drag or SHIFT+ARROW keys).

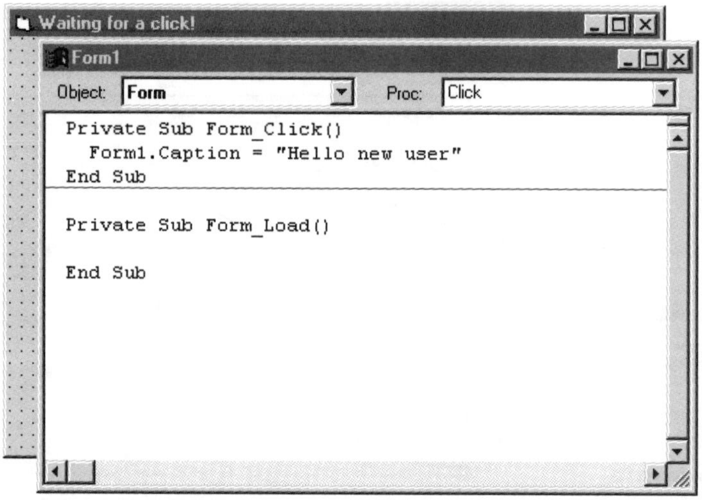

First event procedure coded
Figure 1-4.

(If the form is visible but the code isn't, use F7 to go back to the Code window.)

2. Replace the line of code with the following:
   MsgBox ("Please click on the button")

If you decide to run the project at this point and click inside the form, a little message box pops up that looks like the following. Click on the OK button to make the message box disappear.

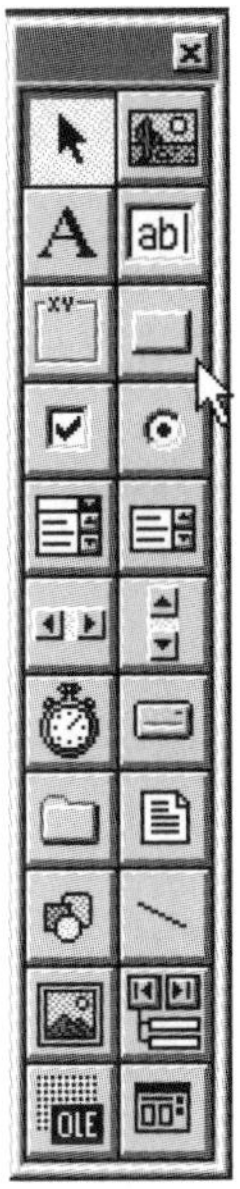

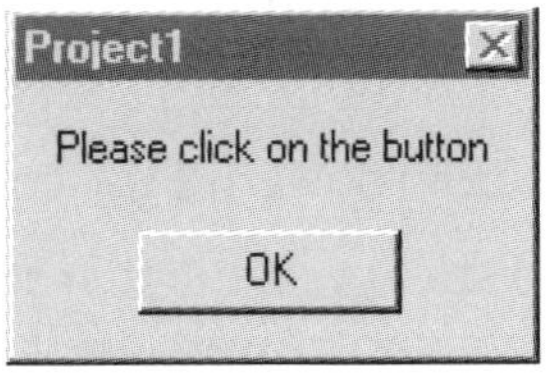

Of course, we haven't added the command button yet. To do that, return to the development environment by using ALT+F4. (Click on the form if it is not visible or press SHIFT+F7

Move to the Toolbox (shown on the left) and double-click on the Command Button icon that the cursor is pointing to in this illustration.

This adds a command button to the center of the screen in the default size and shape. (Chapter 3 will show you how to move and size controls as well as more about the properties of command buttons.) For now, double-click on the command button to open up an event procedure template for the Click event for the Command button.

Type the line **Form1.Caption = "Hello new user!"**, as shown in the following screen:

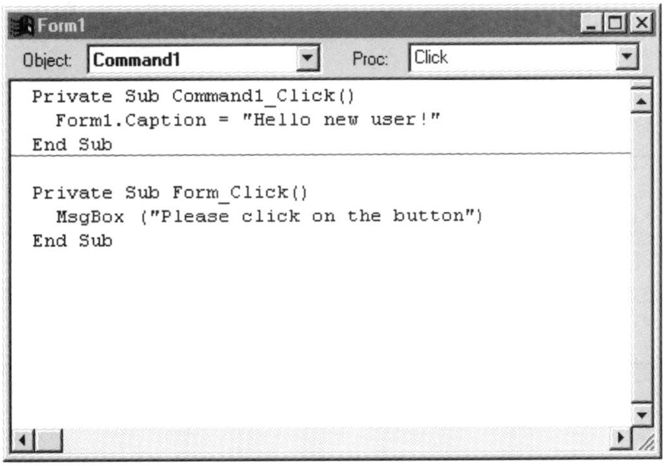

If you run the project, you'll see that the application behaves as previously described. A click on the button changes the caption; a click anywhere else gives the message box!

A More Powerful Project

The previous section showed you three essential steps in Visual Basic development: adding controls to a form, setting properties of Visual Basic objects, and writing simple event procedures. Now let's write a far more sophisticated project—which, surprisingly enough, needs essentially no more code. We hope this project will whet your appetite for Visual Basic and demonstrate how powerful the controls supplied with Visual Basic really are.

Our aim is to show you the first steps you would take to build a graphics file viewer. Using a few controls and a few lines of code, you can have a Windows application that will display any bitmap. Of course you don't yet know how to save the project, bulletproof it, or make it truly user friendly—but it's only the first chapter after all!

So first off, start up a new project by selecting File|New Project.

This time we want to add two controls to the blank form: an *image* control for displaying graphics and a *Common Dialog* control for displaying the file/directory structure. To get an image control onto the form, double-click on the Image control icon (it looks like a landscape with a sun over a mountain) that the cursor is pointing to here:

Next, add a Common Dialog control by double-clicking on the CommonDialog control icon as shown here:

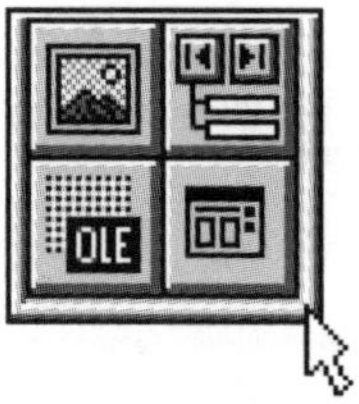

Your screen will look like Figure 1-5.

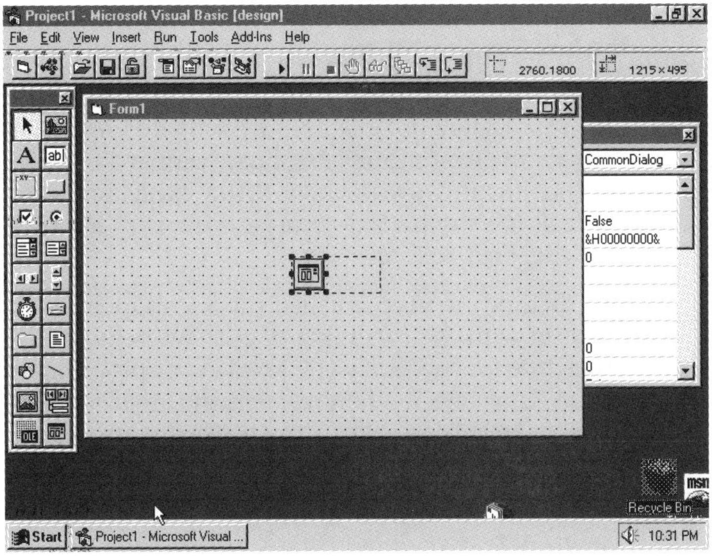

Initial screen for bitmap viewer
Figure 1-5.

We now need to set the *Filter* properties of the CommonDialog control so that only files with the .BMP extension, which indicates a bitmap, will be shown. Make sure the Properties window shows that you are working with the CommonDialog1 control as shown here:

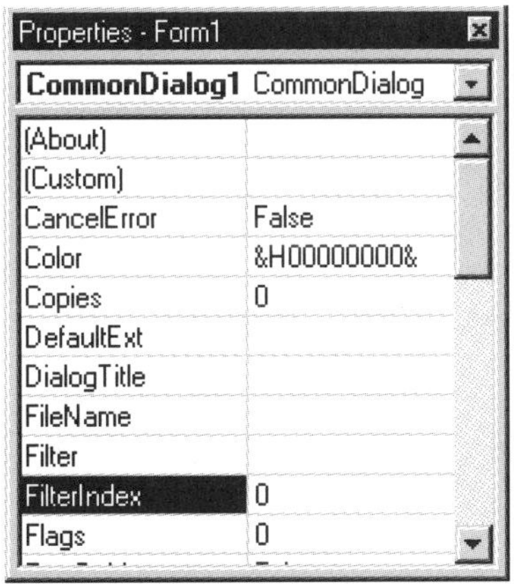

If it doesn't look like this, click inside the CommonDialog icon on the form, as shown in Figure 1-5, and then press F4 again. This lets you work with the properties of the CommonDialog control. Move through the Properties window until you get to the Filter property of this control. Click in the right column and type **Bitmaps|*.bmp**. This will tell the CommonDialog box to display only files that end in *.bmp* (the convention for bitmaps). Next enter the text **Choose bitmap** in the right column of the DialogTitle property.

By the way, if you try to run the project now, nothing will happen. The CommonDialog box needs to be activated in order to be displayed. To activate the CommonDialog box, you need to use a new Visual Basic tool: a *method*. Roughly speaking, in Visual Basic, properties determine what controls *are*, methods determine what they *do*, and events are normally user-triggered actions.

The method we need is called the ShowOpen method, and we will put it together with the other line of code we need inside the Load event procedure for the form. The Load event procedure is a little unusual in that Visual Basic calls it whenever a form is loaded for the first time—which happens in this case when the project starts running.

To get to the event procedure template for Form_Load,

1. Double-click on any blank area in the form. This will open up the event procedure template for the Load event.
2. Now enter the following lines of code so that your event procedure template looks like this:

```
Private Sub Form_Load()
  CommonDialog1.ShowOpen
  Image1.Picture = LoadPicture(CommonDialog1.FileName)
End Sub
```

That's it. If you run this project, you'll be presented with an ordinary Windows dialog box (with the caption "Choose Bitmap") that will be restricted to displaying only files with the .BMP extension. You can navigate among the directories on your drives by clicking and double-clicking as is usual with an CommonDialog box in Windows. Find a bitmap, click on OK, and Visual Basic will display the bitmap on the form.

Tip: You'll find a large number of bitmaps in the directories under C:\VB\BITMAPS.

Of course, this is by no means a bulletproof application: if you select a non-bitmap file, the application will crash. (If you do crash the project, close any message boxes by clicking on the End button in order to get back to the development environment.)

In spite of its fragility, this application shows you various techniques for developing a Visual Basic application that will occur again and again. The interfaces and code will get more sophisticated but the ideas of

- Customizing controls by changing their properties
- Customizing their behavior by using methods

will never change. Moreover, controls in Visual Basic have a lot of built-in functionality. This will become even more obvious as you work with other controls.

Chapter 2

The Visual Basic Environment

This chapter shows you how to use the menus and windows that make up the Visual Basic environment. When you've finished, you'll be comfortable with the online help, the editing tools, and the file-handling utilities built into Visual Basic.

Note: We used the professional edition of Visual Basic for our screen shots. If you have the standard or enterprise edition, your screens will be slightly different.

If you are not completely comfortable with the look and feel of Microsoft Windows applications, this chapter will help. After all, Visual Basic is itself a well-designed Microsoft Windows application, and the way its menus and windows respond is typical of Windows programs. Experienced Microsoft Windows users may want to skim much of this material. Remember, though, that until you are familiar with how a Windows application should look and feel, you can't take full advantage of the power of Visual Basic.

If you are developing an application with Visual Basic for your personal use, conforming to the Windows standard is not essential. However, if others will be using your application, following the Windows standard essentially eliminates the learning curve for using your application. For example, Windows users expect a single click with a mouse to select an item and a double click to activate it.

The default settings built into the design process of a Visual Basic application make it easy to conform to the Microsoft Windows guidelines. Windows default to the proper shape and can be moved and resized as users expect. Similarly, menus respond the way users are accustomed to. Of course, Visual Basic doesn't lock you into these defaults, but it is not a good idea to make changes casually.

Given the power of Visual Basic, with its richness of tools and detailed menus, it's easy to be overwhelmed at first. To help reduce any confusion, this chapter gives you a detailed description of what the environment has to offer.

An Overview of the Main Screen

As mentioned in Chapter 1, when you start up Visual Basic, you are presented with a copyright screen indicating to whom the copy of the program is licensed. After a short delay, you are automatically dropped into the Visual Basic environment, as shown in Figure 2-1.

Note: Visual Basic remembers your last screen arrangement and reuses it. For this reason, your screen may look different from Figure 2-1.

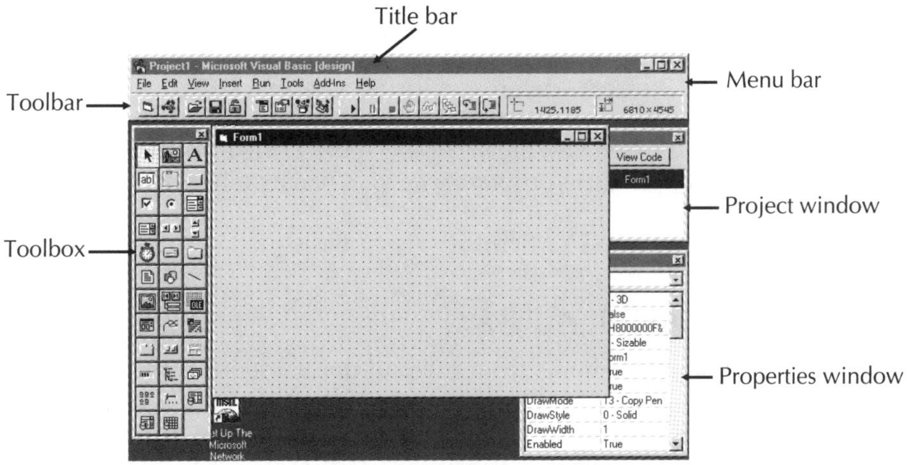

The Visual Basic environment

Figure 2-1.

The screen is certainly crowded. You can see the six parts in the standard Visual Basic environment, although two windows are partially obscured. The Properties window is used to customize a form or control. The Properties window is discussed at length in Chapter 3. Another window, called the Debug window, shows up when you are running or debugging a program; see Chapter 8.

Following is a description of the other parts of the main screen. Subsequent sections of this chapter cover the most commonly used parts of the menus.

Title Bar

The *title bar* is the horizontal bar located at the top of the screen; it gives the name of the application and is common to all Microsoft Windows applications. Interactions between the user and the title bar are handled by Windows, not by the application. Everything below the title and menu bar in a Windows application is called the *client area*. Your application is completely responsible for the look, feel, and response of the objects you place in this area.

In Visual Basic, the title bar starts out by displaying

    Project1 - Microsoft Visual Basic [design]

This is typical of Microsoft Windows applications: in sophisticated programs (like Visual Basic) that have multiple states, the title bar changes to indicate the different states. For example, when you are running a program within the Visual Basic environment, the title bar switches to

Project1 - Microsoft Visual Basic [run]

and when you are *debugging* (correcting errors in a program), temporarily stopping the program, the title bar switches to

Project1 - Microsoft Visual Basic [break]

The Menu Bar

Selecting items from the pull-down menus listed on a *menu bar* is one of the most common ways to unleash the power of a Windows application. The same is true of Visual Basic itself. For Visual Basic, the menu bar gives you the tools needed to develop, test, and save your application. The File menu contains the commands for working with the files that go into your application. The Edit menu contains many of the editing tools that will help you write the code that activates the interface you design for your application, including the search-and-replace editing tools. The View menu gives you fast access to the different parts of your program. The Insert menu gives you access for inserting new objects. The Run menu lets you test your application while developing it. The Tools menu gives you access to the tools used to correct (debug) problems, or *bugs* (Chapter 8 offers a detailed discussion of debugging techniques). The Add-Ins menu gives you access to tools that are added into the Visual Basic environment. Finally, you use the Help menu to gain access to the detailed online help system provided with the program or to run the very basic tutorial included.

Notice that all the menus have one letter underlined. Pressing ALT and the underlined letter opens that menu. Another way to access the menu is to press ALT alone to activate the menu bar. When you do, notice that the File menu item is highlighted. You can now use the arrow keys to move around the menu bar. Press ENTER or DOWN ARROW to open the menu. Once a menu is open, all you need is a single *accelerator key* (also called an *access* or *hot key*) to select a menu option. For example, if the Help menu is open, pressing L brings up the tutorial. Accelerator keys are not case sensitive.

Some menu items have *shortcut keys*. A shortcut key is usually a combination of keys the user can press to perform an action without opening a menu. For example, as is common in Windows applications, pressing ALT+F4 exits Visual Basic without going through the File menu.

The Toolbar

The *toolbar* shown in Figure 2-1 is immediately below the menu bar and was added in Visual Basic 2.0. As is becoming more common in Windows applications, Microsoft added toolbar icons to let you activate common tasks without using the menus. Since every item on the toolbar has a keyboard equivalent, which one you choose is a matter of taste.

Table 2-1 shows what the tools on the toolbar do, reading from left to right.

The Default Toolbar Icons
Table 2-1.

Icon	Name	Purpose
	New Form	Lets you add a new form (customizable window) to a project. This is the same as Insert|Form. See Chapter 3 for information on using multiple forms in your applications.
	New Module	Lets you open a new module for specialized programming code. You'll see how to use them in Chapter 4. This is the same as Insert|Module.
	Open Project	Lets you save an existing Visual Basic project (see the section "Loading and Running Programs" in this chapter). This is the same as File|Open.
	Save Project	Lets you save your Visual Basic project. This is the same as File|Save Project.
	Lock Controls	Locks controls in place to prevent accidental movement.
	Menu Editor	Used to design menus (see Chapter 3). This is the same as Tools|Menu Editor or the shortcut key combination of CTRL+E.
	Properties	Modifies the default size, shape, and color of your Visual Basic objects (see Chapter 3). This is the same as pressing the F4 shortcut or choosing View|Properties.
	Object Browser	Opens the Object Browser dialog box. This is the same as View|Object Browser. The shortcut is F2.

Icon	Name	Purpose
	Project	Switches focus to the Project Window. This is the same as pressing the CTRL+R shortcut or choosing View|Project.
	Start	Lets you run the application. After you design an application, this is the same as choosing Run|Start.
	Break	Pauses a running program. (Programs can usually be continued by using the Run tool or SHIFT+F5.) This is the same as the Run|Break or the CTRL+BREAK combination.
	End	Ends the running program. Same as choosing Run|End.
	Toggle Breakpoint	A debugging tool; see Chapter 8. This places a temporary stop sign at a specific place in your program. Available from the Run menu; the shortcut is F9.
	Instant Watch	Another debugging tool discussed further in Chapter 8. This lets you take a snapshot of what is happening to various parts of your program. Also available from the Tools menu; the shortcut is SHIFT+F9.
	Calls	Shows a list of current procedure calls. A debugging tool; see Chapter 8.
	Step Into	Moves through your program one line at a time. Also a debugging tool, discussed in Chapter 8. Available from the Run menu or with the F8 shortcut.
	Step Over	Used when your program has grown more sophisticated by breaking down specific tasks into different procedures (see Chapter 8). Also moves through your program one line at a time, but treats a procedure as a single step. Also a debugging tool, discussed in Chapter 8. Available from the Run menu; the shortcut is SHIFT+F8.

The Default Toolbar Icons (*continued*)
Table 2-1.

The Toolbox

Located at the left of the screen in Figure 2-1, just below the toolbar, the *toolbox* contains the tools for developing your application. How many tools are available depends on your version of Visual Basic and whether you have added any custom controls. (Figure 2-1 shows the tools supplied with the professional edition of Visual Basic.) You use the toolbox to place command buttons, text buttons, and the other controls in your application.

The Initial Form Window

The initial *Form window* takes up much of the center of the screen. This is where you customize the window that users will see. The Visual Basic documentation uses the term *form* for a customizable window. (See Chapter 3 for more details on the initial Form window.)

Note: This book follows the Visual Basic manuals' convention of using the term "form" to describe a customizable window and objects like command buttons that you can add to it.

The Project Window

Since it is quite common for Visual Basic applications to share code or previously customized forms, Visual Basic organizes applications into what it calls *projects*. Each project can have multiple forms, and the code that activates the controls on a form is stored with the form in separate files. General programming code shared by all the forms in your application can be divided into different modules, which are also stored separately. It is located at the far right of the screen of Figure 2-1. (The Project window is partially obscured by the initial Form window. You can always make it visible by choosing View|Project or CTRL+R.) The Project window contains a list of all the customizable forms and general code (modules) that make up your application. Here's what the initial Project window looks like:

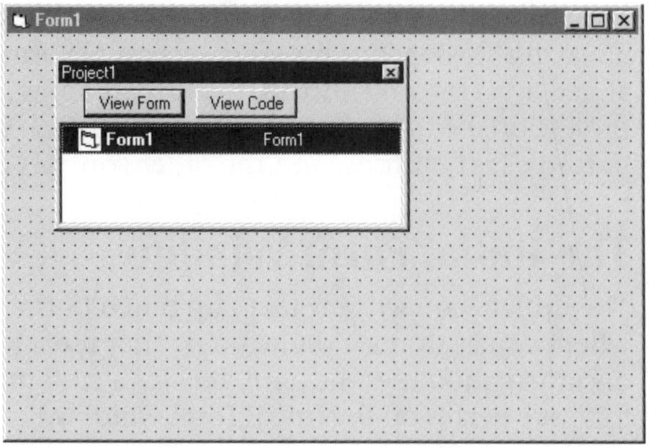

Notice that one item is already listed in the Project window. This is the initial form on which you will build the application. You can click on the View Form button to bring the highlighted form to the forefront. The View Code button will take you to the code associated with the form.

Although Visual Basic stores all the files that go into making up the project separately, it does keep track of where they are. It creates a file, called the *project file*, that tells it (and you, if you look at the file) where the individual files that make up a project are located. Visual Basic creates the Project file whenever you choose Save Project from the File menu (or equivalently, the Save Project tool from the toolbar). It creates a different Project file whenever you choose Save Project As. Project files have the extension .VBP in their filename.

Note: Prior to Visual Basic 4.0, Project files had the extension .MAK.

The Help System

The online help system contains essentially all of the information in the *Language Reference* that comes with Visual Basic. In addition, there are hundreds of example programs and dozens of useful tables.

The online help system contains a very useful feature: it is context sensitive for help. This means that you can press F1 and bypass the help menus to go directly to the needed information. You can get information about any keyword in the Visual Basic programming language, about an error message, or about the parts of the Visual Basic environment.

Once you start up the help system, you can move the help window anywhere you want. You can resize it or shrink it to an icon as needed.

The Help Menu

2

Following is a description of each of the items on the Help menu.

Contents The Contents option, activated by pressing ALT H,C (or C alone if the Help menu is open), tells you how the Visual Basic help system is organized.

Search The Search option, activated by pressing ALT H,S (or S alone if the Help menu is open), lets you search for help on a specific topic.

Obtaining Technical Support This option tells you how to get help from Microsoft. (ALT H,O is the access key combination if the Help menu isn't open; press O if it is.) This option also contains hints on advanced topics.

Tip: If you are a member of CompuServe, Microsoft is very efficient about giving answers to the questions posted by users in its MSBASIC forum. Other users monitor the questions and often provide helpful advice as well. (For instance, the authors of this book frequently log on to this forum and sometimes provides advice.)

Visual Basic Books Online This new feature in Visual Basic launches the Books Online tool, which lets you look—and search—through all the Visual Basic documentation.

Learning Microsoft Visual Basic This is a rather simplistic orientation to Visual Basic.

About The About option gives you the copyright notice and serial number of your copy, tells you to whom the copy of Visual Basic is licensed, and lets you find out information about your system.

More on the File Menu

You will need the main File menu to work with the files that make up your project. This menu includes commands for saving, loading, and printing files. We cover them briefly here and you'll learn more about them in Chapter 3. The File menu also lets you exit Visual Basic. As you've seen, the other way to exit Visual Basic is to use ALT+F4 when the focus is on the main menu bar, and like any Windows application you can also open the control box on the menu bar and choose Close or double-click on the control box.

Note: Under Windows 95 the control box appears as an icon.

Most of the items on the main File menu are useful only when you've started developing your own applications, as discussed in the later chapters of this book. What follows is a brief look at each of the items, which should help you orient yourself.

New Project The New Project option unloads the current project. If you've made any changes to a project since you last saved it, a dialog box like the following pops up, asking you if you want to save your work:

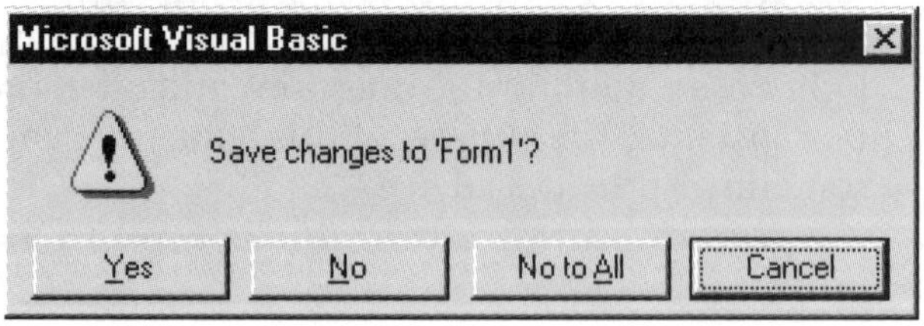

If you answer Yes by pressing ENTER or ALT-Y, you are led to another dialog box for saving files.

Open Project The Open Project option lets you work with an existing Visual Basic application. As the ellipses after the item indicate, choosing this option opens a dialog box.

Save File The Save File option saves the active object to disk. The first time you choose this option, Visual Basic opens a dialog box identical to the one for the Save File As option.

Save File As The Save File As option pops up a dialog box that lets you save the active form or module (general-purpose code) to disk, possibly with a new name. Use this option to keep backup copies of a specific piece of a project on a different disk or to save different versions. You also use this option when part of your current application will be useful in other projects. (In that case, you would use the Add File option to add the file to a different project.)

Save Project The Save Project item saves all the files in the current project and creates the initial Project file. (Recall that a Project file is a list of all the files used in the project plus some other information used by Visual Basic.) The first time you choose this option, the program opens a dialog box identical to the one for the Save Project As option.

Note: In Visual Basic the forms that make up your application are stored in ASCII format, which is readable by other applications. (These are called *text-only files* or simply *text files*.)

Save Project As The Save Project As option pops up a dialog box that lets you save all the files that make up the current project with a new name. It does this by creating a new Project file and saving the files with their current names. You can also use this option to keep backup copies of the project on a different disk or to save different versions of the project.

Add File The Add File option opens a dialog box that lets you incorporate work previously done into your application. You can add already finished forms, general-purpose code (modules), class modules, or even resource files.

Remove File Use the Remove File option to delete the part of your Visual Basic application you're currently working with from the application. This option does not delete the file from the disk where it was stored. For that you'll need to use the Explorer built into Windows 95 or ordinary DOS commands.

Print Setup This lets you select the printer and set the paper and orientation choices.

Print This lets you print either the current form, code in the form, module (code) that you are working with, or all forms and modules in your application. Choosing it opens a dialog box that looks like this:

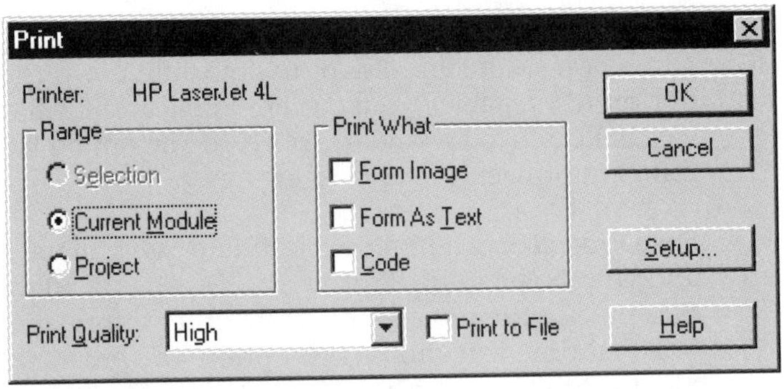

The option (radio) buttons (Selection, Current Module, and Project) determine whether you'll be printing from the part of the application you're currently working with or printing the entire application.

The three check boxes (Form Image, Form As Text, and Code) determine whether you print the forms that make up all or part of the application (what the user sees) or the code that activates the interface.

Make EXE File The Make EXE File option opens a dialog box that lets you create Visual Basic applications that can run in the Windows environment independent of Visual Basic. Stand-alone Visual Basic applications require *dynamic link libraries* (DLL) files and possibly custom control files. Due to Visual Basic's ability to create OLE applications, it is best to use the Setup Wizard discussed in the *Programmer's Guide* chapter, "Distributing Your Application," rather than try to determine the correct file that your application needs.

Make OLE DLL File This is covered in Chapter 10.

Note: This menu option is available only in Visual Basic Professional and Enterprise editors.

The Most Recently Used (MRU) List This keeps track of the four most recently opened Visual Basic projects. If you click on one of the files listed here, Visual Basic automatically loads the project. This makes returning to work in progress easy.

Exit Choosing the Exit option is the usual way to leave Visual Basic. If you've made any changes to the current project, Visual Basic asks you if you want to save them before ending the session.

Tip: Any Visual Basic application that handles files should have a File menu. Also, an important convention for Windows applications is that the last item on this menu should be the Exit command with an ALT+F4 shortcut.

See Chapter 3 for how to create a menu and Chapter 9 for how to work with files.

Editing

Visual Basic comes with a full-screen programming editor. Since it is a programming editor, it lacks features like word wrap and print formatting that even a primitive word processor like Write has. On the other hand, it does add features like syntax checking that can spot certain common programming typos. The Visual Basic program editor also color codes the various parts of your code. For example, Visual Basic commands can be one color, comments another. The colors used are customizable via the Editor page from the Tools menu's Options dialog box. The Visual Basic program editor is activated whenever you are writing or viewing code. The font used in the editor can be changed to suit your needs.

The Edit Menu

The Edit menu contains 15 items. Here are brief descriptions of each of them.

Undo, Redo Undo reverses the last edit you made. Redo reverses the last editing action. The shortcut for Undo is CTRL+Z.

Cut, Copy, Paste You use Cut, Copy, and Paste after you select text. Cut places the text in the Windows clipboard, Copy places a copy of it there, and Paste takes whatever is in the clipboard and pastes it into your Visual Basic application. In particular, you can use this item to exchange information (text or graphics) between another Windows application and Visual Basic.

Paste Link Paste Link is used in exchanging information dynamically between Windows applications; see Chapter 10.

Delete The Delete command removes the selected information but does not place a copy in the clipboard.

Find Choosing the Find option displays a dialog box in which you enter the text (string) you want Visual Basic to search for. Visual Basic searches the entire project for the string. The shortcut is CTRL+F.

Replace The Replace option opens a dialog box with two text boxes. The first is for the text to be found, and the second is for what should replace it. CTRL-H is the shortcut.

Indent Available in a code window. Shift all selected lines to the next tab stop.

Outdent Available in a code window. Shift all selected lines to the previous tab stop.

Bring to Front, Send to Back The Bring to Front option brings the selected object in front of all other objects; the Send to Back option moves the object back when you are developing the project.

Align to Grid Align to Grid is used to accurately position objects on your forms. See Chapter 3 for more on how to use the grid.

Lock Controls The Lock Controls option prevents accidental movement of controls when "checked."

The View Menu

The View menu contains items that deal with displaying and hiding environmental features and the objects and controls that make up your application. Here are brief descriptions of each of the menu items.

Code You use Code to view the source code for the Form file that has focus. The shortcut is F7.

Form You use Form to view the form for the Code file that has focus. The shortcut is SHIFT+F7.

Procedure Definition The Procedure Definition option displays the code window for whatever procedure the cursor is on. The shortcut is SHIFT+F2.

Last Position You use Last Position to jump to previous positions in a code window. The shortcut is CTRL+SHIFT+F2.

Object Browser The Object Browser option displays the Object Browser window. The Object Browser enables you to visually see the scope, inheritance, and references of classes, properties and methods used in your application. The shortcut is F2.

Debug Window You use the Debug Window option to display or bring to the front the Debug Window. The shortcut is CTRL+G.

Project The Project option displays the Project window. You can use the Project to view what files make up your application. The shortcut is CTRL-R.

Properties You use the Properties option to display or bring to the front the Properties window. The shortcut is F4.

Toolbox You use the Toolbox option to display or bring to the front the Toolbox.

Toolbar You use the Toolbar option to toggle the Toolbar on and off.

Color Palette You use the Color Palette option to display or bring to the front the Color Palette window.

The Insert Menu

The Insert menu contains items that let you insert various procedures, windows, code, modules, and so on into your projects. Here are brief descriptions of each of the menu items.

Procedure You use the Procedure item to add a procedure to the code window with the focus.

Form You use the Form item to add multiple windows to your application. See Chapter 3 for more on this option.

MDI Form You use the MDI (multiple document interface) form to make windows act as child windows to a main window. This is discussed in Chapter 10.

Module You use the Module option to add programming code that you'll want to share among all the parts of the application you develop. In

Visual Basic, code is attached to a specific window (form) unless you place it in a module.

Class Module You use the Class Module option to add a module containing the definition of a class that you'll want to share among all the parts of the application you develop. See Chapter 6 for more on Class Modules, which let you use some very basic object-oriented principles in your Visual Basic projects.

File You use File to insert code from a file containing code into the current code module at the point where the cursor is located.

The Add-Ins Menu

The Add-Ins menu gives you access to separate tools that can be seamlessly integrated with Visual Basic. There are two add-ins supplied with various versions of Visual Basic. The Report Manager gives you a fairly complete tool for modifying and building reports that you can use in your program. The other tool included is the Data Manager, which is used for managing databases. You use the Add-In Manager to add and remove add-ins from the menu.

Loading and Running Programs

This chapter ends by leading you through the procedures needed to run an existing Visual Basic program. Visual Basic comes with many interesting sample programs. The one described in this section is the Calculator.

If you choose the Open Project option on the File menu or click on the Open Project tool (the third tool), you are presented with the dialog box shown in Figure 2-2.

Notice in Figure 2-2 that one project file is shown. This is because Visual Basic keeps track of the files that make up a project in a file with a .VBP or .MAK extension (for the "Make file"), and Visual Basic installs one project file in the \VB directory. Of course, you can change the default for the filename extension Visual Basic uses to search by moving to the File name box and typing the new file pattern.

Click on the item marked **samples** in the Directories list box and then move through the subdirectories of the SAMPLES directory until you get to the one marked **calc.** Double-click on it and you are placed in the CALC subdirectory. The Files box now lists the CALC.VBP file, which contains the names and locations of the files that make up the CALC project. When you now double-click on this, Visual Basic loads the Calc project, which is a

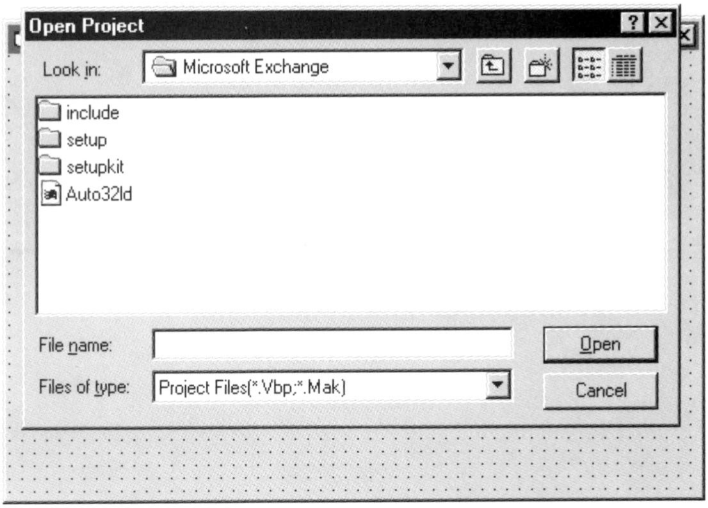

Open Project dialog box
Figure 2-2.

calculator application. You can also select this item by using an arrow key to move to it and then pressing ENTER.

After a short delay (possibly interrupted by a dialog box asking you if you want to save your current work), Visual Basic loads the Calc project. Since this program, written completely in Visual Basic, dramatically shows off the power that will soon be at your fingertips, you might want to press F5 to run it. To end this, or any project when it is running, use ALT+F4.

Chapter 3

Designing a Form: Controls, Menus, and Events

This chapter will show you how to customize forms and the controls you add to them. Changing the appearance of a form or control is most often done by setting properties in the Properties window, and so this chapter starts by showing you how to work with the Properties window. You will also learn how the mouse and the keyboard are used in this context. For example, as you saw in Chapter 1, the mouse is used in adjusting properties of forms and controls. Other uses for the mouse and keyboard are covered here. Next is a survey of the controls, with discussions of some of their associated properties and events. The basics of menu design using Visual Basic's built-in Menu Designer are explained, along with how to save files in ASCII form so that they can be printed out, modified, or viewed in an ordinary word processor.

Note: Even the controls supplied with the standard edition of Visual Basic have, taken together, hundreds of properties. A complete discussion of these controls is beyond the scope of this book. You must be prepared to consult the online help for more information on forms, individual controls, and their associated properties and events.

One way to shorten the learning curve for Visual Basic is to be aware that various types of controls use the same named properties and events. And, in almost all cases, the same name means similar functionality. For example, there is essentially no difference between how one makes a project respond to a click on a form versus on a command button. Similarly, all controls and forms have properties that specify where they are located or a Name property that you use in code to refer to them.

Working with the Properties Window

First, pressing F4 will always bring the Properties window to the top if it is obscured or hidden. Here's a picture of the Properties window.

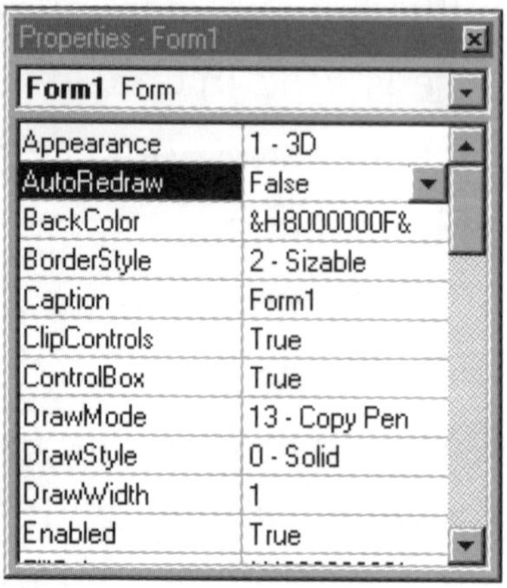

Notice that there is a drop-down list box on top. The item shown is the one whose properties you are currently working with. When you click on the arrow, Visual Basic shows you all the controls that are currently on the form. If the control (or form) that you want to work with is not shown here, simply drop the list down and choose it.

In the sections that follow, we discuss the various methods for setting properties in the Properties window.

Simple Property Editor

With this type of editor, you click in the right, or *value*, column and enter the text or the value there. You can use standard Windows editing techniques for cutting and pasting in these boxes. The archetype is the caption property for a form as shown here:

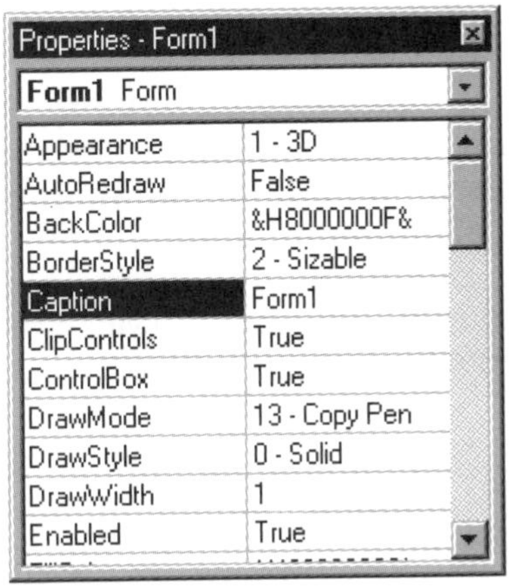

Visual Basic actually checks to make sure that what you entered makes sense. If you enter something that doesn't make sense, Visual Basic will pop up an "Invalid property value" message box and reset the value back to its original value. For example, Visual Basic won't let you enter a string if a number is called for.

Drop-Down List Property Editor

Visual Basic uses this type of property editor when you have a finite number of choices for the value of the property. You have to click in the row for that item in order to see the drop-down arrow. One example of this is the BorderStyle property for a form that controls (as one would expect) what type of border a form has. Here is a picture showing this type of editor with the list of possible values dropped down.

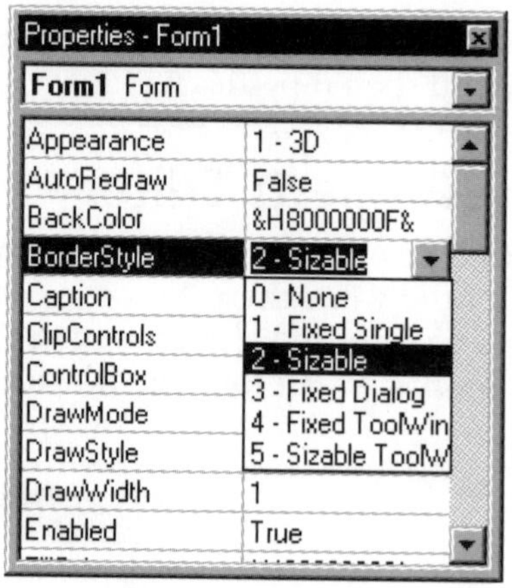

To choose something from the drop-down list of properties available in these types of editors, open the list by clicking the down arrow (or pressing ALT+DOWN ARROW). Then select the item you want. Keep on double-clicking in the value column until the value you want is shown. If you know the value you want, you can also simply enter it.

Note: When you need to work with a color property like ForeColor, clicking on the arrow brings up a palette. Click on the appropriate-colored box to set the color. (See Chapter 11 for more on how Visual Basic works with colors.)

Dialog Box Property Editor

Visual Basic follows the standard Windows convention that an ellipsis means a dialog box is available. The ellipsis shows up when you click in the value column. Click on the ellipsis to reveal the dialog box. (You can also double-click in the value column.). The typical example is the Font property dialog box, as shown here:

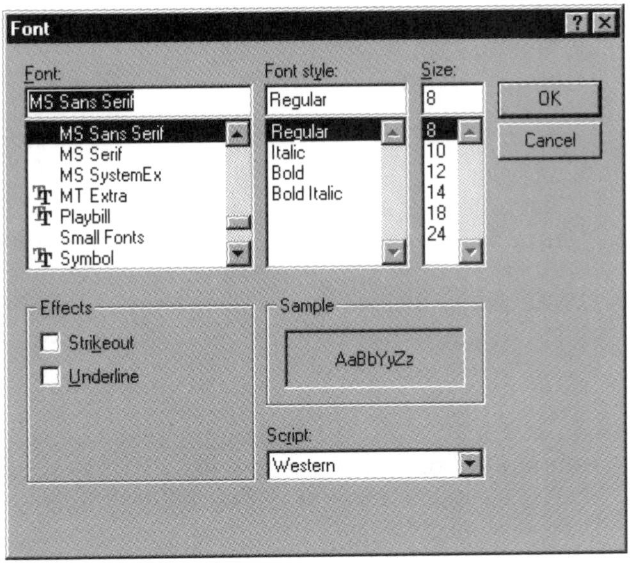

When you have finished adjusting the settings in the dialog box, click OK and they will go into effect.

Forms

Ordinary forms have properties you can set at design time with the Properties window. Forms will also respond to 25 (19 for MDI forms) different events. The purpose of the next few sections is to introduce you to the most important of these properties and events. The treatment of properties and events associated with forms is more thorough than that of controls in the later sections of this chapter. This is because many of these properties and events will recur with similar functionality for the various controls.

Form Properties

Although not quite precise, a good way to think of properties is that they affect the appearance of an object. Properties can be changed at design time or at run time. When they are changed at run time, the syntax takes this form:

```
object.property = new value
```

Note: For more on coding techniques, see Chapter 4.

What follows is a short discussion of the most important properties of a form that you can set at design time. (See Chapter 4 for those that you work with at run time, Chapter 10 for those dealing with linking to other Windows applications, Chapter 11 for more on properties associated with graphics, and Chapter 12 for those dealing with a mouse.)

Note: If a property for forms is not covered here or you want to find out more about one we do discuss, use the online help. The easiest way to do this is to use the context sensitivity built into Visual Basic: choose the property by clicking or moving the cursor to it, then press F1.

Appearance Leave this set at the default value of 1 - 3D to tell Visual Basic to display controls with a three-dimensional look. (Of course, there are some controls that cannot be given this look. Consult the documentation for the specific control if the control seems to appear "flat" when this property is set to be True.)

AutoRedraw This is an extremely important True/False (Boolean) property. It determines whether information displayed on your form persists when the form is repainted. For example, if AutoRedraw is False (the default), then anything on the form will vanish when the form is covered by another form and then uncovered. (See Chapter 11 for more on this important property and for more on graphics in general.)

BackColor, ForeColor As you might expect, these two properties control what color Visual Basic uses for the background and foreground of the object. You can bring up a color palette or set the color directly. To set it directly, you enter the number describing a color using a hexadecimal format (see Chapter 4). To use the color palette, click on the ellipses and then choose the colored box that most closely matches the color you want.

BorderStyle This property determines how the boundary of the form appears. There are five possible values as shown in the following table.

Value	Description
0	No border and so no buttons.
1	*Fixed Single*. The user cannot resize the form with a mouse. You can have a control menu box, a title bar, and Maximize and Minimize buttons, so the user can maximize or minimize the form.
2	*(Default) Sizable*. The user can resize the form with a mouse.
3	*Fixed Dialog*. Generally used for custom dialog boxes and is not resizable by the user. May have a control box but can't include Maximize or Minimize buttons.
4	*Fixed ToolWindow*. Only relevant under Windows 95 (behaves like fixed single under NT or Windows 3.1). This displays the Close button as well as the title bar text in a smaller font. The form will not appear in the Windows 95 task bar.
5	*Sizable ToolWindow*. Also only relevant under Windows 95 (otherwise behaves like sizable). Does not display Maximize or Minimize buttons but is resizable by the mouse. Under Windows 95, gives you a Close button. And, as with Fixed ToolWindow, displays the title bar text in a smaller font and the form does not appear in the Windows 95 task bar.

Note: When you change the setting of the BorderStyle property, you may affect the properties that control the buttons that can appear in the title bar. For example, when the BorderStyle property is set to 0 (None), 3 (Fixed Dialog), 4 (Fixed ToolWindow), or 5 (Sizable ToolWindow), the MinButton, MaxButton, and ShowInTaskbar properties are automatically changed to False.

Caption You saw this property changed in Chapter 1. It determines the text that appears in the title bar.

ClipControls This True/False property determines whether Visual Basic repaints the whole form or just the newly exposed areas. Obviously, it is faster to only paint the newly exposed areas. (See Chapter 11 for more on the problems of painting and repainting screens at run time.)

ControlBox, MaxButton, MinButton The ControlBox property determines whether Visual Basic puts a control box in the left-hand corner. If this is set to False, then the form will no longer respond to the ALT+F4 shortcut combination for closing it, nor will an exit button appear on the title bar. (You would have to provide some other method for closing the form or bring up the Close program dialog box via the CTRL+ALT+DEL combination in order to end the task.)

Enabled, Visible If the Enabled property is changed from the default value of True, the form will no longer respond to any events. Usually this property is manipulated at run time. The Visible property, on the other hand, controls whether the user can even see the form.

Font This property lets you change the fonts for information displayed on the form. Clicking the ellipses brings up an ordinary Windows font dialog box—which fonts are available depends on your system, of course. Using the CurrentX and CurrentY run-time properties of the form, you can control where information appears (see Chapter 4).

FontTransparent This True/False property is used with graphics to determine whether graphics show through text.

Height, Width These properties measure (or set) the height and width of the whole form—including the borders and title bar. Both are measured in *twips*. Theoretically, a twip is 1/20 of a printer point or 1/1440 inch (1/567 of a cm), but how twips translate on a screen depends on the size of the screen. On one 17-inch monitor that we looked at, 4320 twips actually take up five inches and not three. (On the other hand, Windows printer drivers are set up so that when you design an object using twips, you can be sure it will *print out* at the correct measurement. For example, if you want a form to be three inches high when printed, you should make its height 3*1440 twips (= 4320), not worry about how it looks on the screen, and hopefully let the Windows printer drivers take over.)

HelpContextId This property is used when writing a Windows-compatible help system for your application (see Chapter 12).

Icon This property determines the icon used for the program when the form is minimized. Clicking on the ellipses brings up a dialog box that lets you choose the filename for the icon. Visual Basic would include the icon file as part of the application when you create an executable version of it. (Under Windows 95, the icon appears in the upper-left corner of the form and acts as the control box.)

KeyPreview The default for this property is False. If you change it to True, then most keystrokes are processed by the form's Key events first—rather than the control that has the focus. (See Chapter 5 for more on the Key events.)

Left, Top These properties determine where the form is, relative to the left top edge of the screen. It is measured in twips.

MousePointer, MouseIcon The property lets you determine the look of the cursor when the mouse is on the form. There are 15 standard shapes, ranging from the usual arrow or hourglass to more exotic shapes. If you set this value to 99 ("Custom"), then you can use the MouseIcon property to assign a custom mouse pointer to your form.

Name This property is available for every Visual Basic object. The Name property lets you give meaningful names to your Visual Basic objects in order to make programs clearer. Visual Basic sets up a default name like Form1 for the first form, Form2 for the second, and so on.

Note: Naming conventions for objects have inspired quite a lot of flaming. Some people prefer to use a lowercase prefix that indicates the object followed by the meaningful name. Examples of this might be frmAbout or frmInitial. This is the convention that Microsoft suggests, and so we use it in this book. However, there is a lot to be said for using something closer to meaningful English: AboutForm or FormAbout. Rather than getting involved in the argument, we just want to point out the almost obvious fact that meaningful names for objects will make debugging easier—following some documented convention is always a good idea.

The rules for the name of an object are

- Object names can be up to 40 characters.
- The first character must be a letter.
- The rest of the name can include any combination of letters, numbers, and underscores but no spaces.
- The case of the letters in the variable name is irrelevant.

Note: You can use a reserved word (see the online help for a list of them) for an object's name, but this can lead to some really hard-to-find bugs, so it is not recommended.

Picture This brings up a dialog box that lets you place a picture (bitmap, icon, or Windows metafile) on the form.

ScaleMode The ScaleMode property allows you to change the units used in the forms' internal coordinate system. Tired of twips? There are seven other possibilities. You can create your own units by setting it to 0, keep the default twips (this value is 1), or use one of the six remaining choices. A useful setting—especially for graphics—is 3 *pixels* (a picture element—the smallest unit of resolution on your monitor as determined by Windows) as the scale.

ScaleHeight, ScaleWidth The ScaleHeight and ScaleWidth properties let you set up your own scale for the height and width of the form. For example, if you set the value of each of these properties to 100, the form uses a scale that has point 50,50 as its center. (Resetting these properties has the side effect of setting the value of the ScaleMode property back to 0.)

Note: ScaleHeight and ScaleWidth always represent the usable part of the form—the part excluding the borders—regardless of whether you change their values or not.

ScaleLeft, ScaleTop The ScaleLeft and ScaleTop properties describe what value Visual Basic uses for the left or top corner of the form. The original (default) value for each of these properties is 0. Like ScaleHeight and ScaleWidth, these properties are most useful when you are working with graphics. For example, if you are writing a program that works with a graph, you rarely want the top-left corner to be at point 0,0.

ShowInTaskbar This True/False property is used only with Windows 95 applications. It determines whether the form has a representation on the Windows 95 taskbar.

Tag This property isn't used by Visual Basic. It exists solely to provide programmers a way of attaching information to a control.

WhatsThisButton, WhatsThisHelp These two properties are used together in Windows 95–compliant applications in order to give a WhatsThis button on your form. These are most often used with dialog boxes. To show this button:

1. Set the WhatsThisHelp property to be True.

2. Remove the Max and Min buttons (or set the BorderStyle property to Fixed Dialog).
3. Set the WhatsThisButton property to be True.

   The default for both properties is False.

WindowState There are three values for this property. The default, Normal (0), leaves the form neither maximized nor minimized. You normally use code to change this property to one of the other two values: Minimized (1) or Maximized(2).

Form Events

Recognizing events are the key to Visual Basic's power, but if you did not write the code in the appropriate event handler, nothing will happen. The first thing you need to do when writing an event handler is to generate the event procedure template. The general method of generating an event procedure template is to

1. Bring up the code window by pressing F7 or choosing View|Code.
2. Drop down the Proc list box and then click on the name of the event procedure you want to work with.

Figure 3-1 shows an example of the Code window with the event procedure list box dropped down.

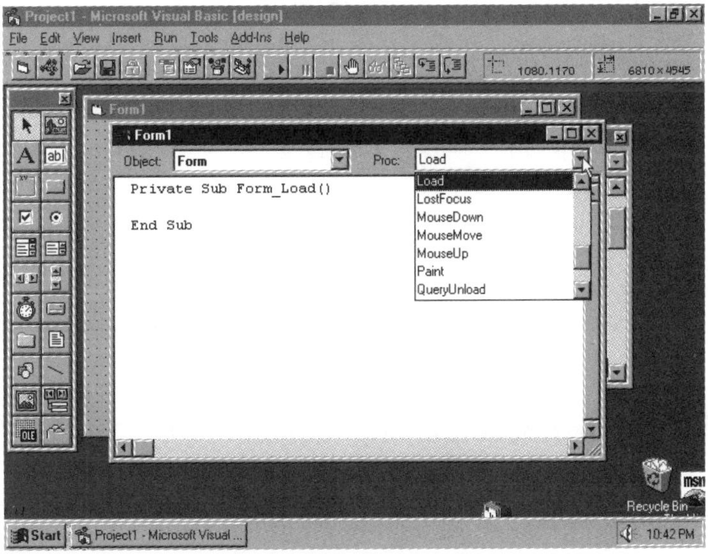

The event procedure list box

Figure 3-1.

Note: If you double-click on a control or a form, Visual Basic pops up the default event procedure template for that object. (For forms, it is the Load event.)

Here are short descriptions of the most important form events:

Initialize, Load, Activate, GotFocus These events can be confused because they are triggered under similar circumstances. It is important that you keep in mind the order in which they are triggered by Visual Basic.

First is the Initialize event. It is triggered first and only once, when the form is first created. *The Initialize event occurs before the Load event.* As its name suggests, the Initialize event is where you place code that you use for setting initial properties of the form.

The Load event is triggered when a form is loaded into memory and occurs after the Initialize event. Usually this code is triggered once only. (However, using code, it is possible to unload and then reload a form, so you can have this event triggered more than once.) When you start a program with a single form, it will generally be loaded automatically—thus triggering this event. (See Chapter 4 for how to deal with multiple form applications.)

The Activate event occurs when a form becomes the active window. As such it can be triggered repeatedly—for example, when the user clicks in a previously inactive window.

Finally, after the Activate event is triggered, Visual Basic will trigger the GotFocus event for the form *only if all visible controls on it are disabled.* (For this reason, people rarely use the GotFocus event for a form.)

Click, DblClick This event is triggered when the user clicks (double-clicks) in a blank area of the form.

Note: The Click event will always be triggered first, even when the user double-clicks.

Deactivate, LostFocus The Deactivate event occurs whenever a form ceases being the active window. As such it can be triggered repeatedly—for example, when the user clicks in another window. (As with GotFocus the LostFocus event for a form is rarely used and will also only be triggered if no controls can receive the focus.)

QueryUnload, Unload, Terminate The QueryUnload is triggered when the user *tries to close* the form—for example, by double-clicking on the control box. You can use this event for clean-up code—or even to prevent the form from closing. The Unload event, on the other hand, is triggered *after* the form closes. The Terminate event is the last event triggered. It occurs when all references to the form are removed from memory. (See Chapter 6.)

DragDrop, DragOver, MouseDown, MouseMove, MouseUp These events are used with code to detect mouse movements. (See Chapter 12.)

KeyDown, KeyPress, KeyUp These events let you determine what the user is doing with the keyboard. (See Chapter 5.)

Resize, Paint The Resize event is triggered whenever the user resizes a form. You usually place code in the resize event procedure to reposition controls as needed. The Paint event is triggered when part of the form is reexposed or after the form has been enlarged (*after* the Resize event).

Note: Both these events are triggered when the form first loads. Also, the AutoRedraw property must be set to False for the Paint event to be triggered.

Controls

Controls are the nuts and bolts of your projects. These are the objects like command buttons and check boxes that make Windows applications easier to use than non-Windows applications. (For those who are familiar with the Windows API, most controls also have a Windows handle so they can be used with Windows API calls—see Chapter 5 for more on how to use the Windows API in Visual Basic.)

Just as with a form, controls have properties that you can set at design time via the Properties window or at run time via code. Many properties, such as Height and Width or Name, work essentially the same way for both forms and controls.

Custom Controls

Visual Basic allows you to add specialized *custom controls* to your project. There are custom controls for everything from multimedia to spell checking to ones that run laboratory equipment. Of course, controls designed for earlier versions of Visual Basic (so-called VBX controls—because the extension used for the filenames is .VBX) can only be used with the 16-bit version of

Visual Basic that comes with the Professional and Enterprise editions. For the 32-bit version of Visual Basic you need to use the newer OLE-compliant, or *OCX*, controls, as they are usually called (also after the extension used for their filenames). The Professional edition of Visual Basic comes with 36 custom controls.

Tip: The "Visual Basic Programmers Journal" is a good source for the latest information about what custom controls are available from third-party vendors.

To add a custom control, choose Tools|Custom Controls. This opens a dialog box that looks like this:

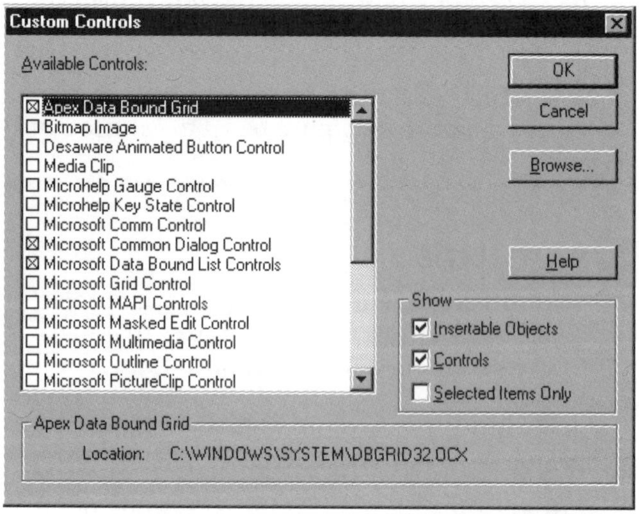

Now check off the control you want to add and click OK. (You can click on the Browse button to search for controls that aren't registered.) Once you add a custom control, Visual Basic places it in the Toolbox like any of the standard controls.

To remove a custom control, again choose Tools|Custom Controls, and remove the checkmark.

Adding Custom Controls Automatically

The following procedure will automatically let you add a custom control to your Visual Basic application development environment.

1. Open the AUTO32LD.VBP project (or AUTO16LD.VBP for the 16-bit version of Visual Basic). This project can be found in the same directory as Visual Basic's executable.
2. Add the custom control to this project.
3. Save this project.

Visual Basic 3 Tip: AUTO32LD.VBP (and AUTO16LD.VBP) are the replacements for the earlier AUTOLOAD.MAK file. Also note that the VBP files for Visual Basic 4.0 are not usually edited by hand—unlike AUTOLOAD.MAK.

To remove a custom control from automatically loading,

1. Open the AUTO32LD.VBP (or AUTO16LD.VBP) project. It can be found in the same directory as Visual Basic's executable.
2. Remove the custom control from this project.
3. Save this project.

An Overview of the Standard Controls

The controls that are standard in the various versions of Visual Basic are displayed in the Toolbox that is usually located to the left of the form. (To make it visible if it is hidden, choose View|Toolbox.) This section gives you an overview of these standard controls. (For which controls will work with databases—so-called "bound" controls—please see Chapter 13.)

Note: This table also supplies Microsoft's suggested prefix for the controls' names—for example, cmdButton would be a use suggested by Microsoft. As always, whether you choose to use their conventions is completely up to you.

Icon	Name (and prefix)	Purpose
	Pointer	Strictly speaking, this isn't a control. It is used to resize or move a control after you have placed it on the form.
	PictureBox (pic)	Used to display graphics. You can both display existing images and draw on picture boxes. Also used as a container for other controls.
	Label (lbl)	Used for text that you don't want the user to change.
	TextBox (txt)	Used for user input.
	Frame (fra)	This is used to group controls (both visually and functionally).
	CommandButton (cmd or btn)	Used for buttons that the user can click on.
	CheckBox (chk)	Used for yes/no choices.
	OptionButton (opt)	Used in groups when there is only one possibility from the group.
	ComboBox (cbo)	Used when you need a combination of a list box and a place to enter a choice. The idea is that you can either choose from the list or enter your own choice directly.
	ListBox (lst)	Used when you want to give the user a fixed list of items to choose from.
	HScrollBar (hsb)	This is a horizontal scroll bar. You can use this to give users an analog tool for moving through a list.
	VScrollBar (vsb)	This is a vertical scroll bar.
	Timer (tmr)	Used to trigger events periodically.

The Standard controls
Table 3-1.

Table 3-1. The Standard controls (*continued*)

Icon	Name (and prefix)	Purpose
	DriveListBox (drv)	Used to display the disk drives available.
	DirListBox (dir)	This is a directory list box
	FileListBox (fil)	Used to display a list of files.
	Shape (shp)	Used for rectangles, circles, and other shapes. Quite sparing of Windows resources.
	Line (lin)	Used to draw lines on a form—also quite sparing of Windows resources.
	Image (img)	Like a picture box, can be used to display a graphical image from a bitmap, icon, or metafile on your form. You cannot draw on an Image control, however, and Image controls use fewer Windows resources than picture boxes.
	Data (dat)	Used to provide access to a database. (See Chapter 13.)
	OLE Container (ole)	Used for OLE—see Chapter 10.
	CommonDialog (cdl)	Gives you access to the Windows common dialog box.
	Grid (grd)	Used for tabular data. (The Grid is a custom control—see below.)
	DBList (dbl)	This is the data-bound list box; also a custom control. (See Chapter 13 for more on data access.)
	DBCombo (dbc)	This is the data-bound combo box; also a custom control. (See Chapter 13 for more on data access.)
	DBGrid (dbg)	This is the data-bound grid control; also a custom control. (See Chapter 13 for more on data access.)

The Professional Edition Controls

The following table gives short descriptions of the controls supplied with the professional and enterprise editions of Visual Basic. Space constraints preclude a discussion of their properties in this chapter (they occasionally appear in examples in the following chapters, however). Consult the documentation supplied or the online help for more information.

Note: Some of these controls will not automatically show up in your toolbox. To add a custom control, choose Tools/Custom Controls, then check-off the box of the custom control you want to add.

Name of Control	Description
3D Check box	3-D replacement for an ordinary check box
3D command button	3-D replacement for an ordinary command button
3D frame	3-D replacement for an ordinary frame
3D group push button	Gives you a group of buttons for a toolbar
3D option button	3-D replacement for an ordinary option button
3D panel	Lets you print 3-D–appearing text
Animated button	Lets you use a series of bitmaps on a button
Communications	Lets you build a communications program
Gauge	Lets you build gauges of various types
Graph	Lets you easily build graphs
ImageList Control	Used for a collection of ListImage objects
Key status	Lets you display or modify the status of the CAPS, INS, NUM and SCROLL LOCK keys
ListView Control	Lets you display visually the items on a list—with associated icons and descriptions if you want.
MAPI message	Used for building MAPI-compliant mail programs
MAPI session	Also used for building MAPI-compliant mail programs
Masked edit	Lets the user enter (but you can restrict the text)

Name of Control	Description
Multimedia MCI	For building multimedia applications
Outline	For building outlines
Picture clip	Provides a way to display multiple images in a single control
ProgressBar	Lets you build a progress bar
RichTextBox	A very useful extension of a text box that allows you to display multiple fonts and large amounts of text
Slider	Similar to horizontal scroll bars
Spin button	Lets you add a spin button for incrementing or decrementing items
SSTab Dialog	Lets you build a tabbed dialog box—like the ones used in Visual Basic itself
StatusBar	Gives you a quick way to add a status bar at the bottom of form
TabStrip	Lets you put divider icons on a form
Toolbar	Lets you easily build toolbars
TreeView	Lets you view data in a treelike arrangement

Note: Some of these controls exist only in the 32-bit version of Visual Basic—consult the online documentation for more information on this.

Adding Controls to a Form

Once you decide which control you want to add to a form, there are a couple of ways to place it there:

- ♦ If you double-click on the control, Visual Basic adds the control in the default size and shape to the middle of the form. (If there are controls already in the center of the form, the new one is placed on top of the previous one.)
- ♦ If you want to add a control at a specific location:
  1. Click on the control.
  2. Click at the spot on the form where you want the upper-left corner of the control to appear.

3. Drag the mouse pointer. As you drag, Visual Basic gives you an outline that shows the size and position of the control. Release the mouse button when you are happy with the control's size and position.

Adding Multiple Controls to a Form

You will often want to add multiple controls of the same type to a form—for example, multiple command buttons or edit boxes.

To add multiple controls of the same type,

1. Hold down the CTRL key.
2. Click on the control in the palette. (You can release the CTRL key after you select the control.)
3. Click at the place on the form where you want the upper-left corner of each copy of the control to appear, and drag to make it the correct size and shape.

Note: If you use this method, be sure to click on the pointer icon in order to go back to the usual method of working with controls.

Container Controls

When you use controls like radio buttons, they need to be kept in groups. That way, Visual Basic knows which ones to turn off when one is turned on. Among standard Visual Basic controls (besides the form itself), both Frames and PictureBoxes can serve as *container* controls. (In the professional edition, the 3-D frame, panel, and tab custom controls can also serve as container controls.) The idea of a container is that all the controls will behave as one at design time—this is sometimes called a *parent-child relationship*. For example, when you move a container control, the child controls move with it.

Note: Properties that measure where a control is, such as Left and Top, are always calculated relative to the boundaries of the container control.

The easiest way to create a container is to add it to the form before you add the child controls. Once you have placed the container on the form, make sure that the container control is selected. Then add controls as you normally would by, for example, clicking inside the container and dragging. (Note that even if the container is in the center of the form, double-clicking on a control will *not* make it a child of the container control.) (You can also set the Container property at run time.)

Note: You can also add multiple copies of the same control to a container control that is currently active by using the CTRL+CLICK method. This is especially useful in making toolbars (see Chapter 12).

Working with Existing Controls

Before you can work with a control that is already on a form, you need to select it. This can be done most easily by simply clicking inside the control. If you are working inside the form, you can also use the TAB key to move the focus among the controls on the form. When a control is selected on a form, small black squares called sizing handles appear on the perimeter. Dragging on them lets you resize the control (see "Resizing and Reshaping Controls" later in the chapter).

Selecting Multiple Controls

You will often need to work with many controls at once—for example, when you have to align them. The easiest way to select multiple controls is

1. Hold down the SHIFT key.
2. Click on each of the controls.

There is one other method for selecting multiple controls that is occasionally useful.

1. Imagine a rectangle that hits only those controls you want to select. Move to one corner of this imagined rectangle and click the left mouse button.
2. Hold the left mouse button down and drag the dotted rectangle until it hits all (and only) the controls you want to select. Then release the mouse button.

Regardless of which way you select a group of controls, when you finish selecting you know you were successful when they all show *gray* sizing handles.

Note: When you have selected multiple controls, the Properties window only shows their common properties. When you change one of the properties listed, all the selected controls are changed accordingly.

For example, to align the edges of a group of controls perfectly, select the controls and set the Left property to the same value; to align the tops, use the Top property.

Moving Controls

To move a control to a different location:

1. Select the control.
2. Place the mouse inside the control, and drag the control to its new location. Be careful not to drag the sizing handles or you will resize it instead of moving it.

Notice that as you manipulate the control, it seems to move in fits and starts, not smoothly. As the old computer joke goes, this is not a bug, it's a feature. The position of controls on a form default so that they are located only at grid points. The Environment page available on the Options menu lets you control this feature, which is called "Align Controls to Grid." You can also make the grid more or less fine by changing options in this dialog box.

Note: When you have selected a group of controls, they all move in tandem.

Finally, if you want to move a control by only one grid line at a time, select the control and then use CTRL and the appropriate arrow key.

Tip: Choosing the Lock controls item on the Edit menu prevents you from inadvertently moving any control on the form.

Resizing and Reshaping Controls

The sizing handles are the easiest way to change the shape and size of a control. To resize a single control, first select it. You should be able to see the black sizing handles. Now drag the appropriate sizing handle.

Note: If you need to resize multiple controls, first select them. Then you can use the Properties window to change the height and width properties.

Deleting Controls

If you need to delete controls on the form, first select them. Then press the DELETE key, or choose Edit|Delete. If you delete a container component, all its child components are cut as well.

Cutting, Copying, and Pasting Controls

Visual Basic lets you cut, copy, and paste controls between forms, or between a form and a container using standard Windows conventions (CTRL+X for cut, CTRL-C for copy, and so on). You can also use the appropriate options on the Edit menu.

Some Individual Controls

This section discusses some common control properties and events that are important when manipulating the focus for controls. We follow this with a discussion of the more common controls. (It is no exaggeration to say that 10 to 15 controls make up the bulk of the visual interface in Visual Basic projects.)

While we discuss some of the most important properties and events that recur for controls, we will not repeat discussions of the many properties and events (such as Color, Cursor, Enabled, Left, Name, Top, Visible, Width, Click, DblClick, and so on) that work essentially the same for forms and controls.

Note: Properties like Left and Top are always calculated relative to the container component.

Focus Properties and Events

Only a single control can be active—that is, have the *focus*—at any given time. (The form has the focus only when no control on it can have the focus.) Visual Basic determines which control to give the initial focus to by first looking at the controls whose TabStop property is set to True. It then moves the focus to the visible and enabled control with the lowest value for the TabIndex property. (Visual Basic sets the TabIndex property numerically according to the order in which you create the controls. You can change the TabIndex property and so the ordering by using the Properties window.)

The two focus events are GotFocus and LostFocus, which are triggered when the control gets or loses the focus, respectively.

Note: Only visible and enabled controls can receive the focus. Frames, labels, menus, lines, shapes, images, and timers can never receive the focus.

Caption Properties and Accelerator Keys Many Windows applications use accelerator keys to quickly move the focus or to click a button. These keys are indicated by an underline in the caption. Users can then press ALT and the underlined letter to click the button or move the focus.

To set up an accelerator key for a Visual Basic control, add an ampersand (&) right before the accelerator (underlined) letter. For example, if you set the caption property of a command button to &Quit, the user can then use ALT-Q instead of clicking on the button to activate its OnClick event procedure.

Command Buttons, 3D Command Buttons, Animated Buttons

Placing buttons on a form so that the user can click on them in order to do something is very common in Windows applications (although many controls can detect the Click event and so have a Click event procedure associated to them).

Note: 3-D Command Buttons and Animated Buttons are available only in the Professional and Enterprise editions. Generally speaking, they work similarly to ordinary command buttons—except that 3-D Command Buttons look a little fuller and Animated Buttons give you the option of using an image (or images, for an animation) on the button.

Most of the properties of command buttons are already familiar to you. Two special properties of command buttons are described next.

Cancel Sometimes you want to have the pressing of the ESC key trigger an event. For this to happen, set the Cancel property of the command button to be True. Once you have done this, Visual Basic triggers the Click event handler for this button whenever the user presses the ESC key.

Default The Click event for a *default* button (one whose Default property is True) is triggered whenever the user presses the ENTER key. To make a button the default button, set the button's Default property to be True.

Note: If the user presses ENTER when a button has the focus, then Visual Basic triggers the Click event for that button. This happens whether or not you have set up a default command button.

TextBoxes, RichTextBoxes, MaskedEdit boxes

Text boxes are the primary method for accepting input and displaying output in Visual Basic. (If you have the Professional edition, the MaskedEdit and RichTextBox custom controls also perform these functions, although the former runs only on the 32-bit version of Visual Basic.) In fact, printing too many lines of text to a form will often lead to a run-time error, and in any case you can't scroll back through the form for lines that may have slipped off the top. All three text boxes never treat what a user types in as a number; this means that getting numeric information to a Visual Basic program requires transforming a string of digits into a number by using a built-in function or Visual Basic's built-in automatic conversions (see Chapter 4).

There are more than 40 properties for text boxes. Many of them should be familiar to you. As before, the Name property is used only for the code you write; the user never sees it. The Font property gives you a dialog box for setting font properties, and in this case they will affect what the user enters or sees. (Unlike RichTextBoxes, which support multiple fonts in the same box, ordinary text boxes allow you only one font for all the text in the box.)

There are three properties you have not seen before and one property that works differently for text boxes than for forms. The three new properties are Text, MultiLine, and ScrollBars. The BorderStyle property also works differently for text boxes than for forms.

Note: For information on the properties of the RichTextBox and MaskedEditBoxes, consult the Custom Control reference in the online help. Two points you may want to note are that (a) RichTextBoxes do not have the size limitations of ordinary text boxes and (b) using RichTextBoxes for editor applications will make their file handling easier (see Chapter 9).

Text The Text property is the analog of the Caption property for a command button or a form. The Text property controls the text the user sees. When you create a text box, the default value for this property is set to the default value for the Name property for that control—Text1, Text2, and so on. If you want a text box to be empty when the application starts up, select the Text property and blank out the original setting.

ScrollBars The ScrollBars property determines if a text box has horizontal or vertical scroll bars. These are useful because Visual Basic allows you to accept long or multiple lines of data from a single text box; roughly 32,000 characters is the usual limit. There are four possible settings for the ScrollBars property:

Value	Meaning
0	This is the default value. The text box lacks both vertical and horizontal scroll bars.
1	The text box has horizontal scroll bars only (limits text to 255 characters).
2	The text box has vertical bars only.
3	The text box has both horizontal and vertical bars.

MultiLine The MultiLine property determines if a text box can accept more than one line of text. (It is usually combined with resetting the value of the ScrollBars property.) When this property is True, the user can always use the standard methods in Microsoft Windows to move through the text box: the arrow keys, HOME, CTRL+HOME, END, and CTRL+END. Visual Basic automatically word-wraps when a user types more than one line of information into a text box with MultiLine set to True—unless you've added horizontal scroll bars to the text box.

Note: Users can use the ENTER key to separate lines unless you've added a default command button to the form. If you have a default command button, the user has to press CTRL+ENTER to break lines.

BorderStyle There are only two possible settings for the BorderStyle property for a text box. The default value is 1, which gives you a fixed single border. If you change the value of this property to 0, the border disappears.

MaxLength This property determines the maximum number of characters the text box will accept. The default value is 0, which (somewhat counterintuitively) means there is no maximum other than the roughly 32,000-character limit for multiline text boxes. Any setting other than zero will limit the data the user can enter into that text box to that number of characters.

PasswordChar As you might expect from the name, this lets you limit what the text box displays (although all characters are accepted and stored). The convention is to use an asterisk (*) for the password character. Once you set this property all the user sees is a row of asterisks. This property is often combined with the MaxLength property to add a password feature to your programs.

Locked If this is set to False, the user cannot edit what is displayed in the text box.

Event Procedures for Text Boxes

Text boxes can recognize 17 events. Events like GotFocus and LostFocus work exactly as before. Three others—KeyDown, KeyUp, and KeyPress—are for monitoring exactly what the user types and are covered in Chapter 5. The Change event lacks the flexibility of the key events, as you'll see in Chapter 5, but it is occasionally useful. Visual Basic monitors the text box and triggers this event procedure whenever a user makes any changes in the text box. For example, you can warn people that they should not be entering data in a specific text box, blanking out what they typed.

Caution: Be very careful not to put any code in the Change event procedure that changes the contents of the text box. This will cause the system to continually trigger the event until the program crashes. (This is usually called an *event cascade.*)

Labels

Labels are used for text that identifies the controls they are next to—for example, you will want to label text boxes. They can also be used to display text that users can't edit.

Tip: You can use a label to give an accelerator key to controls that do not have a caption property (like edit boxes). The idea is that when the user uses the accelerator key, the control that follows it in tab order receives the focus.

Alignment There are three possible ways to align text. For example, if you set the value of this property to 0 (the default), Visual Basic will left-justify the text.

AutoSize, WordWrap If the AutoSize property is set to True, the label automatically resizes horizontally to fit the text. If WordWrap is True, the label will grow vertically to fit the caption.

BorderStyle, BackStyle The BorderStyle property has two possible values. The default is 0 (no border) Set the value to 1, and the label resembles a text box. This is occasionally useful when your program displays results. The BackStyle property determines whether the label is transparent or opaque.

ListBox and ComboBox Controls

Both the ListBox and ComboBox controls let you display a scrollable list of items that users can select from. The difference is that the user *cannot change the entries in a list box.* (Combo boxes provide an edit area in which the user can enter information.) You usually use code in order to enter the items in these controls, but Visual Basic now allows you to enter them directly via the List property in the Properties window at design time. To do this,

1. Choose the List property.

2. Enter the items, pressing CTRL+ENTER after each one.

Here are short discussions of the most important properties of these controls that you may want to set at design time.

Columns and MultiSelection The Columns property controls the number of columns in a list box. If the value is 0 (the default), you get a normal single-column list box with vertical scrolling. If the value is 1, you get a single-column list box with horizontal scrolling. If the value is greater than 1, you allow (but do not require) multiple columns, which show up only when the items don't fit into the list box. (To force multiple columns, reduce the height of the list box accordingly.) The MultiSelect property controls whether the user can select more than one item from the list. There are three possible values for this property:

Type of Selection	Value	How It Works
No multiselection allowed	0	
Simple multiselection	1	A mouse click or pressing the spacebar.
Extended multiselection	2	SHIFT+CLICK extends the selection to include all list items between the current selections; CTRL+CLICK selects or deselects a single item.

Sorted This property applies to both controls. It determines if Visual Basic keeps the items sorted as you add more items to the list or combo box.

Style This property lets you determine the style of the combo box. There are three possibilities. The default value (0) (Dropdown Combo) gives you the usual drop-down list with an edit area. If the value of the Style property of a combo box is 1 (Simple Combo), the user sees the combo box with the list already dropped down.

Notice that in both these cases, the user still has a text area to enter information. On the other hand, the final possible choice for the Style property for combo boxes, a value of 2 (Dropdown List), gives you a drop-down list box with no edit area.

CheckBox and RadioButton Controls

Use check boxes when you want to provide nonexclusive options to the user. You then use code to determine if the user checks or unchecks a specific check box (using the value of the Value property). On the other hand, use a group of radio buttons when you need to present mutually exclusive choices to the user. Whenever a user clicks on one radio button in a group, the other buttons are switched off. In any case, as one would expect, when the user clicks on a box or button, Visual Basic also triggers the Click event for that control.

Note: Since radio buttons work as a group, the only way two radio buttons on a form can be checked at the same time is if they are in separate container controls.

Tip: Professional edition owners have the possibility of adding 3-D custom control versions of these controls—they look somewhat better.

Timers

Use a Timer control whenever you want something—or "nothing," such as a pause—to occur periodically. For example, you might want to have a program that "wakes up" at intervals and checks stock prices. On a more prosaic level, if you want to display a "clock" on a form, you might want to update the clock's display every minute or even every second (see "The Timer Event" later in this chapter for the one line of code this takes).

Timers are not visible to the user; the icon appears only at design time. For this reason, where you place or how you size the timer control at design time is not important. Although timers are an important tool for Visual Basic programmers, they shouldn't be overused. In fact, Windows restricts all the applications (not just the Visual Basic ones running at one time) to 16 timers. Do not go overboard on the timer control, since too many will use up a large share of precious Windows resources.

Enabled Enabled is a Boolean (True/False) property that determines whether or not the timer should start ticking. If you set this to True at design time, the clock starts ticking when the form loads. ("Ticking" is meant metaphorically; there's no noise unless you program one.) Also, because timer controls are invisible to the user, he or she may well be unaware that a timer has been enabled. For this reason, you may want to notify the user that a timer is working by means of a message box, an image control, or a picture box with a clock icon inside of it.

If you set the Enabled property to False at design time, the timer control starts working only when you switch this property to True in code. Similarly, you can disable a timer inside code by setting its Enabled property to False.

Interval The Interval property determines how much time Visual Basic waits before calling the Timer event procedure (see the next section). The interval is measured in milliseconds, and the theoretical limits are between 1 millisecond and 65,535 milliseconds (a little more than one minute and five seconds). The reason these are only theoretical limits is that the underlying hardware reports the passage of only 18 clock ticks per second. Since this is a little less than 56 milliseconds per clock tick, you can't really use an Interval property any less than 56, and intervals that don't differ by at least this amount may give the same results. (You can, however, use API functions, described in Chapter 5, for smaller time intervals.)

The smaller you set the Interval property, the more CPU time is spent waking up the Timer event procedure. If you set the Interval property too small, your system performance may slow to a crawl.

Note: An Interval property of zero disables the timer.

The Timer Event Visual Basic tries to trigger the Timer event procedure as often as you have set the Interval property. But since the CPU may be doing something else when the time determined by the interval elapses, you cannot be guaranteed that Visual Basic will call the Timer event procedure exactly when you want it. (Visual Basic will know when the interval has elapsed; it just may need to finish what it is doing before activating the Timer event.) If the time has elapsed, Visual Basic will call the Timer event procedure as soon as it is free to do so. You can use code to determine if more time has elapsed than you planned.

For example, suppose you want to develop a project with a clock that will update itself every second. To design the form, follow these steps:

1. Add a label and a timer to a blank form.
2. Set the AutoSize property of the label to be True and the font size to be 18. Set the Interval property of the timer control to be 1,000 (1,000 milliseconds = 1 second).

Now write the following code in the Timer event procedure for the Timer1 control:

```
Private Sub Timer1_Timer()
    Label1.Caption = Now
End Sub
```

Visual Basic will call this event procedure and update the clock's time roughly every second because the Interval property was set to 1,000. (See Chapter 5 for more on the date/time functions we used in this example.)

Tip: If you want to have a Timer event procedure do something less frequently than about once a minute (the maximum setting for the Interval property), you need to add a static variable to the Timer event procedure. This variable will let you keep track of the number of intervals that have elapsed. See Chapter 4 for more on these kinds of variables.

Grid Controls

The Grid control lets you build tables of textual data. We only cover the basic properties of grids here. Many of the properties of grids are only useful at run time. For example, the Text property both lets you put items in the cells and gives you access to the items in each cell. (Although we give some examples of using a grid at run time in later chapters, for more on the run-time properties and on working with grids, please see the online help. Only the design time properties of the Grid control are covered here.)

Note: The grid control is a custom control and if it is not automatically added, you must add it manually. It is called the "Microsoft Grid Control." We only cover the design-time properties of the Grid control here.

Cols, Rows These properties determine the number of rows and columns in the grid. The default values for each of these properties is two.

FixedCols, FixedRows, FixedAlignment Often when you are working with a grid, you will want to use certain cells to display information at all times. For example, regardless of how the user scrolls through a spreadsheet, you may want to display the column headings. Fixed rows and columns are always displayed in gray and must be at the top and left sides of the grid.

GridLines, ScrollBars These two properties control whether grid lines, which make it easier to see cell boundaries, and scroll bars appear. The default is to show grid lines and to have both horizontal and vertical scroll bars.

The Events for Grid Controls

Grids respond to many of the standard events; for example, you can use the Click event to determine whether the user has clicked inside the grid and the KeyPress event to send what a user is typing inside the grid directly to the currently selected cell. Visual Basic provides you with two events unique to grids that you may want to use. They are described below.

RowColChange This event is triggered when the current cell changes.

SelChange This event is activated when the selected region changes.

Designing Menus

Think of menu items as specialized controls that you add to your forms. Menu items respond only to a Click event. Designing the right kind of menus will make your applications much more user friendly. Visual Basic lets you build multilevel menus and add pop-up menus as well.

Menus that contain submenus are usually called *hierarchical* (or *cascading*) menus. Of course, using too many levels of menus can make the application confusing to the user. Four are almost certainly too many; two or three levels are what you usually see. The user knows that a submenu lurks below a given menu item when he or she sees an arrow following the menu item.

Tip: Instead of using lots of submenus, consider designing a custom dialog box for the options.

To add a menu to your form, use the Menu Design window available from the Tools menu on the Visual Basic main menu bar. The Menu Design window looks like the one in Figure 3-2. What follows is a short description of each of the components of this dialog box.

Caption What you type in the Caption text box is what the user sees. The caption also shows up in the text area inside the dialog box. Unlike other

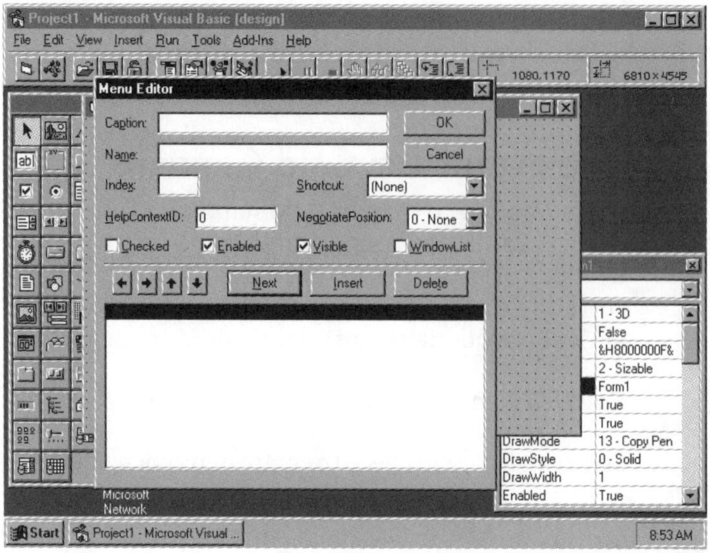

The Menu Design window
Figure 3-2.

Visual Basic controls, menu items do not have default captions. As with other controls, you use an ampersand (&) in the caption to give the item an access key.

Tip: If you set the Caption property for a non–main menu to a hyphen (-), a separator bar shows up.

Name Each menu item must have a control name. Unless the menu items are part of a control array (see Chapter 6 for more on control arrays), they must have different control names. The Microsoft convention is to use a *mnu* prefix for menu item control names.

The OK and Cancel Buttons Click the OK button when you have finished designing the menu. Click the Cancel button if you decide not to build the menu. Even after you've finished designing a menu and clicked on the Done button, you can return to the Menu Design window and make changes.

The Index Box Use the Index box if you want to make a menu item part of a control array (see Chapter 6).

The Shortcut Box The Shortcut box gives you a drop-down list box from which you can choose accelerator keys to your menu items. Recall that accelerator keys are either function keys or key combinations that activate a menu item without the user having to open the menu at all. (The shortcut key is automatically added to the caption.)

Tip: The ALT+F4 shortcut to close a window is not an allowable shortcut key. Response to this key combination is built into the form unless you remove the control box at design time. If you have a File menu and a control box on the form and want to show ALT+F4 as a shortcut for the Exit item, place this shortcut as part of the caption and use the QueryUnload event to call the Click procedure of the Exit item.

Window Lists Window lists are used when you have MDI windows. (See the section "MDI Forms" in Chapter 12.)

HelpContextId This is used when you are working with the Help compiler—available in the Visual Basic Professional and Enterprise editions.

The Checked Check Box The Checked check box determines whether a checkmark shows up in front of the menu item. It is much more common to switch the Checked property to True when a user selects the item while the program is running than to set it at design time.

The Enabled Check Box The Enabled check box determines the value of the Enabled property of the menu item. A menu item that is Enabled will respond to the Click event. An item that has this property changed to False—either at design time by toggling the box off or at run time via code—shows up grayed.

The Visible Check Box The Visible check box determines the value of the Visible property of the menu item. If a menu item is made invisible, all its submenus are also invisible and Visual Basic moves the menu items to fill in the gap.

The Arrow Buttons The arrow buttons work with the current menu items. The menu item you're currently working with is highlighted in the large text window below the arrow buttons. Submenus are indicated by the indentation level in this text window. The left and right arrow buttons control the indentation level. Clicking on the left arrow button moves the highlighted item in one level; clicking on the right arrow button moves it one indentation level deeper. You cannot indent an item more than one level deeper than the item above it. If you try, Visual Basic will not let you leave the Menu Design window until you fix it.

Clicking on the up arrow button interchanges the highlighted menu item with the item above it; clicking on the down arrow button interchanges the highlighted item with the item below it. The up and down arrows do not change the indentation pattern of an item.

The Next Button Clicking the Next button moves you to the next menu item or inserts a new item if you are at the end of the menu. The indentation of the new item is the same as the indentation of the previous item.

The Insert Button Clicking the Insert button inserts a menu item above the currently highlighted menu item.

The Delete Button Clicking the Delete button removes the currently highlighted item. You cannot use the DEL key to remove menu items.

Pop-Up Menus One of Windows 95's conventions is that a right mouse click brings up a context-sensitive menu. In order for a pop-up menu to exist, you must first create it as an ordinary menu—complete with captions and names for the item. Visual Basic allows any menu with at least one item to be a pop-up menu.

Tip: If you don't want the user to see it on the main menu bar, set the Visible property of the top-level menu item to False. (For more on pop-up menus, see the section on Mouse events in Chapter 12.).

The ASCII Representation of a Form

Unlike earlier versions of Visual Basic, Visual Basic 4 saves all its form files in ASCII (text) format. The ASCII representation of a form is an extremely useful debugging tool. Using it, you can easily make sure the properties of the form and its controls are exactly what you want.

Tip: You can modify the properties of a form or its controls using an ordinary text editor on the ASCII representation.

To see what the ASCII representation of a form looks like, do the following:

1. Start up a new project.
2. Add a form and set the caption to "ASCII".

3. Add a command button in the default size, in the default location, and using the default name of Command1 by double-clicking.
4. Add a Click procedure to the command button with the single line of code: **Print "You clicked me!"**
5. Save the form file under the name ASCII.FRM.

Now, if you examine the file in another word processor like Windows 95 Word Pad, you'll see something like this. (The values for height and width and other aspects will depend on your machine.)

```
VERSION 4.00
Begin VB.Form Form1
   Caption          =   "ASCII"
   ClientHeight     =   4140
   ClientLeft       =   1140
   ClientTop        =   1515
   ClientWidth      =   6690
   Height           =   4545
   Left             =   1080
   LinkTopic        =   "Form1"
   ScaleHeight      =   4140
   ScaleWidth       =   6690
   Top              =   1170
   Width            =   6810
   Begin VB.CommandButton Command1
      Caption          =   "Command1"
      Height           =   495
      Left             =   2760
      TabIndex         =   0
      Top              =   1800
      Width            =   1215
   End
End
Attribute VB_Name = "Form1"
Attribute VB_Creatable = False
Attribute VB_Exposed = False
Private Sub Command1_Click()
  Print "You clicked me"
End Sub
```

The idea of the ASCII form representation is simple: it contains a textual description of the form's properties followed by the code that is attached to the form.

(For more on the ASCII representation of a form, please consult Appendix A of the *Programmers Guide*.)

Chapter 4

Fundamentals of Visual Basic Programming

By now you have a feel for what a Visual Basic application looks like. You've seen how to customize forms by adding controls, and you've started writing the event procedures that are the backbone of a Visual Basic application. But as you've probably realized, the event procedures you've seen didn't do much. To do more, you must become comfortable with the sophisticated programming language built into Visual Basic.

If you are familiar with QuickBASIC, Pascal, C, or even QBASIC, you'll have an easier time of it, and the next chapters will go pretty quickly. If you are familiar only with the older interpreted BASIC found on PCs (GW-BASIC, BASICA), you'll want to read these chapters much more carefully. In any case, there are subtle differences between Visual Basic programming and conventional programming that can trip up even experienced programmers, so you probably don't want to skip these chapters.

The Anatomy of a Visual Basic Program

It can't be stressed enough that the key to Visual Basic programming is recognizing that Visual Basic generally processes code only in response to events. If you think of a Visual Basic program as a set of independent parts that "wake up" only in response to events they have been told to recognize, you won't go far wrong; but if you think of the program as having a starting line and an ending line and moving from top to bottom, you will. In fact, unlike many programming languages, executable lines in a Visual Basic program must be inside procedures or functions. Isolated executable lines of code don't work. For illustration purposes, this book may show you fragments of a program, but they are not meant to, nor can they, work independently.

Even if you know a more conventional programming language very well, you shouldn't try to force your Visual Basic programs into its framework. If you impose programming habits learned from older languages on your Visual Basic programs, you're likely to run into problems.

The Code Window

You always write code in the Code window. Figure 4-1 shows the Code window with the Object list box pulled down for the calculator application that comes with Visual Basic. As you have seen, this window opens whenever you double-click a control or form. You can also click the View Code button from the Project window or choose View|Code or press F7 to open the Code window.

The Code window has a caption that lists the form (the calculator in Figure 4-1), two list boxes, and an area for editing your code. The left list box, called *Object,* lists all the controls on the form, plus an object called *general* that holds common code that can be used by all the procedures attached to the form. You'll see more about this kind of code in the sections in this chapter titled "Changing the Defaults for Types" and "Constants."

The right-hand list box, named *Proc,* is the Procedure list box. As you have seen, this list box shows all the events recognized by the object selected in the Object list box. If you have already written an event procedure, it shows up in bold in the Procedure list box.

Statements in Visual Basic

When you enter a statement in Visual Basic, Visual Basic uses the same advanced technology pioneered in QuickBASIC to analyze and process it. This happens immediately after you press ENTER. Many typos are detected by

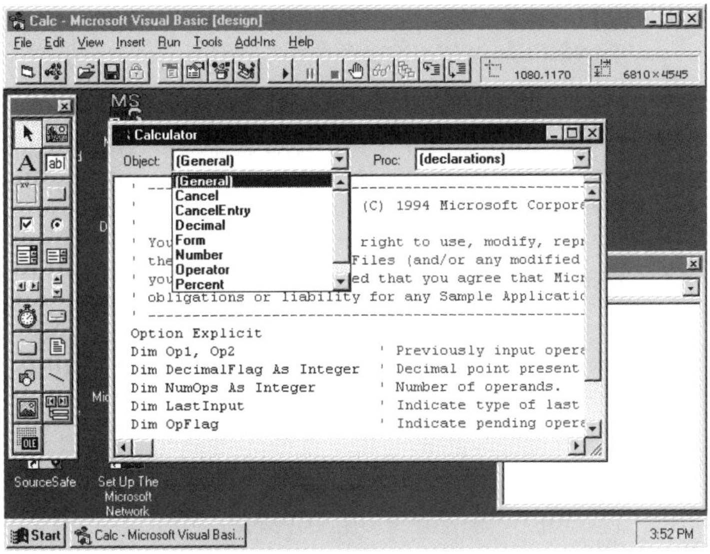

Code window with the calculator application
Figure 4-1.

Visual Basic at this stage. If a statement you enter can't be analyzed, a message box pops up that often helps you find out what caused the problem.

Unless they are within quotation marks, case and spacing are ignored by Visual Basic. Nonetheless, Visual Basic does try to impose its own conventions. It capitalizes the first letter of command words and often adds extra spaces for readability. For example, no matter how you capitalize the command word Print—PRint, Print, print, and so on—pressing ENTER will change it to Print. It's a good idea to stick to a standard method of spacing and capitalization in your code.

Statements in Visual Basic rarely use line numbers, and each statement generally occurs on its own line. You can combine statements on one line by placing a colon (:) between them. Lines are limited to 1023 characters and can be extended to the next line by using the underscore character (_) as the last character in the line. If you use a line with more characters than can fit in the window, Visual Basic scrolls the window toward the right as needed.

Sometimes in this book you'll see lines that easily fit this limit but are longer than can fit on one line of a printed page. We will use the underscore as the line continuation character whenever possible. (The underscore does not work as a line continuation character inside quotes. In this case you will have to continue until the closing quote.) In any case, we will "outdent" the line. Here are some examples of these conventions:

```
  MsgBox "You have to click a button for anything to happen" _
306, "Test Button"
```

```
  Print "This is an example of a line with quotes that won't fit on a
single line of the page."
```

If you were entering these lines in Visual Basic, in the first example you could either omit the underscore and continue typing or use the underscore and press ENTER after it. In the second example you would continue until you get to the closing quote.

Remark Statements

Remark (or Rem) statements are put into programs to explain what code does. It's easy to question why comments are important—until you try to modify or fix a program someone else wrote or even a program you wrote months ago. Remark statements are neither executed nor processed by Visual Basic. As a result, they do not take up any room in the compiled code. There are two ways to indicate a remark statement. The usual way to indicate a comment is with a single quote.

```
Private Sub Command1_Click ()
  'A comment describing the procedure would go here
 End Sub
```

(You can also use the older **Rem** keyword.)

You can also add comments to the ends of lines. In this case it is easier to use the single quotation mark because the Rem form requires a colon before it.

The End Statement

When Visual Basic processes an End statement, the program stops. The various Unload events are not triggered, and if you are developing a program, you are dumped back into the development environment. The effect is exactly the same as choosing the End option on the Run menu. In a stand-alone program, after the End statement, all windows opened by the program are closed and the program is cleared from memory.

You can have as many End statements within a Visual Basic program as you want, but it is good programming practice to restrict the number of events that end a program.

Assignment and Property Setting

Giving values to variables and resetting properties are two of the most common tasks in Visual Basic code. Visual Basic uses an equal sign for both these operations; for example,

```
InterestRate = .05
```

You can also use the optional keyword **Let** that was common in earlier versions of BASIC:

Let *Variable*Name = *value*

Assigning to Properties

If you want to change a property setting for a Visual Basic object, place the object's name followed by a period and then the name of the property on the left side of the equal sign, and put the new value on the right-hand side:

object.*property* = *value*

For example, suppose you have a text button (control name of Text1) and want to blank it out in code rather than use the properties bar. You need only have a line like this in an event procedure:

```
Text1.Text = ""
```


Since there is nothing between the quotation marks, the text assigned to this property is blank. Similarly, a line like

```
Text1.Text = "This is the new text."
```

in an event procedure changes the setting for the text property to the text in the quotation marks.

You can change the setting of a property via code as often as you need to. For example, if you wanted to change the caption on a command button called Command1, you would place a line like this in an event procedure:

```
Command1.Caption = "Put new caption here."
```

Similarly, if you wanted to make a button called Command5 the first button in Tab order, you would add a line like this to an event procedure:

```
Command5.TabIndex = 0
```

Now suppose you want a form called Form1 to move around when various command buttons (btnLeft, btnRight, and so on) are clicked. Here is an example of one of the event procedures you would need:

```
Sub btnLeft_Click ()
  Form1.Left = Form1.Left - 75
End Sub
```

Look at the key line "Form1.Left = Form1.Left – 75." On the left-hand side of the assignment statement is the property that gets the value, but it seems that the property occurs on the right-hand side as well. What happens is that Visual Basic first analyzes the right-hand side of any assignment to extract a value from it. In this case it looks at the current position of the left side of the form and calculates the number of twips it is from the left. It then subtracts 75 from this number. Only after it has done this does it look to the left side. Visual Basic now changes the old value of the "Left" property to a new one.

Every Visual Basic object has a default property (for example, text boxes have the Text property). When referring to the default property, you don't need to use the property name. For example, you can enter

```
Text1 = "This is new text"
```

However, this approach can lead to less readable code and requires you to remember what the default property of the control is. Thus, in spite of the very small gain in speed this approach yields, this book doesn't emphasize this feature of Visual Basic.

Boolean Properties

Properties that take only the value True or False are called *Boolean properties,* after the English logician George Boole. Boolean properties specify whether a command button is visible, is enabled, or is the default cancel or command button. Visual Basic has built-in constants for these important property values. A statement such as

```
Command1.Visible = False
```

in an event procedure hides the command button. The control stays hidden until Visual Basic processes the statement

```
Command1.Visible = True
```

If you want the TAB key to skip over a control while a program is running, change the TabStop property to False:

```
Control.TabStop = False
```

Internally, Visual Basic uses the values 0 for False and –1 for True for property settings (actually, any nonzero value will work for True). The usual way to toggle between Boolean properties is with the Not operator. For example

```
Command1.Visible = Not(Command1.Visible)
```

Note: For the Not operator to work properly in toggling a Boolean property between on and off, you must use the built-in True constant or a value of –1 for True.

Variables

Variables in Visual Basic hold information (values). Whenever you use a variable, Visual Basic sets up an area in the computer's memory to store the information. Variable names in Visual Basic can be up to 255 characters long and, provided the first character is a letter, can include any combination of letters, numbers, and underscores. The case of the letters in the variable name is irrelevant and all characters in a variable name are significant. BASE is the same variable as base. However, Visual Basic always changes the form of the names of your variables to reflect the capitalization pattern you last used. If you use Mortgageinterest, mortgageinterest, and MortgageInterest successively as variable names, when you move off the line Visual Basic will automatically change all occurrences to MortgageInterest because this was the last one you used.

Tip: This feature is often useful in detecting typos in variable names. If you think a misspelled variable name is causing a problem, change one occurrence to all caps, move off the line, and scan the program to see if all the occurrences of the variable name have been changed. If you find one that wasn't changed, you will know that variable name contains a typo. Correct the error and then change the variable name back to the form you want; all occurrences of the name will change again as well. For another way to detect typos and variable names, see the section "Requiring Declaration of Variables" later in this chapter.

Choosing meaningful variable names helps document your program and makes the inevitable debugging process easier. Meaningful variable names are an excellent way to clarify the point of many kinds of program statements.

You can't use names reserved by Visual Basic for variable names: for example, Print is not acceptable as a variable name. However, you can embed reserved words within a variable's name. For example, PrintIt is a perfectly acceptable variable name. Visual Basic will present an error message if you try to use a reserved word as a variable name, usually immediately after you press ENTER.

The most common convention for variable names is to use capitals only at the beginning of the words that make up the parts of it (for example, MortgageInterest, not Mortgageinterest). This convention is called *mixed case variable names*. This is the convention used in this book, as most people find it much more readable. Some people add underscores as well (for example, Mortgage_Interest)—this style is not used in this book because it wastes space and occasionally causes problems in debugging.

Variable Types

Visual Basic handles 11 standard types of variables. It is also possible to define your own variable types, as you will see in Chapter 5. There are two other variable types that you will see in Chapter 5. The 11 standard variable types are described here.

String String variables hold characters. One method to identify variables of this type is to place a dollar sign ($) at the end of the variable name: AStringVariable$. String variables can theoretically hold up to 65,535 characters, although a specific machine may hold less due to memory constraints, overhead requirements for Windows, or the number of strings used in the form.

One of the most common uses of string variables is to pick up the information contained in a text box. For example, if you have a text box named Text1, then

```
ContentOfText1$ = Text1.Text
```

assigns the string contained in the text box to the variable named on the left-hand side.

Byte Byte variables hold relatively small integer values, between 0 and 255. The Byte data type has no type-declaration character.

Boolean Boolean variables are stored as 2-byte numbers, but can only hold the value True or False. Boolean variables have no type-declaration character.

Date Date variables are stored as 8-byte numbers with possible values in the range January 1, 100 to December 31, 9999. Date has no type-declaration character.

Object Object variables hold address information that refer to OLE Automation objects. The Object type has no type-declaration character. (See Chapters 6 and 10 for more on objects.)

Integers Integer variables hold relatively small integer values, between –32,768 and +32,767. Integer arithmetic is very fast but is restricted to these ranges. The identifier used is the percent sign (%):

```
AnIntegerVariable% = 3
```

Long Integers The long integer variable is a type that was introduced in QuickBASIC. It holds integers between –2,147,483,648 and +2,147,483,647. The identifier used is the ampersand (&). Long integer arithmetic is also fast, and there is very little performance penalty on 386DX, 486DX, or Pentium machines for using long integers rather than ordinary integers.


```
ALongIntegerVariable& = 123456789
```

Single Precision For single-precision numbers, the identifier is an exclamation point (!). These variables hold numbers that are approximations. They can be fractions, but you can be sure of the accuracy of only seven digits. This means that if an answer comes out as 12,345,678.97, the 8.97 may or may not be accurate. The answer could just as likely be 12,345,670.01. Although the accuracy is limited, the size (range) of these numbers is up to 38 digits. Calculations will always be approximate for these types of variables. Moreover, arithmetic with these numbers is slower than with integer or long integer variables.

Double Precision Double-precision variables hold numbers with 16 places of accuracy and allow more than 300 digits. The identifier used is a pound sign (#). Calculations are also approximate for these variables. You can rely only on the first 16 digits. Calculations are relatively slow with double-precision numbers. Double-precision variables are mainly used in scientific calculations in Visual Basic—because of the data type described next.

Currency Currency variables are a type that will be new to GW-BASIC and QuickBASIC users. They are designed to avoid certain problems inherent in switching from binary fractions to decimal fractions. (It's impossible to make 1/10 out of combinations of 1/2, 1/4, 1/8, 1/16, and so on.) The currency type can have 4 digits to the right of the decimal place and up to 14 to the left of the decimal point. Arithmetic will be exact within this range. The identifier is an "at" sign (@)—*not* the dollar sign, which identifies strings. While calculations other than addition and subtraction are about as slow as for double-precision numbers, this is the preferred type for financial calculations of reasonable size. (For those who are interested, this type uses 19-digit integers, which are then scaled by a factor of 10,000. This gives you 15 places to the left of the decimal point and 4 places to the right.)

The Variant Type The variant data type is designed to store all the different possible Visual Basic data received in one place. It doesn't matter whether the information is numeric, date/time, or string; the variant type can hold it all. Visual Basic automatically performs any necessary conversions so you don't (usually) have to worry about what type of data is being stored in the variant data type. On the other hand, as you'll see in the next chapter, you can use a built-in function to determine whether data stored in the variant type is numeric, date/time, or string. This function lets you easily check user entries to see whether they match the format you want. Using variants rather than the specific type is a little slower because of the conversions needed, and some programmers feel relying on automatic type conversions leads to sloppy programming.

Fine Points of Variables

Unlike many other versions of BASIC, in Visual Basic you cannot use variables like A% and A!, which differ only in the type identifier, in the same program. Using them produces a duplicate definition error when you try to run your program.

The first time you use a variable that you haven't specified as belonging to one of the built-in types, Visual Basic temporarily assigns it a default value of "empty" and gives it the variant type. The "empty" value disappears the moment you assign a value to the variable.

Every other type of variable also has a default value. For string variables, this is the null (empty) string—the one you get by assigning " " to a string variable. For numeric variables, the default value is zero. You should only rely on the default values if this is documented (by a Remark statement, for example) in your program. Otherwise, you risk creating a breeding ground for hard-to-find bugs. It is therefore quite common to use the first statements in an event procedure to initialize the variables.

The Dim Statement for Types

Many people prefer not to use the identifiers to specify the type of a variable. Instead they use the Dim statement. Here are some examples:

```
Dim I As Integer
Dim TextBox As String
Dim Interest As Currency
```

The technical term for these statements is *declarations*. You can combine multiple declarations on a single line but you must include the type with each variable:

```
Dim Year as Integer, Rate As Currency, Name as String
```

Declaring the types of variables used in an event procedure before using them—and commenting as needed, of course—is a good programming habit. It can make your programs more readable since it is easy to skip over the single-character identifiers. Most people prefer the following to using the variables Years%, Rate@, and Currency@:


```
Sub btnCalculate_Click
  ' This procedure calculates mortgage interest
  Dim Years As Integer
  Dim Rate As Currency
  Dim Amount As Currency
.
End Sub
```

You can also say Dim Years%, Rate@, and so on if you prefer using a type identifier.

Note: If a variable is declared in a Dim statement, then trying to use variables with the same name but a different type identifier at the end of the variable will cause a "Duplicate definition" error when the program is run.

For example, if you use the statement Dim Count As Integer to declare the integer variable Count, then the variables Count$, Count!, Count#, and Count@ may not be used. Count% may be used, however, and is recognized by Visual Basic as just another way of denoting the variable Count.

Finally, to give a variable the variant data type, just use the Dim statement without any As clause or identifier:

```
Dim Foo     'makes Foo have the variant data type
```

You can also use

```
Dim Foo As Variant
```

which is preferable to many programmers since it makes it clear what type the variable has.

Note: Microsoft likes to use a prefix to identify the variable's type— for example, sName for a string variable. This convention makes for harder-to-read code so it's not used here.

Requiring Declaration of Variables

One of the most common bugs in programs is the misspelled variable name. Most versions of BASIC (and Visual Basic itself) allow you to create variables "on the fly" by merely using the variable name in your program. This is unlike such strongly typed languages as Pascal.

However, when you create variables on the fly, you can easily misspell a variable name, and a misspelled variable name will almost certainly yield a default value that causes your program to behave incorrectly. Such an error is among the most difficult to eradicate—because you need to find the misspelled variable name.

One way to avoid this problem is to force all variables to be declared. Then you will be notified if a variable name is spelled incorrectly in a procedure. The designers of Visual Basic give you this option but do not force you to use it.

To turn on this option, add the command Option Explicit in the declaration section for the form or code module. After Visual Basic processes this command, it will no longer allow you to use a variable unless you declare it first.

Note: You can also use the Environment page of the Options dialog box on the Tools menu to require variable declaration.

Scope of Variables

Programmers refer to the *scope* of variables when they want to talk about the availability of a variable used in one part of a program to the other parts of a program. In older programming languages, where *all* variables were available to *all* parts of the program, keeping variable names straight was always a problem. If, in a complicated program, you had two variables named Total, the values could—and would—contaminate each other. The solution in modern programming languages like Visual Basic is to isolate variables within procedures. Unless you specifically arrange it, changing the value of a variable named Total in one procedure will not affect another variable with the same name in another procedure. The technical explanation for this is that variables are *local* to procedures unless specified otherwise. In particular, an event procedure will not normally have access to the value of a variable in another event procedure.

As always, it is not a good programming practice to rely on defaults. If you want to be sure a variable is local within an event procedure, use the Dim statement inside the event procedure.

Sharing Values Across Procedures

Of course, occasionally you will want to share the values of variables across event procedures. For example, if an application is designed to perform a calculation involving one interest rate at a time, that rate should be available to all the procedures in a form. Variables that allow such sharing among all the code in a form are called, naturally enough, *form-level variables*. (You can also have true global variables when you have a multiform application—see the next chapter for more on these.)

You put the Dim statements for form-level variables in the Declarations section. For example, if you open the Code window, select (declarations) for the (general) object, and enter

```
Dim InterestRate As Currency
```

then the following is true:

- The value of the variable named InterestRate will be visible to all the procedures attached to the form.
- Any changes made to this variable in one event procedure will persist.

Obviously, the last point means you have to be careful when assigning values to form-level variables. Any information passed between event procedures is a breeding ground for programming bugs. Moreover, these errors are often hard to pinpoint.

Although most programmers don't think it is a good idea, you can use the same variable name as both a local and a form-level variable. Any Dim statements contained in a procedure take precedence over form-level declarations—they force a variable to be local. Therefore, you lose the ability to use the information contained in the form-level variable. Duplicating the names makes the form-level variable invisible to the procedure. Visual Basic doesn't tell you whether a form-level variable has been defined with the same name as a local variable.

Tip: Some programmers like to prefix form-level variables with the letter "f" (for example, fInterest) and global variables with the letter "g" (for example, gInterest). This makes it easier to tell at a glance what are form-level variables and what are global variables. See Chapter 5 for more on global variables.

Having Values Persist

When Visual Basic invokes an event procedure, the old values of local variables are wiped out. They go back to their default values. (As mentioned before, you are often better off if they are reinitialized.) Such variables are called *dynamic variables*. However, dynamic variables are not enough for all programming situations. For example, suppose you need to keep track of how many times a command button has been clicked. If the counter is always set back to zero, you're in trouble. You *could* have the values persist by using a form-level variable, but it is generally a good idea to reserve form-level variables only for sharing information. Most programmers choose this method only if other event procedures needed the count.

The solution is to use *static variables*. These variables are not reinitialized each time Visual Basic invokes a procedure. Besides being ideal for counters, they are ideal for making controls alternatively visible or invisible (or for switching between any Boolean properties, for that matter) and as a debugging tool.

To make a variable static within a procedure, replace the keyword **Dim** with the keyword **Static**:

```
Static Counter As Integer, IsVisible As Boolean
```

Here is an example of an event procedure for a command button that counts the clicks and displays the number:

```
Private Sub Command1_Click()
  'This procedure uses a static variable to count clicks
  Static Counter As Integer      ' Counter starts at 0
  Counter = Counter + 1
  Print Counter
End Sub
```

The first time you click, the counter starts out with its default value of zero. Visual Basic then adds 1 to it and prints the result. Notice that by placing the Print statement after the addition, you are not off by 1 in the count.

Occasionally, you want all local variables within a procedure to be static. To do this, add the keyword **Static** before the word "Sub" that starts any procedure:

```
Static Sub Command1_Click()
```


Strings

Since information in Visual Basic text boxes is always stored as text, strings are far more important in Visual Basic than in ordinary BASIC. To put two strings together (*concatenate* them), use a plus sign (+). For example, if

```
Title$ = "Queen "
Name$ = "Elizabeth "
Numeral$ = "I"
```

then

```
"Queen Elizabeth I" = Title$ + Name$ + Numeral$
"Queen Elizabeth II" = Title$ + Name$ + Numeral$ + Numeral$
```

The + joins strings in the order in which you present them. Thus, unlike when you add numbers together, order is important when you use the + sign to join two strings together. You can use the + sign to join together two strings before Visual Basic will make the assignment statement. Here is an example using the variables defined above:

CurrentQueen$ = Title$ + Name$ + Numeral$ + Numeral$

Tip: If you need to concatenate other Visual Basic data, use an ampersand (&) in place of the +. For example, C=A% & B$ concatenates an integer variable and a string variable by changing them both to variants. (You can also use the & for concatenating strings.)

ASCII/ANSI Code

A computer doesn't have one kind of memory for text and another for numbers. Anything stored in a computer's memory is changed into a number (actually, a binary representation of a number). The program keeps track of whether or not the memory patterns are codes for text. Usually, the code for translating text to numbers is called the ASCII code (American Standard Code for Information Interchange). The ASCII code associates with each number from 0 through 255 a displayable or control character, although Windows cannot display all 255 ASCII characters, using a more limited set of characters called the ANSI character set. The control characters and such special keys as TAB and line feed have numbers less than 32. The value of the function Chr$(*n*) is the string consisting of the character of ASCII value *n* in the current font. The statement

Print Chr$(*n*)

either displays the character numbered *n* in the ANSI sequence for that font or produces the specified effect that the control code will have on your screen—or both. For instance, the statement

Print Chr$(169)

prints the copyright symbol (©) on the screen if you are using the Courier font.

The following code uses the ASCII/ANSI value for the quotation mark, 34, to display a sentence surrounded with quotation marks.

```
Print Chr$(34);
Print "Quoth the raven, nevermore.";
Print Chr$(34)
```

The output of this command looks like this:

```
"Quoth the raven, nevermore."
```

The preceding output also can be produced by the statement

```
Print """Quoth the raven, nevermore.""";
```

since Visual Basic—unlike many other forms of DOS BASIC—treats " " " as the literal quotation mark inside Print statements.

Visual Basic has a function called *Asc* that takes a string expression and returns the ASCII/ANSI value of the first character. If the string is empty (the null string), using this function generates a run-time error.

As you'll see later in this chapter, ASCII/ANSI order is what Visual Basic uses by default to compare strings when you use relational operators like < or >. The most important use of the ASCII/ANSI codes is for the KeyPress event procedure, which also is covered in Chapter 5.

Note: Internally, the 32-bit version of Visual Basic uses a 2-byte Unicode for its characters. Except for handling binary files (see Chapter 9), using Unicode is transparent to the programmer.

Tip: It is much faster to build up the string first and then change the Text property once than to change the Text property repeatedly.

Fixed-Length Strings

A fixed-length string is a special type of string that plays an important role in Chapter 9. These variables are created with a Dim statement. Here is an example:

```
Dim ShortString As String * 10
```

This sets up a string variable (in spite of not using the identifier). However, this variable will always hold strings of length 10. If you assign a longer string to ShortString, as shown here,

```
ShortString = "antidisestablishment"
```

what you get is the same thing as

```
ShortString = "antidisest"
```

As you can see, the contents of the variable are changed because the right part of the string is cut off. Similarly, if you assign a shorter string to ShortString, like this,

```
ShortString = "a"
```

then you still get a string of length 10—only this time the variable is padded on the right.

Numbers

Numbers in Visual Basic cannot use commas to delineate thousands. They *can* use a decimal point, unless they are integers. If you need to give a numeric value to a variable, place the number on the right-hand side of the assignment statement. If you assign a number with a decimal point to an integer variable, it is automatically rounded off. If you assign a number larger than the limits for the given variable, Visual Basic gives you an error message at run time. Here are some examples:

Number	Acceptable Variable Type
3001	OK for all numeric variables
3000001	OK for all but short integer variables
30000.01	OK for all but integer variables (rounded off for them and long integer variables)
3,001	Illegal because it uses a comma

To change a string of digits to a number, use the built-in function Val:

Val("3001") = 3001

You will find the Val function essential in all your Visual Basic applications, because all input received from text boxes is in the form of strings (text). Unlike other forms of BASIC, Visual Basic does not provide a way to enter numbers directly.

The Val function reads through the string until it encounters a nonnumeric character (or a second period). The number you get from it is determined by where it stopped searching:

Val ("30Something") = 30

Similarly, you will want to change a number back to a string of digits when you want to display it in a text box. There are many ways to do this, depending on the form you want the number to take. The function Str is the simplest. It converts a number to a string but doesn't clean it up in any way. It also leaves a space in front of positive numbers.

To polish the display, the Str function is often replaced by the Format function. (See the Format item in the online help for more details.) The Format function is very versatile. Among its many features, this function lets you cut off extraneous digits and display a (large) number with commas or a leading dollar sign.

Note: Another possibility is storing information in the variant data type. If you assign a variable that holds numeric information currently stored in the variant data type to a numeric variable, then Visual Basic will perform the conversion automatically. However (unlike when you use the Val command, for example), you must be careful that the variable of the variant data type holds something with no extraneous characters or extra periods beyond the one allowed. Otherwise, an error message will appear. (Our feeling is that it is both sloppy programming and a breeding ground for bugs, if you rely on Visual Basic's built-in variant data type to do the conversion for you.)

Operations on Numbers

The following table gives you the symbols for the five fundamental arithmetic operations:

Operator	Operation
+	Addition
–	Subtraction (and to denote negative numbers)
/	Division
*	Multiplication
^	Exponentiation

For integers and long integers, there is one symbol and one keyword for the arithmetic operations unique to numbers of these types:

Operator	Operation
\	Integer division (this symbol is a backslash)
Mod	The remainder after integer division

The ordinary division symbol (/) gives you a value that is a single-precision, double-precision, or currency answer, depending on the objects involved. The backslash (\), on the other hand, throws away the remainder in order to give you an integer. For example, 7\3 = 2. Since a / gives either a single- or double-precision answer, use a \ or the Mod operator if you really want to work with integers or long integers.

The Mod operator is the other half of integer division. This operator gives you the remainder after integer division. For example, 7 Mod 3 = 1. When one integer perfectly divides another, there is no remainder, so the Mod operator gives zero: 8 Mod 4 = 0.

The usual term for a combination of numbers, variables, and operators from which Visual Basic can extract a value is a *numeric expression.*

Parentheses and Precedence

When you do calculations, you have two ways to indicate the order in which you want operations to occur. The first way is by using parentheses, and you may well prefer this method. Parentheses let you easily specify the order in which operations occur. Something like 3 + (4 * 5) gives 23 because Visual Basic does the operation within the parentheses (4 times 5) first and only then adds the 3. On the other hand, (3 + 4) * 5 gives 35 because Visual Basic adds the 4 and the 3 first to get 7 and only then multiplies by 5.

Visual Basic allows you to avoid parentheses, provided you carefully follow rules that determine the precedence of the mathematical operations.

The following list gives the order (hierarchy) of operations:

exponentiation (^)
negation (making a number negative)
multiplication and division
integer division
the remainder (Mod) function
addition and subtraction

Think of these as being levels. Operations on the same level are done from left to right, so 96 / 4 * 2 is 48. Because division and multiplication are on the same level, first the division is done, giving 24, and then the multiplication is done. On the other hand, 96 / 4 ^ 2 is 6. This is because the exponentiation is done first, yielding 16, and only then is the division done.

More on Numbers in Visual Basic

If you've tried any calculations involving large numbers in Visual Basic, you've probably discovered that it often doesn't bother printing out large numbers. Instead, it uses a variant on *scientific notation*. For example, if you ask Visual Basic to print a 1 followed by 25 zeros using a statement like Print 10 ^ 25, what you see is 1E+25.

If you are not familiar with this notation, think of the E+ as moving the decimal place to the right, and adding zeros if necessary. The number of places is exactly the number following the "E." If a negative number follows the "E," move the decimal point to the left. For example, 2.1E–5 gives you .000021. You can enter a number using the E notation if it's convenient; Visual Basic doesn't care whether you enter 1000, 1E3, or 1E+3. To make a number double precision, use a "D" instead of an "E."

If you assign the value of a single-precision variable to a double-precision variable, you do not suddenly increase its accuracy. The number may have more—or even different—digits, but only the first six or seven can be trusted. When you assign a value of one type to a variable of a different type, Visual Basic does a type conversion if it can. If it cannot figure out a way to do this that makes sense, it generates an error at run time.

When you use numbers in your program and do not assign them to a variable of the variant type, Visual Basic assumes the following:

- If a number has no decimal point and is in the range –32768 to 32767, it's an integer.
- If a number has no decimal point and is in the range for a long integer (–2,147,483,648 to 2,147,483,647), it's a long integer.
- If a number has a decimal point and is in the range for a single-precision number, it is assumed to be single precision.
- If a number has a decimal point and is outside the range for a single-precision number, it is assumed to be double precision.

These built-in assumptions occasionally lead to problems. This is because the realm in which an answer lives is determined by where the questions live. If you start out with two integers, Visual Basic assumes the answer is also an integer. For example, a statement like

```
Print 12345*6789
```

starts with two integers, so the answer is assumed to also be an integer. But the answer is too large for an integer, so you would get an overflow error. The solution is to add the appropriate identifier to at least one of the numbers. Use the statement

```
Print 12345&*6789
```

and Visual Basic treats both 12345 and the answer as long integers.

You can also use a built-in function to force a type conversion.

Conversion Function	What It Does
CBool	Makes an expression a Boolean
CByte	Makes an expression a byte
CInt	Makes a numeric expression an integer by rounding
CLng	Makes a numeric expression a long integer by rounding
CSng	Makes a numeric expression single precision
CDate	Makes a date expression a date
CDbl	Makes a numeric expression double precision
CCur	Makes a numeric expression of the currency type
CStr	Makes any expression a string
CVar	Makes any expression a variant

Numeric conversions will be performed only if the numbers you're trying to convert are in the range of the new type; otherwise, Visual Basic generates an error message. Using the numeric conversion functions has the same effect as assigning the numeric expression to a variable of the type specified.

Constants

A program is easiest to debug when it's readable. Try to prevent the MEGO ("my eyes glaze over") syndrome that is all too common when a program has lots of mysterious numbers sprinkled about. It's a lot easier to read a line of code like

```
Calculate.Visible = True
```

than one like

```
Calculate.Visible = -1
```

As mentioned before, Visual Basic has two constants built in for True and False to let you do this.

More generally, Visual Basic's *named constant* feature allows you to use mnemonic names for values that never change. Constants are declared just like variables, and the rules for their names are also the same: 40 characters, first character a letter, and then any combination of letters, underscores, and numerals. Our convention is to use all capitals for constants.

If you have only one form or want the constants visible to the event procedures for only one form, put them in the (declarations) section for the (general) object. You can also define a constant within a procedure, but this is less common, and only that procedure would have access to the constant.

You set up a constant by using the keyword **Const,** followed by the name of the constant, an equal sign, and then the value:

```
Const PIE = 3.14159
```

You can set up string constants:

```
Const LANGUAGE = "Visual Basic Version 4.0"
```

You can even use numeric expressions for constants—or define new constants in terms of previously defined constants:

```
Const PIEOVER2 = PIE/2
```


What you can't do is define a constant in terms of Visual Basic's built-in functions or the exponentiation operator. If you need the square root of ten in a program, you need to calculate it before you can write

```
Const SQUAREROOTOFTEN = 3.16227766
```

Visual Basic uses the simplest type it can for a constant, but you can override this by adding a type identifier to a constant. For example,

```
Const THISWILLBEALONGINTEGER& = 37
```

forces Visual Basic to treat the constant 37 as a long integer instead of an ordinary integer. (Constants are not affected by any definers you set up.) Even if you use a type identifier at the end of the constant when you define it, you don't need to use the identifier in the program. Using the preceding example, all subsequent occurrences of this constant can be

```
THISWILLBEALONGINTEGER
```

As mentioned, our convention is to use all caps for constants, but this is not required. Moreover, references to constants don't depend on the case.

Note: Visual Basic has built-in predefined global constants you can incorporate into your programs. They are usually given a prefix of vb (lowercase). For example, when you use the MsgBox function you can use built-in constants like vbOKOnly to get only an OK button. (Check the online help for these built-in constants. You can also use the Object Browser discussed in Chapter 6 to examine them.)

Another example of a useful built-in constant is vbCrLf which can be used to give you a new line when you place separate lines in a multi-line text box or add breaks between lines in a message box. (vbCrLf gives you the carriage return plus a line feed character automatically.)

Repeating Operations

Suppose you need to repeat an operation. In programming (as in real life), you may want to repeat the operation a fixed number of times, continue until you reach a specific predetermined goal, or continue until certain initial conditions have finally changed. In programming, the first situation is called a *determinate loop* and the latter two are called *indeterminate loops*. Visual Basic allows all three kinds of loops, so there are three different control structures in Visual Basic for repeating operations.

Determinate Loops

Suppose you want to print the numbers 1 to 10 on the current form inside an event procedure. The simplest way to do this is to place the following lines of code inside the procedure:

```
For I% = 1 To 10
  Print I%
Next I%
```

In the preceding example, the line with the **For** and **To** keywords is shorthand for "for every value of I% from 1 to 10." You can think of a For-Next loop as winding up a wheel inside the computer so the wheel will spin a fixed number of times. You can tell the computer what you want it to do during each spin of the wheel.

For and **Next** are keywords that must be used together. The statements between the **For** and the **Next** are usually called the *body* of the loop, and the whole control structure is called, naturally enough, a *For-Next loop*.

The keyword **For** sets up a counter variable. In the preceding example, the counter is an integer variable: I%. In this example, the starting value for the counter is set to 1. The ending value is set to 10. Visual Basic first sets the counter variable to the starting value. Then it checks whether the value for the counter is less than the ending value. If the value is greater than the ending value, nothing is done. If the starting value is less than the ending value, Visual Basic processes subsequent statements until it comes to the keyword **Next**. At that point it adds 1 to the counter variable and starts the process again. This process continues until the counter variable is larger than the ending value. At that point, the loop is finished, and Visual Basic moves past it.

Tip: Although you can use variables of any numeric type for the counters, choose integer variables whenever possible. This allows Visual Basic to spend as little time as possible on the arithmetic needed to change the counter and so speeds up the loop.

Finally, you may have noticed that the body of the For-Next loop is indented. As always, the purpose of the spacing in a program is to make the program more readable and therefore easier to debug. The designers of Visual Basic made it easy to consistently indent code. The Visual Basic editor remembers the indentation of the previous line, and every time you press ENTER, the cursor returns to the spot directly below where the previous line started. To move the cursor back, you can use the LEFT ARROW key. Or if you get into the habit of using the TAB key to start each level of indentation, you can use the SHIFT-TAB combination to move backward one tab stop. (If you've used the TAB key, you can undo the indentation pattern for a block that you've used by selecting the block of text and then pressing SHIFT-TAB.)

More on For-Next Loops

You don't always count by ones. Sometimes it's necessary to count by twos, by fractions, or backward. You do this by adding the **Step** keyword to a For-Next loop. The **Step** keyword tells Visual Basic to change the counter by the specified amount rather than by 1, as was done previously. For example, a space simulation program would not be complete without the inclusion, somewhere in the program, of the fragment

```
For I% = 10 To 1 Step -1
  Print "It's t minus"; I%; "and counting."
Next I%
Print "Blastoff!"
```

When you use a negative step, the body of the For-Next loop is bypassed if the starting value for the counter is smaller than the ending value.

Caution: Loops with fractional **Step** values will run more slowly than loops with integer **Step** values.

You can use any numeric type for the **Step** value.

Nested For-Next Loops

Suppose you want to allow not only a range of interest rates in a mortgage table but also a range of dollar amounts—say with horizontal scroll bars to move through the information. For each dollar amount, you want to run through an entire range of interest rates. This is a typical situation: You have an inner loop that does something interesting in a particular case, and you want to alter the situation to address a slightly different case. Placing one loop inside another is called *nesting* loops.

A fragment such as

```
For I% = 2 To 12
  Print 2*I%
Next I%
```

gives you the "twos table." To get an entire multiplication table, you need to enclose this loop with another one that changes the 2 to a 3, the 3 to a 4, and so on. The loop looks like this:

```
For J% = 2 To 12
  For I% = 2 To 12
    Print I%*J%,
  Next I%
  Print
Next J%
```

The rule for nesting For-Next loops is simple: the inner loop must be completed before the Next statement for the outer loop is encountered. You can have triply nested loops, quadruply nested loops, or even more. You are limited only by how well you understand the logic of the program, not by Visual Basic.

An Example: The Screen Object and Available Fonts

Another good example of a For-Next loop gives you a list of the fonts available to Windows. You can do this by using a simple For-Next loop to analyze a property of the *Screen object*. The Screen object is one that you will use frequently within Visual Basic. For example, it will let you manipulate forms by their placement on the screen. For our example you need two properties of the Screen object. The first is the FontCount property, which gives you the number of available fonts that the printer or screen has available:

```
NumberOfScreenFonts = Screen.FontCount
NumberOfPrinterFonts = Printer.FontCount
```

The second is the Fonts property. Screen.Fonts(0) is the first font for your display, Screen.Fonts(1) is the second, and so on, up to Screen.Fonts (Screen.FontCount –1), which is the last. All this information is determined by how Microsoft Windows was set up and by the hardware and software you have.

To run this program, create a new project with a blank form. Add the Click procedure given here, press F5, and then click anywhere in the form.


```
Sub Form_Click()
  Dim I As Integer

  Print "Here is a list of the fonts for your display."
  For I = 1 To Screen.FontCount - 1
    Font.Name = Screen.Fonts(I)
    Print "This is displayed in ";Screen.Fonts(I)
  Next I
End Sub
```

To report on the fonts that Windows can pull out of your printer, change the keyword **Screen** to the keyword **Printer**.

Indeterminate Loops

Loops often need to either keep on repeating an operation or not, depending on the results obtained within the loop. Such loops are indeterminate—that is, not executed a fixed number of times—by their very nature. You use the following pattern when you write this type of loop in Visual Basic:

Do
  Visual Basic statements
Until *condition is met*

A simple example of this is a password fragment in a Form_Load procedure that starts an application. If you compiled a project to a stand-alone program with a Form_Load procedure that looks like this,

```
Sub Form_Load()
'Password protection

  Do
    X$ = InputBox$("Password please?")
  Loop Until X$ = "Vanilla Orange"
End Sub
```

it would be more difficult for anyone who didn't know the password to use this program.

It's important to remember that the test for equality is strict: typing **VANILLA ORANGE** would not work, nor would typing **Vanilla orange**. Another point worth keeping in mind is that the test is done only at the end of the loop, when Visual Basic processes the Until statement.

When you write an indeterminate loop, something must change; otherwise the test will always fail and you'll be stuck in an infinite loop. To stop an infinite loop, you can use the CTRL+BREAK combination or choose Run|End or use the End tool on the toolbar.

The Relational Operators

Of course you will usually need ways to check for something besides equality. You do this by means of the *relational operators*. The relational operators are listed here.

Symbol	Checks (Tests For)
<>	Not equal to
<	Less than
<=	Less than or equal to
>	Greater than
>=	Greater than or equal to

For strings, these operators test for ANSI order. This means that "A" comes before "B," but "B" comes before "a" (and a space comes before any typewriter character). The string "aBCD" comes after the string "CDE" because uppercase letters come before lowercase letters. (The online help contains a complete ANSI table that you can find by using the Search button and looking for the ANSI character set.) The ANSI codes from 0 to 31 are for control combinations and include the BACKSPACE and ENTER keys.

Note: You can make all comparisons in the code attached to a form insensitive to case by putting the statement Option Compare Text in the Declarations section of the form. Use Option Compare Binary to return to the default method of comparing strings by ANSI order. The Option Compare Text uses an order determined by the country set when you install Windows.

The Do While Loop

Visual Basic has other kinds of loops. These loops consist of replacing the keyword **Until** with the keyword **While**. (Of course, you can always change a **Do Until** into a **Do While** by reversing the relational operator.) For example,

```
Do
Loop Until X$ <>""
```


is the same as

```
Do
Loop While X$ = ""
```

Do Loops with And, Or, Not

When you have to combine conditions in a loop you use the **Or**, **Not**, and **And** keywords. These three keywords work just like they do in English. You can continue a process as long as both conditions are True or stop it when one turns False. However, it becomes increasingly confusing to try to force a combination of the **And**, **Or**, and **Not** operators into loops that they don't seem to fit. For example, suppose you want to continue a process while a number is greater than zero and a text box is empty. It is much easier to say

```
Do While Number > 0 And Text1.Text = ""
```

than to say

```
Do Until Number <=0 Or Text1.Text <> ""
```

although they both mean the same thing.

Note: To preserve compatibility with interpreted BASIC, Visual Basic allows a variant on the Do While loop (that is, the test at the top): the While/Wend loop.

Making Decisions

At this point, all your programs can do is to decide whether or not to repeat a group of statements. They can't, as yet, change which statements are processed depending on what the program has already done or what it has just encountered. The next few sections take care of this. All the commands in these sections deal with turning an outline containing a phrase like

If *condition* Then *Do something else...*

into Visual Basic code. Visual Basic uses the If-Then statement in much the same way that you do in normal English. For example, to warn a user that a number must be positive, use a line like this:

```
If X < 0 Then MsgBox "Number must be positive!"
```

More generally, when Visual Basic encounters an If-Then statement, it checks the first clause (called, naturally enough, the If clause) and checks whether it's True. If that clause is True, the computer does whatever follows (called the Then clause). If the test fails, processing skips to the next statement.

The If-Then is also used to determine which button was pressed in a message box. To do this, assign the value of the MsgBox function to a variable and then use an If-Then to check the value. For example,

```
X% = MsgBox ("Yes/No?", vbYesNo)
If X% = vbYes Then Print "Yes button clicked."
```

Notice that you need to use parentheses when using MsgBox in this way. The online help gives the values needed to check for the other kinds of buttons. (Also see the section on Message Boxes and Input Boxes later in this chapter.)

You can also use the keywords **And**, **Or**, and **Not** in an If-Then. These let you check two conditions at once. For example, suppose you have to check if a number is between 0 and 9:

```
If Digit >=0 And Digit <= 9 Then Print "OK"
```

More often than not, you will want to process multiple statements if a condition is True or False. For this you need the most powerful form of the If-Then-Else, called the Block If-Then. This lets you process as many statements as you like in response to a True condition. The block If-Then looks like this:

If *thing to test* Then
 lots of statements
Else
 more statements
End If

Now, you do not put anything on the line following the keyword **Then**; press ENTER immediately after typing it. This bare "**Then**" is how Visual Basic knows it's beginning a block. The **Else** is optional; putting it there (again alone on a line) means that another block will follow, to be processed only if the If clause is False. However, whether the **Else** is there or not, the Block If must end with the keywords **End If.**

4

What Is It?

You can easily use If-Then to determine whether the user has entered a string in the form of a date or a number. The procedure depends on the variant data type combined with two Boolean functions (functions that return either True or False). For example, the built-in function IsDate tells you whether an expression can be converted to a date. Consider the following code that checks whether the contents of a text box are in the right form to be used as a date:

```
Dim DT     ' DT is a variant
DT = Text1.Text
If IsDate(DT) Then
  ' do whatever you want with the date
Else
  MsgBox "Please enter the text in the form of a date!"
End If
```

Similarly, you can use the IsNumeric function to determine whether a variable can be converted to a number. This gives you a quick way of checking for extraneous characters in a string of digits,

Finishing Up with the If-Then

You often need to continue testing within the confines of the original If-Then. This is done with the keywords

ElseIf-Then

For example:

```
If A = B Then
  Print A
ElseIf A < B Then
  Print A
  A = A + 2
ElseIf A > B Then
  Print B
  B = B + 2
End If
```

Now everything is tied together. And just like in the If-Then-Else, Visual Basic activates, at most, one clause. In particular, if A < B, then Visual Basic processes only the second clause. And when it is done with that, it bypasses any other ElseIfs that may be contained in the block; it goes immediately to the statement following the End If. (By the way, you could replace the final ElseIf with a simple Else—if you've eliminated all the other possibilities.)

A block If-Then can have as many ElseIfs as you like but only one Else (as the last clause). The limits are determined by how much you can process rather than what Visual Basic can do.

Combining the If-Then with Loops

Suppose you need to check that there is exactly one file with a .TXT extension in the current directory. To do this, you have to use the Dir$ function, but you need to allow two ways to leave the loop. Here is a fragment that does this:

```
NameOfFile$ = Dir$("*.TXT")
NumberOfFiles = 0
Do Until NameOfFile$ = "" Or NumberOfFiles > 1
  NumberOfFiles = NumberOfFiles + 1
  NameOfFile$ = Dir$
Loop
If NumberOfFiles = 0 Then Print "No Files Found"
If NumberOfFiles > 1 Then Print "Too Many Files"
```

Notice that Visual Basic enters the loop only if it finds an example of the file. You have to allow for the loop never being entered at all. Once the loop is entered, you have Visual Basic add 1 to the file count.

You can use the If-Then to give you a way to write a loop that "tests in the middle." For this, you combine the If-Then with a new command: the Exit Do. Whenever Visual Basic processes the Exit Do statement, it pops you out of the loop, directly to the statement following the keyword **Loop.**

More generally, Visual Basic allows you to set up a potentially infinite loop at any time; just omit the tests in a Do loop, leaving an unadorned Do at the top and an equally unadorned Loop at the bottom. Once you've done this, the loop will end only when Visual Basic processes an Exit Do statement. (During program development, you can always end the program prematurely from the Run menu, and you can also use the toolbar or CTRL+BREAK combination, of course.)

Note: There is a version of the Exit command for leaving a For-Next loop as well; in this case, it takes the form **Exit For**.

Select Case

Suppose you were designing a program to compute grades based on the average of four exams. If the average was 90 or higher, the person should get an A; 80 to 89, a B; and so on. This is such a common situation that Visual Basic has another control structure designed exactly for it. It's called the Select Case. To use this command, you start with something you want to test. For example, suppose you want to test if a character is a vowel. You could write

```
If Char$ = "A" Or Char$ ="a" Then Print "Vowel"
```

and so on.

Using the Select Case control structure, combined with the UCase$ command to turn the letter into uppercase, you can write

```
Select Case UCase$(Char$)
  Case  "A", "E", "I", "O", "U"
    Print "Vowel"
  Case  "Y"
    Print "Y is a problem - sorry"
End Select
```

The Select Case command makes it clear that a program has reached a point with many branches; multiple If-Thens do not. And the clearer a program is, the easier it is to debug.

What follows the keywords **Select Case** is a variable or expression, and what Visual Basic is going to do depends on the value of the variable or expression. The keyword **Case** is shorthand for "In the case that the variable (expression) is," and you usually follow it by a relational operator.

The keyword **To** allows you to give a range of values.

```
Case 90 To 99
  MsgBox("You get an A")
Case 80 To 89
   MsgBox("You get a B")
```

Finally, you can use a Case Else at the end of the Select Case statement to deal with all the remaining situations.

Working with Objects at Run Time

There are both objects and properties of objects that you must use code to work with—neither the properties nor the objects themselves are available via the Properties window. For example, if you wanted to find out what Windows is assuming for the height of the screen, you would look at the Height property of the Screen object—and the Screen object and its associate properties are available only at run time. Similarly, you can control a printer (through the Printer object) only at run time.

Note: It is possible to create instances of Visual Basic objects at run time. See Chapter 6 for more information on how to do this.

Methods

If you want your Visual Basic objects to actually do anything, you most often need to work with its built-in methods. For example, if you want to set the focus to a specific control at run time, you need to use the SetFocus method:

```
Command2.SetFocus
```

Since there are literally hundreds of methods, it would be impossible to cover them all. You must be prepared to work with the online help to see if a component has a method that does what you want. As with properties, your task is made easier by the fact that methods with the same name tend to work in similar ways. For example, the Move method applies to all visible controls and lets you move and resize the control any way you want.

The Font Properties in Code

Which fonts and font sizes you can use depends on what kind of hardware is available to the system in which you run the application. Visual Basic lets you find out this information by analyzing the Fonts property of the Screen or Printer objects.

To assign a font name in code, use the Name property of the Font object and place the name in quotation marks on the right-hand side of an assignment statement:

```
ObjectName.Font.Name = "Modern"
ObjectName.Font.Name = "Helv"                    'Helvetica
```

4

All objects that display text let you set these properties. These include forms, command buttons, labels, and text boxes. Of these, only forms (and picture boxes) let you combine different fonts. If you change these properties at run time for any other control, all the old text switches to the new font as well. The rule is that if text is specified by a property (like the Caption property for command buttons), changing a font changes the previous text. On the other hand, if you display text by using the Print method, the changes are not retroactive and therefore go into effect only for subsequent Print statements.

You can change all the font properties via code. Except for Font.Size, they are all Boolean properties (True or False). As with Font.Name, any control that displays text lets you set these properties of the Font object. For example:

```
ObjectName.Font.Size = 18              '18 point type
ObjectName.Font.Bold = True
ObjectName.Font.Italic = True
ObjectName.Font.Strikethru = False
ObjectName.Font.Underline = False
```

As with changing fonts, only forms (and picture boxes) let you mix these font properties.

Forms, Picture Boxes, and the Printer have one other font property you may occasionally find useful: FontTransparent. If you set this to True, background graphics and background text will show through the text displayed in the transparent font.

These properties can be combined in almost any way you want. If your hardware and software support it, you can have 18-point bold italic script type in a control if that seems appropriate.

Visual Basic 3 Tip: Visual Basic 4 still supports the older font properties such as FontBold, FontSize, and so on, although Microsoft suggests replacing them with the equivalent properties of the Font object.

Message Boxes and Input Boxes

Using special-purpose message boxes for displaying information is quite common in a Windows application. You have already seen that the most basic mechanism for doing this in Visual Basic is the version of the MsgBox function whose syntax is MsgBox(*string*). Unfortunately, all this version of the MsgBox function does is display a box with the string and an OK button. (The name of your application's executable file is the caption of the message box.)

Note: All message boxes are modal. This means they must be closed before the application will continue.

Getting more information to the user—for example giving the user buttons to click on to provide information to the program—is also possible with a message box. However, before we look at the general syntax for dealing with this message box, look at the following code snippet:

```
If MsgBox('Do you really want to terminate the program?',_
vbYesNo+vbExclamation) = vbYes then End
```

As you might expect, this presents the user with a box that looks like this:

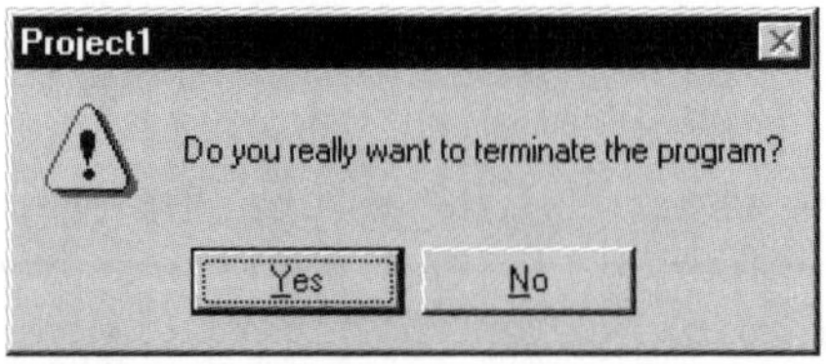

Notice the Yes and No buttons. When the user clicks a button, Visual Basic returns a value that depends on the button. In our example, if the user clicks on the Yes button, Visual Basic would return the value given by the built-in constant vbYes. If he or she clicked on the No button, the function would have the value vbNo. We then test to see what the value is by checking if it is equal to the constant vbYes. If it is we terminate the application.

ReturnValue = MsgBox(*prompt* [, *buttons*] [, *title*] [, *helpfile*] [, *context*])

Since this is pretty typical of an online help entry, let's spend a little time going over the various pieces. First, the information passed to a function in Visual Basic is usually called a *parameter*. (You'll learn a lot more about parameters in Chapter 5.) Optional parameters are indicated by enclosing them in square brackets. In this case only the prompt parameter is required. If you use an optional parameter, you must separate it by commas. If you skip a parameter, you must still use the extra comma.

Note: In certain cases, including the MsgBox function, you can use what are called named arguments to avoid dealing with the commas for optional arguments. See the next chapter for more on named arguments.

Here are short discussions of the parameters for the MsgBox function.

Prompt Parameter This is a string or string expression that Visual Basic displays as the text in the message box. Since it is a string, it is limited to 1024 characters. You can use the carriage return/line feed combination to separate lines if necessary.

Buttons Parameter This determines the type of message box that appears. There are three different groups of symbolic constants that you can combine. (They are separated by blank lines in the following table.)

Symbolic Constant	Value	Result
vbOKOnly	0	Displays OK button only
vbOKCancel	1	Displays OK and Cancel buttons
vbAbortRetryIgnore	2	Displays Abort, Retry, and Ignore buttons
vbYesNoCancel	3	Displays Yes, No, and Cancel buttons
vbYesNo	4	Displays Yes and No buttons.
vbRetryCancel	5	Displays Retry and Cancel buttons

Symbolic Constant	Value	Result
vbCritical	16	Displays Critical Message icon
vbQuestion	32	Displays Warning Query icon
vbExclamation	48	Displays Warning Message icon
vbInformation	64	Displays Information Message icon
vbDefaultButton1	0	Makes the first button the default
vbDefaultButton2	256	Makes the second button the default
vbDefaultButton3	512	Makes the third button the default

You can control the appearance of the message box by adding at most one value from each group. For example, if you set the Button parameter to vbOKCancel + vbCritical + vbDefaultButton2, you get a message box that looks like the following. (Notice how the focus is on the second "Cancel" button.)

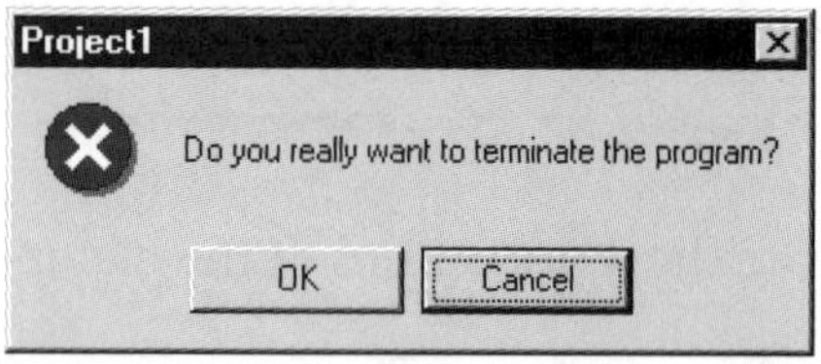

In general the first group of values describes the number and type of buttons, the second group gives the icon used in the message box, and the third group determines which button is the default.

Note: If the MsgBox has a Cancel button, when the user presses the ESC key, this will have the same effect as clicking on the Cancel button.

Finally, there is a fourth group of values for the Button parameter that controls the modality of the message box. The default is that the message box is "application modal." This means the user cannot resume working with that application until he or she closes the box. If you add 4096 (or the symbolic constant vbSystemModal) to the value of the Button parameter, the user will not be able to switch to *any* other application.

Note: When you specify both the helpfile and help context ID, the user can press F1 to see the Help topic corresponding to the context.

Title This parameter is a string expression that you want displayed in the title bar of the dialog box. (If you omit this parameter, Visual Basic uses the application name.)

HelpFile This is a string expression that identifies the Help file for context-sensitive help for the dialog box. (See Chapter 12 for more on Help files.)

Context This is the Help Context ID number (again see Chapter 12).

Values Returned from a MsgBox

The following table summarizes the return values from the message box. You simply have to test for equality with the appropriate symbolic constant.

Symbolic Constant	Value	Button Chosen
vbOK	1	OK
vbCancel	2	Cancel
vbAbort	3	Abort
vbRetry	4	Retry
vbIgnore	5	Ignore
vbYes	6	Yes
vbNo	7	No

Input Boxes

Text boxes are the normal way for a Visual Basic application to accept data. (For those who know ordinary BASIC, there is no direct analog of the Input statement.) There is one other method that is occasionally useful. The InputBox function displays a modal dialog box on the screen. This is the principal advantage of input boxes; it is sometimes necessary to insist that a user supply some necessary data before letting him or her move on in the application. The disadvantages are that the dimensions of the input box are fixed beforehand and that you lose the flexibility that text boxes provide. Here is an example of an input box:

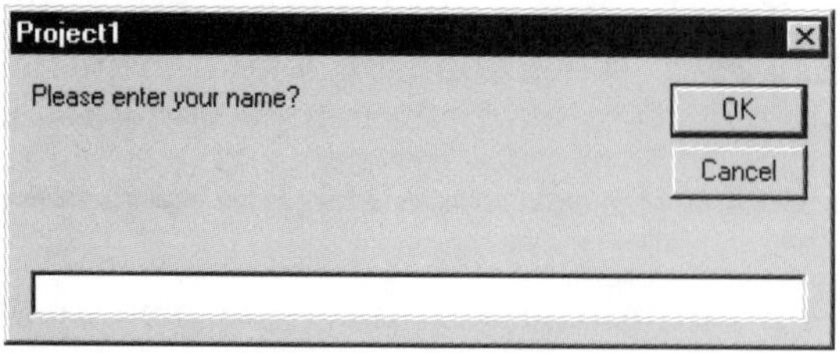

As you can see, input boxes have a title bar and four components, three of which are controls. The first is the prompt, "Please enter your name?" There are always two command buttons labeled OK and Cancel. Finally, there is a text box at the bottom. Visual Basic always places the focus here when it processes a statement containing an InputBox function. The simplest syntax for the InputBox function is

```
StringVariable = InputBox( prompt$)
```

where the prompt is a string or string variable. This gives a dialog box that is roughly centered horizontally and one-third of the way down the screen.

Now the user types whatever he or she wants in the text box. Pressing ENTER or clicking the OK button causes whatever is in the text box to become the value of the string variable. Pressing ESC or clicking the Cancel box causes Visual Basic to assign the null string to the variable. The full syntax for the InputBox function is

InputBox(prompt [, *title*][, *default*][, *xpos*][, *ypos*][, *helpfile, context*])

Here are short descriptions of these items.

prompt	The prompt parameter is a string or string variable whose value Visual Basic displays in the dialog box. It is limited to roughly 255 characters. The prompt doesn't wrap, and you have to explicitly add line separators.
title	The title parameter is optional and gives the caption used in the title bar. There is no default value; if you leave this out, nothing is displayed in the title bar.
default	The default parameter is also optional. It lets you display default text in the Edit box, where the user will be entering information.
xpos,ypos	This parameter is also optional. Both *xpos* and *ypos* are integral numeric expressions: *xpos* is the distance in twips between the left edge of the input box and the left edge of the screen, and *ypos* is the distance in twips between the top of the box and the top of the screen.

helpfile	The helpfile parameter is also optional. It is a string value to identify the help file to use. If a helpfile parameter is specified, then the context parameter must also be specified.
context	The context parameter is a numeric expression that is the help context ID number assigned to a help topic. If context is specified, then the helpfile parameter must also be specified.

Projects with Multiple Forms

As your applications grow more complicated, you won't want to restrict yourself to applications that are contained in only a single form. Multiple forms will add flexibility and power to your applications. This is over and above solving the problems you've already seen with controls blocking out text that you've printed to a form. To add additional forms to an application you're designing, choose Insert|Form.

The Project window lists all the forms by name with an .FRM extension. Visual Basic stores each form as a separate file and uses the .VBP file to keep track of where they are stored. The new form is placed by default in the center of the screen—usually blocking out the original form. As you can imagine, when you are customizing more than one form at design time, the screen begins to get cluttered.

Tip: The easiest way to bring a form to the foreground so you can work with it is to open the Project window and double-click the form name or select the form by name and click the View Form button.

Writing Code for Multiple Forms

Although forms do not have a control name that you use for writing code for event procedures, they do have a Name property that you can use to refer to other properties of the form. Setting this property to something meaningful via the Properties window makes it easier to refer to the different properties or apply a method to the form. The default value for this property starts at Form1 for the first form, Form2 for the second, and so on. Using the default value means you have to refer to properties when you code, like this:

```
Form3.Height = Screen.Height/2    'cut the default height in 2
```

If Form3 was your "Help Form," for example, the code will be a lot easier to read if you set the form name to HelpForm and write

```
HelpForm.Height = Screen.Height/2  'set height to half normal
```

or using Microsoft's convention:

```
frmHelp.Height = Screen.Height/2
```

Form names are used only in code to refer to properties and methods; they are not used for event procedures. For example, to apply the Cls (clear screen method) to the preceding form, you would write

```
frmHelp.Cls
```

On the other hand, regardless of how you name a form, the Click procedure template for the form itself will always look like this in the Code window:

```
Private Sub Form_Click ()

End Sub
```

This will rarely cause problems since event procedures for a form are attached to the form.

Although you do not need the form name to refer to properties of the current form, using the form name sometimes makes your code cleaner. This is because code for one form can affect controls on another form. Suppose your HelpForm had a Quit button you wanted to disable via code within an event procedure attached to a different form. It is safer (and clearer) to write

```
frmHelp.Quit.Enabled = False
```

even in event procedures attached to the frmHelp than to use

```
Quit.Enabled = False
```

although both have the same effect. The general syntax is

FormName.ControlName.Property = Value

where a period separates the form name from the control. (You can also use the exclamation point as in Visual Basic 3.0, although Microsoft discourages this because it may not be allowed in future versions of Visual Basic.)

Finally, global constants are available to all the code attached to the project.

How to Handle Multiple Forms at Run Time

Visual Basic displays at most one form when an application starts running. This is called the *startup form.* Any other forms in your application must be explicitly loaded and displayed via code. The startup form is usually the initial form that appears when you begin a new project. If you want to change this, choose Tools|Options and then go to the Project page. All you need to do now is select the form (by name) that you want to be the startup form by clicking on the down arrow in the Startup Form drop-down list box and choosing the form you want.

The four keywords to handle forms are described here.

Show The **Show** keyword shows the form on the screen. To do this, Visual Basic first checks that the form is loaded into memory. If it is not, then it loads the form first. The basic syntax for the Show method is

FormName.Show

The Show method also moves the form to the top of the desktop if it was covered by another form. **Show** can also be used in the FormLoad event of any form to display information without needing to set Auto Redraw to True.

Load The **Load** keyword places the form into memory but does not display it. Visual Basic also loads the form into memory whenever you refer to its properties or controls in code. Because of this, the main reason to load a form prior to showing it is to speed up response time. The trade-off is that you use up more memory. Its syntax is

Load *FormName*

When Visual Basic loads a form, it sets all the properties of the form to the ones you initially made at design time and invokes the Form_Load event procedure.

Hide The **Hide** keyword removes the form from the screen but doesn't unload it from memory. The controls are not available to the user, but you can still refer to them in code. The values of the form-level variables do not disappear. As with loading a form, hiding a form trades response time for memory. The syntax is

FormName.Hide

Unload The Unload removes the form from memory. All information contained in its form-level variables is lost. The syntax for this command is

Unload *FormName*

Tip: When a form is unloaded, Visual Basic generates the QueryUnload event. This event procedure is a good place to put code you want to be activated at the end of the useful life of the form—for example, when the user chooses Close from the control box or the ALT+F4 combination.

Keeping the Focus in a Form (Modality)

Message boxes require that users close them before they can work with a form. This property is often useful for a form as well. For example, you may want to make sure a user has digested the information contained in a form before he or she shifts the focus to another form in the application. This property is called *modality* in the Microsoft Windows documentation. You make a form modal by adding an option to the Show method that displays the form. If you have a line of code in a procedure that reads

```
FormName.Show vbModal
```

then Visual Basic displays the form rigidly. No user input to any other form in the application will be accepted until the modal form is hidden or unloaded. Once a form is shown by using the modal setting, a user cannot move the focus to any other form until the modal form is hidden or unloaded. In particular, neither mouse clicks nor keypresses will register in any other form. Usually you have a default command or cancel button on a modal form.

Tip: A dialog box is usually a modal form with a fixed double border.

Forms default to be nonmodal, but you can also use the following code to force them to be nonmodal:

```
FormName.Show vbNormal
```

Displaying Information

Since you now know how to add other blank forms to your applications, you are in a better position to display information in an application. This is because controls on a form can obscure any information Visual Basic displays by using the Print method. The general syntax for the Print method applied to a form is

FormName.Print *expressions to print*

Where Visual Basic displays the information depends on the current value of two properties of a form, called *CurrentX* and *CurrentY*. CurrentX refers to the horizontal position, and CurrentY to the vertical position, where it will display information. The units used are determined by the scale set up with the various scale methods you saw in Chapter 3.

Note: You can print to a PictureBox in exactly the same way as you print to a form.

Whenever you use the Cls method to clear a form or picture box, Visual Basic resets the CurrentX and CurrentY values to zero. Using the default setting for the various scale properties would mean that the next Print statement puts information in the top left-hand corner of the form or picture box. If you have changed the scale (for example, by using the ScaleLeft and ScaleTop properties), Visual Basic will use whatever location on the form is now represented 0,0.

You set the CurrentX and CurrentY properties the same way you'd set any property:

FormName.CurrentX = *Value*
FormName.CurrentY = *Value*
Picture1.CurrentX = *Value*

The value may be any numeric expression from which Visual Basic can extract a single-precision value.

Note: Many Visual Basic programmers prefer to use picture boxes for general printing and text and labels for text printing instead of printing directly to a form. If you have the Professional Edition, the RichTextBox control is a great choice for 32-bit applications as well.

Positioning text

Normally, after Visual Basic processes a statement involving the Print method, it moves to the next line. You also use an empty Print statement to add a blank line. If you want to suppress the automatic carriage return, place a semicolon at the end of the statement. Each time you use a comma in a Print method (statement), Visual Basic displays the data to the next print zone (set to be the width of 14 average characters apart).

The Tab function lets you move to a specific column and start printing there. The Tab function also uses the average size of a character in the current font to determine where the columns are. Its syntax is

Print Tab(*ColumnNumber%*);

ColumnNumber% is an integral expression. If the current column position is greater than its value, Tab skips to this column on the next line. If the value is less than 1, Visual Basic moves to the first column. In theory, you can have values as large as 32,767 for the column. But since Visual Basic doesn't wrap around to the next line, you wouldn't really want to do this.

The Spc function has a similar syntax to the Tab function:

Spc(*Integer%*)

This function inserts the specified number of spaces into a line starting at the current print position.

However, unless you are using a nonproportional font, you are better off using the CurrentX and CurrentY properties than the Tab or Spc commands to position text. The keys to using CurrentX and CurrentY effectively are the TextHeight and TextWidth properties, which let you determine the width and height of the text before setting the CurrentX and CurrentY properties.

Note: To position text inside a multiline text box, you need to insert spaces and newline characters. Text boxes do not support direct positioning of text.

The Printer Object

Visual Basic uses the printer you set up when you installed Microsoft Windows. Visual Basic makes it easy to use whatever resolution, font properties, and so on, that the printer driver in Windows can coax from the printer.

First, the PrintForm command sends a screen dump of a form to the printer. If your application has more than one form, you have to use the form name in this command:

FormName.PrintForm

Because this command does a bit-by-bit dump of the whole form (including captions and borders), it lacks flexibility. Moreover, most printers have higher resolution than the screen.

Most of the printer commands in Visual Basic are *page oriented*. This means that Visual Basic calculates all the characters (actually dots) that will appear on a page before it sends the information to the printer. This allows you to have complete control over the appearance of the printed page.

The usual way to send information to a printer is the Print method applied to the Printer object. For example, because the Print method is page oriented, you can set the CurrentX and CurrentY properties to precisely position text or even dots on a page.

The syntax used to send text to the printer is similar:

Printer.Print *text*

Semicolons and commas also work the same way they did for forms.

You control the font properties in the same fashion. For example:

```
Printer.Font.Name = "Script"              'Use script font
Printer.Font.Size = 18                    '18 point type
```

As with printing to forms, font changes are not retroactive. They affect only text printed after Visual Basic processes the change.

Useful Properties and Methods for the Printer

If you check the online help, you'll see that there are 40 properties and 12 methods for the Printer object. Most of the ones that are unfamiliar to you, such as DrawMode, apply to Graphics (see Chapter 11). The vast majority, however, should be familiar to you since you've seen them for forms. What follows are short descriptions of some printer properties and methods you will use most often. (Check the online help for the printer properties we don't cover here.)

ColorMode This property lets you determine whether a color printer prints in color or monochrome.

Copies This property lets you set the number of copies to be printed.

Height, Width These properties give you the height and width of the paper in the printer as reported by Windows. This is measured in twips, regardless of how you set the scale properties. You obviously can't change these at run time; they are *read-only* properties. One example of how you might use these properties is to make sure that someone has switched to wider paper before printing something that would not fit on the usual 8 1/2 ×11-inch paper. (For 8 1/2 × 11-inch paper, Visual Basic reports an available width of 12,288 twips and an available height of 15,744 twips.)

EndDoc This method tells Windows that a document is finished. The syntax is

Printer.EndDoc

This releases whatever information there is about the page or pages still in memory and sends it to the Microsoft Windows print manager for printing.

NewPage This method ends the current page and tells the printer to move to the next page. The syntax is

Printer.NewPage

Page This property keeps track of the number of pages printed in the current document. The counter starts over at 1 after Visual Basic processes a statement with EndDoc. It increases by 1 every time you use the NewPage method or when the information you send to the printer with the Print method didn't fit on the previous page. A common use of this property is to print a header at the top of each page.

PrintQuality This is used to set the quality of the printed output—if the printer driver supports it. The syntax is

Printer.PrintQuality = *value*

where you can use four built-in constants ranging from vbPRPQDraft or vbPRPQHigh. You can also set the value to the number of dots per inch if the printer (and its driver) supports this.

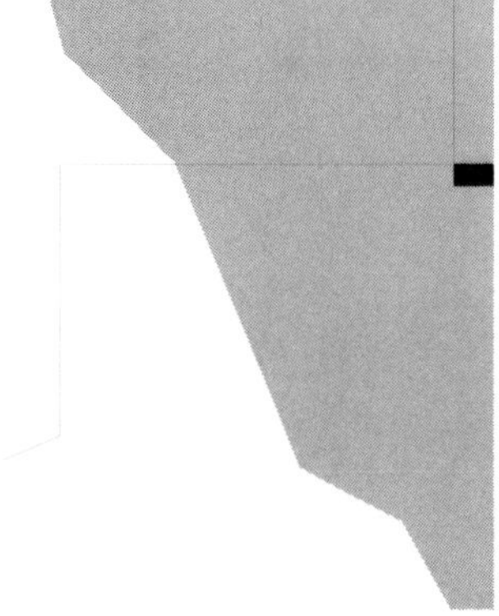

Chapter 5

Advanced Programming Techniques

The last chapter showed you the essentials of Visual Basic's built-in programming language. This chapter takes you further along the road to mastering it. First, you will learn how to handle arrays. Then there's a bit more discussion of the variant data type and how to extend Visual Basic's built-in types by constructing your own types. Next is a short treatment of one way to mimic pointers via arrays. (Visual Basic doesn't support true pointers—unfortunately). Then there's a brief look at Visual Basic's built-in functions and procedures. Following that, there's a section on writing your own functions and procedures. The chapter concludes with a bit more discussion of the anatomy of a project. For example, you'll see how to add modules for code alone and true global (Public) code to a project. After that, there is a short discussion of how to use the functions built into Windows, how to call functions from external libraries that you may have written in languages like C, and what you need to know to more efficiently use Visual

Basic's compiler when you generate stand-alone programs. The last section explains the (infamous) GoTo.

Arrays

To Visual Basic, a list (often called a *one-dimensional array*) is just a collection of variables, each one of which is identified by two things:

- The name of the list
- The position of the item in the list

In Visual Basic the name of a list must follow the rules for variable names. For an item in the list, the notation is simply the name of the list followed by a number in parentheses that indicates the position. For example, the third errand on an errand list might be stored as Errand(3).

Lists can't be open ended in Visual Basic. While the limits are quite large, you must tell Visual Basic how much memory to set aside for the list before you use it. There are two kinds of lists in Visual Basic: fixed lists, where the memory allocation never changes; and dynamic lists, where you can change size on the fly. The advantage of a fixed list is that memory is set aside at the beginning of the program; you run a much smaller risk of running out of memory while the program is running. The advantage of dynamic lists is the flexibility they give. You can change the size in response to what the program has encountered.

Both kinds of lists may be made visible to the whole application, to a specific form or module, or only within an event procedure. To set up a fixed list in the form that will be available to all the procedures in the form, place a statement like

```
Dim Errand(13) As String
```

in the Declarations section of the form. This actually sets up a 14-element list for strings visible to every procedure on that form. The items would be stored in Errand(0) through Errand(13).

To set up a dynamic list in a form, place a statement like

```
Dim Errand() As String
```

in the Declarations section of the form or module. You then use the ReDim statement inside a procedure to allocate the space:

```
Sub NameOfProcedure()
..Dim Number As Integer

' set the value of Number
  ReDim Errand(Number) As String
End Sub
```

Each time Visual Basic processes a ReDim statement, the information in the array is lost.

Note: You can also use the ReDim statement in a procedure without needing a Dim statement in the Declarations section of the form or module first. In this case, space is allocated for that list only while the procedure is active; it disappears as soon as the procedure is exited.

A variation of the ReDim statement can be used to increase the size of a dynamic list while retaining any information already stored in the list. The statement

```
ReDim Preserve Errand(NewSize) As String
```

can be placed in a procedure to increase the number of entries in the array Errand( ) to NewSize + 1 without losing data already stored in the list.

Finally, you can set up a local fixed array inside a procedure by using the **Static** keyword. As with static variables, the information you store in a list defined by static dimensioning remains intact. You cannot use a variable inside the parentheses when you do static dimensioning.

Lists with Index Ranges

Some people never use the entry numbered 0 of a list; they just find it confusing. (And if you are not going to use it in a program, it certainly wastes space.) For this reason, Visual Basic, to keep compatibility with interpreted BASICs, has a command that eliminates the entry numbered 0 in all lists dimensioned in the module or form. It is the Option Base 1 statement. This statement is used in the Declarations section of a form (or Standard module) and affects all lists in the module. All new lists dimensioned in that form or module now begin with item 1. After Option Base 1, Dim Errand(30) sets aside 30 spots rather than 31.

As usual, Visual Basic goes one step beyond interpreted BASICs. Suppose you want to write the input routine for a bar graph program for sales in the years 1980 through 1995. You could write something like

```
Static SalesInYear(15) As Single
For I = 0 To 15
  Sales$=InputBox("Enter the sales in year "+ (1980 + I))
  SalesInYear(I) = Val(Sales$)
Next I
```

However, this code requires 15 additions (one for each pass through the loop). The trick is to use the keyword **To** to define the list, as in the following:

```
Dim SalesInYears(1980 To 1995)
```

and then change the code in the above example in the obvious way.

In general, the keyword **To** marks the range, smaller number first (from 1980 to 1995, in this case), for this way of declaring an array. You can use the **To** keyword with any statement that declares an array (Dim, ReDim, Static, Private, ReDim Preserve, and so on).

Arrays with More Than One Dimension

You can also have arrays with more than one dimension; they're usually called multidimensional arrays. Just as lists of data lead to a single subscript (one-dimensional arrays), tables of data lead to double subscripts (two-dimensional arrays). For example, suppose you want to store a multiplication table in memory—as a table. You could do this as:

```
Static MultTable(1 To 12,1 To 12) As Integer
Dim I As Integer, J As Integer
For I = 1 To 12
  For J = 1 To 12
    MultTable(I, J) = I*J
  Next J
Next I
```

Visual Basic allows you up to 60 dimensions with the Dim statement and 8 with the ReDim statement.

Tip: Although you normally use a For-Next loop to iterate through the elements in a list or array, you can also use the For Each construct whose syntax takes the form:

```
For Each element In the array
    statements]
    [Exit For]
    [statements]
Next [element]
```

The Erase Statement

As your programs grow longer, the possibility that you'll run out of space increases, although, given Visual Basic's rather large limits and Windows 95 memory management, it's never very likely. In particular, arrays do not take up space in the 64K data segment used for each individual form data. Only four bytes are used out of this 64K segment for each array!

Visual Basic allows you to reclaim the space used by a dynamically dimensioned array. You do this with the Erase command. For example,

```
Erase Errands
```


would erase the Errands array and free up the space it occupied.

If an array was not dimensioned dynamically (that is, was not dimensioned using the ReDim statement inside a procedure), then the Erase command simply resets all the entries back to zero for numeric lists (and to the null string for string lists or to null for variants). Using the Erase command on a fixed (static) list gives a fast method to "zero out" the entries. (It sets them to the null string for string arrays.)

Assigning Arrays to Variants: The Array Function

Occasionally you will want to store an array in a variant. It is a little less than elegant to do this, but since you can't assign one array to another, this technique can sometimes be very useful. For instance, it gives you a very quick way to swap the contents of two arrays, as the following example shows:

```
Dim I As Integer
ReDim A(1 To 20000) As Long
ReDim B(1 To 20000)
For I = 1 To 20000
  A(I) = I
  B(I) = 2 * I
Next I
Dim Array1 As Variant, Array2 As Variant, Temp As Variant
Array1 = A(): Erase A()
Array2 = B(): Erase B()
Temp = Array1
Array1 = Array2
Array2 = Temp
```

At this point the variants Array1 and Array2 contain the original arrays in reverse order, and the memory for the original arrays has been reclaimed. Since momentarily you have two objects instead of one, this technique can be a bit memory-hungry. On the other hand, if you need to swap two arrays, this is a whole lot faster than copying the 20,000 entries one by one!

Note: If you store an array in a variant, use the ordinary index to get at it. For example, after you run the above, Array1(5) would have the value 10.

Occasionally you need to create an array in a variant directly. For this you use the Array function whose syntax is

Array(*arglist*)

where the *arglist* argument consists of an arbitrary list of items separated by commas.

Types Revisited

Since variant variables make it easy to avoid dealing with explicit variable types, some programmers, reveling in their freedom from strongly typed languages, are tempted to use them for everything. It's important to note that most experienced Visual Basic programmers feel this should be avoided. Using variant variables when their special properties are not needed often exacts a performance penalty and will occasionally lead to subtle bugs. It is far better for the programmer to be in control of the type of his or her variables and than the compiler!

This having been said, there are, of course, times when variants are useful. You saw above how they can be used with arrays to quickly swap the contents of two arrays. As another example, the built-in IsDate and IsNumeric functions let you check if data stored in a variant can be safely converted to a date or a number. This makes it easier to evaluate whether the data a user enters is of the correct form. For example:

```
Dim Foo As Variant
Foo = Text1.Text
If Not(IsNumeric(Foo)) Then
  Text1.Text = ""
  MsgBox "Please enter a number!"
End If
```

Tip: Using the VarType function (see the online help) combined with an If-Then gives you a way to go beyond the built-in IsDate and IsNumeric functions to build your own IsCurrency function, IsBoolean functions, and so on. (Variants can hold any Standard data type except fixed-length strings.)

There are four special variant values: Empty, Error, Nothing, and Null. *Empty* means the variant variable hasn't been initialized. (Thus a variant containing Empty is 0 if it is used in a numeric expression, and a zero-length string ("") if it is used in a string expression.) *Null,* on the other hand, requires initialization:


```
Dim Foo As Variant
Foo = Null
```

Null is used to indicate that the variable contains no valid data; as such, it is extremely useful in working with databases. *Nothing* is used with objects (see the next chapter), while *Error* is used when you want to indicate that an error condition has occurred but you do not want to use Visual Basic error-trapping facilities (see Chapter 7) to work with it (for example, because you want to handle this error directly).

User-Defined Types (Records)

Suppose you want to have a three-dimensional array for 100 employees in a company. The first column is to be for names, the second for salaries, and the third for social security numbers. This common situation can't be programmed in a multidimensional array except by using the variant data type. The problem is that variants use more memory and are slower as well. For both speed and memory reasons, you might prefer to set up three parallel lists—the first for the names, the second for salaries, and the third for social security numbers (they're being stored as strings to include the dashes), as shown here:

```
Dim Names$(100), Salary!(100), SocSec$(100)
```

Having done this, you now would use the same pointer (that is, the row number) to extract information from the three lists. The way around this extra work is to use a new structure called a user-defined *type* or a *record*. Essentially, a record is a type of "mixed" variable that you create as needed. It usually mixes different kinds of numbers and strings. Visual Basic makes it easy to avoid maintaining parallel structures or using arrays of variants.

Here's the first step: in the Declarations section of the form, enter

```
Type  VitalInfo
    Name As String
    Salary As Long
    SocialSecNumber as String
End Type
```

This defines the type. Each of the different parts of the record is called a *field*. From this point on in the program, VitalInfo is just as good a variable type for variables as single-precision, double-precision, variants, and so on.

Now, to make (set up) a variable of "type" VitalInfo, all you have to do is declare it using Dim, Private, Static ReDim, and so on.

```
Dim YourName as VitalInfo
Static YourFriend As VitalInfo
ReDim MyNames(1 To 100) As VitalInfo  'for an array of 100 records
```

To fill the type, you assign values to the various fields using the (.) you have seen for properties:

```
YourName.Name = "Howard"
YourName.Salary = 100000
YourName.SocSecNumber = "036-78-9987"
```

The With Statement

You can use the With statement as a convenient method for quickly getting at the parts of a record. For example,

```
With YourName
  .Name = "Howard"
  .Salary = 100000
  .SocSecNumber = "036-78-9987"
End With
```

lets you avoid some typing and is more efficient.

Tip: You can also use the With statement with properties of objects. For example:

```
With txtBox
  .Height = 2000
  .Width = 2000
  .Text = "This is a text box"
End With
```

Pointers

Well, there aren't any—so the question is how to imitate them if you need to create data structures like linked lists or trees that use them. There is no perfect solution because you will need to go through some contortions to dispose of the memory allocated.

This having been said, the only way to create analogues to pointers in Visual Basic is to create an array of records and use one or more of the fields in the record to hold the row of the next item. You need to keep on using ReDim Preserve to build up the object and assign the memory. For example, if you wanted to create a binary tree:

```
Type DataInBinaryTree
  Data As String
  LeftChild As Integer  'row where left child is
  RightChild As Integer 'row where right child is
End Type
```

In this example, the two fields LeftChild and RightChild act as pointers to the row containing the child. To build the tree, for example, you start with an array of records of this type of size 1.

```
ReDim Data(1 To 1) As DataInBinaryTree
```

Each time you need to enter the next item you have to

1. Update the counter of the number of items.
2. Use ReDim Preserve to enlarge the array of records.
3. Fill in the "pointer" rows as needed (use a –1 for a pointer to null).

Note: The only way to reclaim memory from these imitation pointers is to copy the array of records to a new array of records (or a variant)—after eliminating the entry you want to remove.

Built-In Functions

There are hundreds of functions built into Visual Basic. The information about the most common functions is summarized in the three tables that follow. Table 5-1 gives short descriptions of the most common functions that do not have to do with date, time, or string information. Table 5-2 provides short descriptions about the date/time functions, and Table 5-3 provides information about the string functions.

Note: For more on individual functions (including the exact syntax needed for them), please consult the online help. Choosing Functions to get an alphabetical list and then the individual function from the list is one quick way to get the information.

Function	Purpose
Abs	Finds the absolute value of a number
Atn	Finds the arctangent
Cos	Finds the cosine
Exp	Raises e (2.71828 . . .) to the given power
Fix	Returns the integer part of a number
FV	Future value
Hex	Gives the hex equivalent
Int	Finds the greatest integer
Ipmt	Interest paid over time
IRR	Internal rate of return
Log	Common logarithm
MIRR	Modified internal rate of return

Some of the More Common Functions
Table 5-1.

Function	Purpose
Nper	Time to accumulate (disburse) an annuity
NPV	Net present value
Pmt	Pay out for annuity
Ppmt	Returns the principal paid out in an annuity payment
PV	Present value
Rate	Interest rate per period for an annuity
Rnd	Calls the random number generator
Sgn	Returns the sign of a number
Sin	Returns the sine of the number
SLN	Straight-line depreciation
Sqr	The square root function
SYD	Sum of year's depreciation
Tan	The tangent of an angle in radians
Timer	Returns the number of seconds since midnight

Some of the More Common Functions (*continued*)
Table 5-1.

Table 5-2 gives you a list of the most common string functions:

Function	Description
Asc	Returns the character code corresponding to the first letter in a string
InStr	Returns the position of the first occurrence of one string within another
LCase	Converts a string to lowercase
Left	Finds or removes a specified number of characters from the beginning of a string
Len	Gives the length of a string
LTrim	Removes spaces from the beginning of a string
Mid	Finds or removes characters from a string
Right	Finds or removes a specified number of characters from the end of a string
RTrim	Removes spaces from the end of a string
Str	Returns the string equivalent of a number (the numeral)
StrComp	Another way to do string comparisons
StrConv	Converts a string from one form to another
String	Returns a repeated string of identical characters
Trim	Trims spaces from both the beginning and end of a string
UCase	Converts a string to uppercase

The Most Common String Functions
Table 5-2.

Table 5-3 gives you the functions for handling date and times.

The Logical Operators on the Bit Level

The logical operators (Not, And, Or, and so on) are really functions that work on the bit (binary-digit) level. Suppose you are given two integers, X and Y. Then X And Y makes a binary digit 1 only if both binary digits are 1; otherwise, it is zero. For example, if

X = 7 in decimal	= 0111 in binary
Y = 12 in decimal	= 1100 in binary

then X And Y = 0100 in binary (4 in decimal) because only in the third position are both bits 1. Because And gives a 1 only if both digits are 1, Anding with a number whose binary digit is a single 1 and whose remaining digits are all zeroes lets you isolate the binary digits of any integer. For example:

X And 1	Tells you whether the least significant (rightmost) binary digit is on. You get a zero if it is not on.
X And 2	Since 2 in decimal is 10 in binary, a zero tells you that the next significant (second from the right) binary digit is off.

Function	Description
Date	Returns the current date (what is shown in the system clock)
DateAdd	Lets you add a specified interval to a date
DateDiff	Lets you subtract a specified interval from a date
DateSerial	Returns a date corresponding to the specified day, month, and year
DateValue	Takes a string and returns a date
Day	Tells you what day a string or number represents
Hour	Tells you what hour a string or number represents
Minute	Tells you what minute a string or number represents
Month	Tells you what month a string or number represents
Now	Returns the current time and date
Second	Tells you what second a string or number represents
Time	Tells you the current time in the system clock
TimeSerial	Returns a variable of date type for the given time
Weekday	Tells you what day of the week a date corresponds to
Year	Tells you what year a date corresponds to

The Date/Time Functions
Table 5-3.

This process is usually called *masking* and is the key to using the KeyUp and KeyDown event procedures.

Named Arguments

The InputBox function that you have already seen is one of the many Visual Basic built-in functions that support what are called *named arguments*. Named arguments give you a more elegant way of dealing with functions that have many parameters. (Unfortunately, not every Visual Basic built-in function supports named arguments—check the online help for those that do.)

Note: Only functions from the Visual Basic for Applications library support named arguments.

Here's an example of an InputBox function using named arguments:

```
MyInput  = InputBox(prompt:="Example", Default:= "A default value", _
xpos:=100, ypos:=200)
```

In general, as this example shows, named arguments use a **:=** (colon plus an equal sign), together with the name of the argument. (While the spelling of the argument must match perfectly, case is irrelevant.) Like any arguments, you separate named arguments from each other by a comma.

Note: Even with named arguments you can still only omit optional arguments.

User-Defined Functions and Procedures

In Visual Basic the distinction between the two is simply that functions return values and procedures do not. (People often use the term *subprogram* if they want to refer to both at the same time.)

To add a user-defined procedure function to the current form:

1. Open the Code window by double-clicking anywhere in the form or by pressing F7.
2. Choose Insert|Procedure.

The New Procedure dialog box will pop up, as shown here.

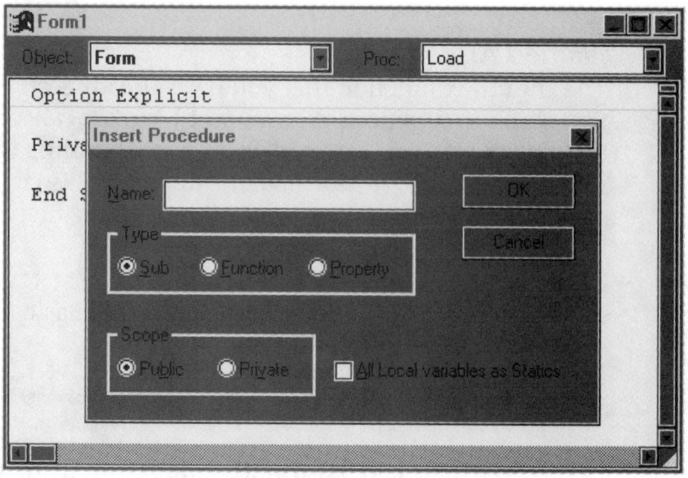

Set the radio button to the type of procedure you want. (For property procedures, see the next chapter.) The Public/Private buttons control the scope of the subprogram—see the section "Standard(Code) Modules" that follows. Once you enter the name, click on OK, and a template for the procedure or function pops up.

Note: You can also start a new procedure by typing the keyword **Function** or the keyword **Sub** followed by the name of the procedure anywhere in the code window and then pressing ENTER or the DOWN ARROW.

Functions

Suppose you want to write a function that would allow you to chop out any substring. To do this, we use Instr to find out where the string is and then use Right$, Left$, and Mid$ to do the cutting. Here's the function:

```
Function CutSmall$ (Big$, Small$)
  'local variables
  Dim Place As Integer, Length As Integer

  Place = Instr(Big$, Small$)
```

```
  Length = Len(Small$)
  If Place = 0 Then
    CutSmall$ = Big$
  Else
    CutSmall$ = Left$(Big$, Place-1)+Mid$(Big$, Place+Length)
  End If
End Function
```

The general form of a Function definition is as follows:

```
Function FunctionName (parameter1, parameter2, ...)
  statements
  FunctionName = expression
End Function
```

where parameter1, parameter2, and so on, are variables. The first line is usually called the *function header*. The variables inside the header are referred to as the parameters of the function. The types of the parameters can be specified by type-declaration tags or with phrases of the form As *type*. Function names must follow the same rules as variable names. The statements are usually called *the body* of the function.

If *FunctionName* (*argument1, argument2, . . .*) appears in a Visual Basic statement, then the memory location of *argument1* is assigned to *parameter1*, the memory location of *argument2* is assigned to *parameter2*, and so on. Since Visual Basic defaults to sending a memory location and not a value (passing by reference), any changes you make to the parameters inside the body of the function will be preserved.

5

After this, Visual Basic executes the statements in the function definition; the last value assigned to *FunctionName* inside the body of the function definition is the one used for the statement involving the *FunctionName* (*argument1, argument2, . . .*). The argument entries *argument1, argument2,* and so on, can be constants, variables, or expressions.

The type of value returned by a function is specified with a type-declaration tag (%, !, &, #, or $) appended to the function name, an As clause at the end of the Function header, or a DefType statement appearing above the function definition. Lines in your programs usually will not use a form such as

```
FunctionName (arg1, arg2, arg3)
```

Although in Visual Basic 4 the call to a function need not be part of an expression or statement. (It is most often placed in an assignment statement.)

Note: Usually you can call a function only when you use the same number of arguments as there are parameters in the function definition. The types must be compatible as well. Visual Basic allows you to create your own subprograms with optional or a varying number of arguments. See the section on this that follows.

Sub Procedures

Function procedures can be made to do almost anything, provided that what you want to do is get an answer—a value—out of them. Visual Basic distinguishes itself from languages like C in that you *do not* use functions for everything. Instead, you use a Sub procedure when you do not want to take raw data, massage it, and then return a single value. You would not use a function to find both the maximum and minimum elements in a list, for example.

You tell Visual Basic you want to define a Sub procedure in much the same way you would with a Function procedure: use Insert|New Procedure. A procedure must have a header that gives its parameters and takes the form

```
Sub SubprocedureName(parameter1, parameter2, ...)
  statement(s)
End Sub
```

When Visual Basic executes statements of the form

```
SubprocedureName argument1, argument2,...
```

or

```
Call SubprocedureName (argument1, argument2, ...)
```

just as with functions, the *memory locations* of the arguments are passed to the corresponding parameters, and the statements inside the Sub procedure are executed. Since Visual Basic defaults to sending a memory location and not a value (passing by reference), any changes you make to the parameters inside the body of the procedure will be preserved.

When the End Sub statement is reached, execution continues with the line following the call to the Sub procedure.

Tip: To quickly work with any Sub or Function procedure attached to your form, pop up the Object Browser. Make sure the Object Browser says you are working with your Project in the Libraries/Projects list box. To work with a specific subprogram, move through this dialog box until the subprogram you want to work with is highlighted, and press ENTER.

Passing by Reference/Passing by Value

There are two ways to pass a variable argument to a procedure or function: passing by value and passing by reference. The default in Visual Basic as mentioned above is to pass information by reference. When an argument variable in a subprogram is passed by reference, any changes to the corresponding parameter inside the procedure will change the value of the original argument when the procedure finishes. When passed by value, the argument variable retains its original value after the procedure terminates—regardless of what was done to the corresponding parameter inside the procedure. Argument to functions and procedures are always passed by reference unless surrounded by an extra pair of parentheses or the **ByVal** keyword is used in declaring the function or subprogram. (You can use ByRef to indicate that a variable is passed by reference.)

Note: Visual Basic 4 can change the type of arguments when you pass by value. This "evil type coercion" can lead to subtle bugs. Forewarned is forearmed!

Leaving Functions or Procedures Prematurely

You don't have to give every function an explicit value. Sometimes you are forced to exit a function prematurely.

```
Function BailOut (X) As Single
  If X < 0 Then
   Exit Function
  Else
.
.
  End If
End Function
```

(Use Exit Sub to leave a procedure prematurely.)

Using Lists and Arrays with Procedures

Visual Basic has an extraordinary facility to use lists and arrays in procedures and functions. It's easy to send any size list or array to a subprogram. To send an array parameter to a procedure or function, put the name of the array and include the open parenthesis. For example, assume that List# is a one-dimensional array of double-precision variables. Array$ is a two-dimensional string array, and BigArray% is a three-dimensional array of integers. Then,

```
Sub Example(List#(), Array$(), BigArray%(), X%)
```

would allow this Example procedure to use (and change) a list of double-precision variables, an array of strings, a three-dimensional array of integers, and a final integer variable. Note that just as with variable parameters, list and array parameters are placeholders; they have no independent existence.

Visual Basic makes this process of dealing with arrays as parameters more practical by including the functions LBound and UBound. LBound gives the lowest possible index and UBound the highest in a list. For example, you can easily write the following function to find the maximum element in a list.

```
Function FindMax(A() As Single)
  ' local variables Start, Finish, I
  Dim Start As Integer, Finish As Integer, I As Integer

  Start = LBound(A)
  Finish = UBound(A)
  Max = A(Start)
  For I = Start  To Finish
    If A(I) > Max Then Max = A(I)
  Next I
  FindMax = Max
End Function
```

In general, LBound(*NameOfArray*, *I*), UBound(*NameOfArray*, *I*) gives the lower (upper) bound for the *I*'th dimension. For a list (one-dimensional array), the *I* is optional, as in the preceding example.

Subprograms with a Variable or Optional Number of Arguments

Visual Basic permits you to have optional arguments in functions and procedures you define yourself. Optional arguments must be of the Variant data type and must be the last arguments in a function or procedure. For example, you might have a Sub procedure that looks like this:

```
Sub ProcessAddress(Name As String, Address As String, City As String, _
State As String, ZipCode As String, Optional ZipPlus4 As Variant)
```

In this case the last argument (for a Zip+Four code) is optional.

Note: You can have as many optional arguments as you want. They all must be variants and they must be listed after all the required arguments in the procedure (or function) declaration.

You can also have procedures and functions that accept an arbitrary number of arguments. For this you use the **ParamArray** keyword with an array of variants, as in the following example:

```
Function AddThemUp(ParamArray VariantNumbers()) As Single
  Dim Total As Single
For Each Number in VariantNumbers()
  Total = Total + Number
  AddThemUp = Total
End Function
```


Tip: Functions and Procedures that use the **Optional** or **ParamArray** keyword will work slower than those with a fixed number of arguments of a specific type. Save these kinds of procedures and functions for when you really need them.

Recursion

Recursion is a general method of solving problems by reducing them to simpler problems of a similar type. The general framework for a recursive solution to a problem looks like this:

```
Solve recursively (problem)
  If the problem is trivial, do the obvious
  Simplify the problem
 Solve recursively (simpler problem)
  (Possibly) combine the solution to the simpler problem(s)
  into a solution of the original problem
```

A recursive subprogram constantly calls itself, each time in a simpler situation, until it gets to the trivial case, at which point it stops. For the experienced programmer, thinking recursively presents a unique perspective on certain problems, often leading to particularly elegant solutions and therefore equally elegant programs. (For example, most of the very fast sorts, such as QuickSort, are recursive.)

For Visual Basic programmers, besides sorting routines, one common use of recursion is when you need to deal with the subdirectory structure of a disk. For example, if you wanted to delete a file but didn't know where it was, you would need to search on deeper and deeper subdirectories until you had exhausted all the subdirectories on that disk.

There are actually two types of recursion possible and both are supported in Visual Basic. The first is where the subprogram only calls itself. This is called *direct recursion*. Using direct recursion in Visual Basic is simple. Just call the subprogram the way you would call any subprogram. The second type is called, naturally enough, *indirect recursion*. This occurs, for example, when a subprogram calls another subprogram, which in turn calls the first subprogram.

Note: Visual Basic keeps track of the information used in a recursive procedure in its stack. The stack is limited (roughly 40K) in the 16-bit Visual Basic but much less so in the 32-bit version (1 MB). (You can get at most 240 recursive calls in the 16-bit version.) If you find a recursive procedure generating the "Out of stack space" error, your only alternatives are to either recast the recursive procedure as an iterative one if this is possible, or to create your own stack by using arrays. This, of course, requires quite a lot of programming!

As an example, let's look at the greatest common divisor (GCD) of two integers. (For those who have forgotten their high school mathematics, this is defined as the largest number that divides both of them. It's used when you need to add fractions.) Therefore:

GCD(4,6) = 2 (because 2 is the largest number that divides both 4 and 6)

GCD(12,7) = 1 (because no integer greater than 1 divides both 12 and 7)

Around 2,000 years ago, Euclid gave the following method of computing the GCD of two integers, *a* and *b*:

If *b* divides *a*, then the GCD is *b*. Otherwise, GCD(*a*,*b*) = GCD(*b*, *a* mod *b*)

(Recall that the mod function gives the remainder after integer division.) For example,

GCD(126, 12) = GCD(12, 126 mod 12) = GCD(12, 6) = 6

Here's the code for a recursive GCD function:

```
Function GCD (P as Long, Q As Long) As Long
 If Q mod P = 0 Then
    GCD := P
  else
    GCD := GCD(Q, P mod Q);
    End If
End Function
```

Here the pattern is to first take care of the trivial case. If you are not in the trivial case, then the code reduces it to a simpler case—because the mod function leads to smaller numbers. (In this example, there is no need to combine results as there would be in, say, a sorting routine.)

Building Larger Projects

When you start building larger projects with Visual Basic you will probably want to reuse code as much as possible. For this reason you will often want to store procedures and functions you create in their own modules rather than leave them attached to a form. The next section, "Standard Code Modules," explains the techniques needed for doing this.

Visual Basic 3 Tip: Standard modules used to be called code modules in Visual Basic 3.

In general, the Project window gives you access to all the project's form modules, Standard (code) modules, and Class modules (see Chapter 6). If you are using a resource file (see the following), this is listed here as well. Each time you click on the View Code button in the Project window, you open a code window for the highlighted form or Standard module. You can open individual Code windows for as many forms or modules as you want.

Tip: If you find yourself using certain custom controls all the time, you might want to make them part of your toolbox automatically. This is done by changing the AUTO32LD.VBP (AUTO16LD.VBP for 16-bit development) project file. All you have to do is load this project file, add the new controls to the toolbox, and then save the AUTO*LD.VBP project files.

(Visual Basic uses the various AUTO*LD.VBP projects to determine what it loads automatically.)

Note: The Enterprise edition of Visual Basic integrates Microsoft's Source Safe product to make using a group to build Visual Basic projects safer (and more productive). See the documentation that comes with Source Safe for more on how to integrate it into your projects. Source Safe is just one of the many add-ins that you can use in Visual Basic 4 to make projects easier to develop or manage. (See the online help for more on add-ins.)

Standard (Code) Modules

A Standard (code) module is the place where you put code you want accessible to all code in a project. Standard modules have no visual components. Standard modules are also useful for reusing code. (Just save the code in a Standard module and then add it to another project.) You add a new Standard module by choosing Insert|Module; you add an existing one by using File|Add File. The convention is that Standard modules have a .BAS extension.

The Code window for a Standard module looks much like the Code window attached to a form. You can have two types of declarations for variables in the General section of a Standard module:

- For variables visible only to procedures in the Standard module
- For variables you want visible everywhere in the project

For the former, use the **Private** keyword; for the latter, the **Public** keyword.

```
Private LocalToStandardModule As Integer
Public GlobatToProject As Integer
```

Visual Basic 3 Tip: You can use the older **Global** keyword instead of **Public** if you prefer.

Of course, just as form-level declarations can be superseded by declarations in procedures, public (global) declarations will be superseded by declaring a form- or procedural-level variable.

The Sub and Function procedures in code modules default so that they are available to the whole project. To make them only available to the code in the Standard module, you must use the **Private** keyword before the subprogram header. (It is a good idea to use the **Public** keyword even if, strictly speaking, it isn't needed.) For example:

```
Private ALocalProcedure (Foo As Variant)
Public AGlobalProcedure(Foo As Variant)
```

Tip: Although you may have many code modules and put global variables in each of them, it makes debugging easier if you keep all global (Public) variables in a single code module.

When you use a Sub or Function procedure inside another procedure, Visual Basic follows very simple steps to determine where to look for it:

1. Visual Basic first looks at procedures attached to the current form or module.
2. If the procedure is not found in the current form or module, Visual Basic looks at all code modules attached to the project.

The second of these options explains why the name of a procedure must be unique throughout all code modules. On the other hand, you certainly can have the same procedure name attached to two different forms; otherwise, forms could not have their own Form_Load procedures. (If you need to call an event procedure from another form or module declare it Public instead of Private.)

The DoEvents Function

Usually you want Windows (and Visual Basic) to constantly monitor the environment for events to respond to. On the other hand, there can be a lot of idle time that you can use, for example, to do time-consuming numeric calculations or sorts. However, you don't want a Visual Basic application to stop responding to events completely. For example, this is something you may want to do when you write a procedure that wastes time, as you saw earlier in this chapter. Obviously, you need a way to tell Visual Basic to periodically respond to events in the environment and return to the calculation when nothing else needs to be done.

The function that does this is called DoEvents. Whenever Visual Basic processes a statement containing this function, it releases control to the Windows operating system to process all the events that have occurred. (Windows keeps track of events in an events queue and keypresses in the SendKeys queue.) Obviously, you should not use the DoEvents function inside an event procedure if it is possible to reenter the same event procedure again. For example, a Click event procedure may be called again by the user's clicking the mouse. If you forget about this possibility, your program may be caught in an infinite regression.

Note: Do Events is much more important when using the 16-bit version of Visual Basic than the 32-bit version.

The DoEvents function actually gives you the number of forms loaded for the application.

Tip: Regardless of whether you are using the 16- or 32-bit version of Visual Basic, you will want to use the DoEvents function inside a subprogram that is making a time-consuming numeric computation (or is engaged in any CPU-intensive task). Set up a timing loop or a counter so that Visual Basic periodically processes a DoEvents function to check what events may have taken place while it was calculating. The little extra time that Visual Basic uses to manage the timing loop inside the function is well worth it.

Sub Main

You don't always have to have a form be loaded when an application created with Visual Basic starts. Occasionally it is useful to have code executed first. This is done by placing a special Sub procedure in a code module called Sub Main. You can have only one Sub Main in each project. Once you add a Standard module and a Sub Main to it, you can make Visual Basic execute the Sub Main before loading any forms. (In fact, if you use a Sub Main you will have to handle loading and showing the forms yourself.)

To specify Sub Main as the startup code:

1. Choose Tools|Options.
2. Select the Project page.
3. Select Sub Main from the Startup Form drop-down list box and click on OK.

Tip: By combining a Sub Main with the DoEvents function, you can process code in what is usually referred to as idle time—time when the CPU is otherwise inactive.

Using the Windows API

Microsoft Windows consists of libraries of many hundreds of specialized functions. These are called Application Programming Interface (API) functions. Most of the time, Visual Basic is rich enough in functionality that you don't need to bother with API functions. But some tasks, like rebooting the user's computer, cannot be done with Visual Basic code.

Note: If you use API functions at all carelessly, your system will lock up and you will have to reboot. You should have the "Save before run" option set when experimenting with API functions.

Another problem is that API functions are cumbersome to use and often require a fair amount of work before the information is usable by your Visual Basic program.

Before using a DLL function within a Visual Basic program, you must add a special declaration to the Declarations section of a Standard (code) module. For example, to find out what kind of chip is being used in the system, place the following statement in the Declarations section of a Standard module:


```
Declare Function GetWinFlags Lib "Kernel" () As Long
```

This tells Visual Basic that you will be using the Windows API function GetWinFlags, which is contained in the Kernel library ("Lib" stands for "library"). Since this is a function, you would expect it to return a value—in this case, a long integer because of the As Long clause. To use this function, you need to isolate individual bytes of the long integer by using masking techniques. For example, if the first byte of the value of this function is &H4 (decimal 4), then the chip used by the computer is an 80386.

Note: It is extremely important that the Declare statement for an API function be exactly as Windows expects. Leaving off a **ByVal** keyword will almost certainly lock your system. Also, in the 32-bit version of Microsoft Windows, names of functions in dynamic-link library (DLL) are case sensitive; those in the 16-bit version are not.

One nice feature of Visual Basic Professional or Enterprise editions is that they supply a file with all the Declare statements for the Windows API functions. You can copy and paste this information inside your program freely. (Look for the API viewer in the Visual Basic program group.) Obviously, for any serious use of API functions, having the necessary documentation (with the correct Declare statements!) is essential.

Mixed-Language Programming

Using a dynamic link library created with another language, such as C, is similar to using one of the Windows DLLs. You will need to use a Declare statement to tell Visual Basic about the function you want to use.

Note: Most DLLs expect the values to be passed by value (**ByVal**) rather than by reference (**ByRef**). The one usual exception is arrays that are passed by reference.

The full syntax for the Declare statement looks like this for a Sub program in a DLL (one that doesn't return a value):

```
[Public | Private ] Declare Sub name Lib "libname" [Alias " _
aliasname" ][([arglist])]
```

For a function (something that returns a value), use

```
[Public | Private ] Declare Function name Lib "libname" [Alias " _
aliasname" ]  [([arglist])][As type]
```

Most of the elements in a Declare statement (Public, Private, and so on) should be familiar to you. For the new ones, the Lib argument is just bookkeeping—it tells Visual Basic that a DLL is being called. The libname argument is the name of the DLL that contains the procedure you will be calling. The **Alias** keyword is used when the procedure has another name in the DLL but you don't (or can't) use it (probably because it conflicts with some reserved word in Visual basic itself). The aliasname argument is then the name of the procedure in the DLL. The Alias is what you will call it in Visual Basic.

Table 5-4 gives you a list of the most common C types, their Window's equivalent, and what you would use in a Visual Basic Declare.

Resource Files

Although no version of Visual Basic comes with the ability to build resource files, Visual Basic does have the ability to use one resource file per project.

Visual Basic Equivalents for Declare Statements
Table 5-4.

Window Type	C Type	Visual Basic Declare Type
BOOL	int	ByVal Boolean
BYTE	unsigned char	ByVal Byte
WORD	unsigned int	ByVal Integer
DWORD	unsigned long	ByVal Long
LPSTR	char far*	ByVal String
HANDLE	WORD	ByVal Integer
HWND	HANDLE	ByVal Integer
HDC	HANDLE	ByVal Integer

Resource files are used for storing strings, pictures, and other data that you need in the project. They are useful for internationalizing your project or simply for increasing performance or the information your project can hold. This is because data stored in a resource file is loaded only when needed.

When you create the EXE file, the resource file is linked into the EXE. You access the information in a resource file with the resource functions described in the following table:

LoadResString	Loads a string
LoadResPicture	Loads a bitmap, icon, or cursor.
LoadResData	Loads data and returns a byte array

See the online help for more information about these functions.

Note: For information on how to create a resource file, consult the Windows SDK or the documentation supplied with the resource compiler in Visual C++.

To add a resource file to your project:

1. Choose File | Add.
2. Select Resource Files (*.RES) in the List Files of Type box.
3. Select the resource file you want to add to the project, and choose OK to close the Add File dialog box.

Compiler Essentials

When you are first developing your project in the design environment, Visual Basic offers you the choice of compiling your whole project when you choose Run | Run (or press F5 or choose the Run tool), or just compiling what it needs to get the project running. Similarly, you can have Visual Basic compile the project during idle time. Both of these options speed up the response time to choosing Run | Run—they have no effect on the final EXE file. You can change these options by choosing Tools | Options and then working with the Advanced page in this dialog box.

At some point, however, you will want to compile your project into a stand-alone application. First and foremost: *Visual Basic's compiler does not generate true stand-alone executables.* It generates an intermediate *p-code* that needs to be interpreted by a run-time library. The run-time libraries are called VB40016.DLL (for 16-bit operating systems) or VB40032.DLL (for 32-bit operating systems). The appropriate version of the run-time file must be in \WINDOWS\SYSTEM, a directory on the user's path, or in the same directory as the executable itself (useful for a program on a floppy).

Note: You may also need other .DLL files, depending on the project. If you use custom controls, for example, you will need to distribute the various OCX files or VBX files for 16-bit development.

The run-time libraries are quite large: over 900K for the 32-bit version of Visual Basic, and over 700K for the 16-bit version. On the other hand, the p-code executables created with Visual Basic are quite small. The one for the sample calculator project is only 14,848 bytes. Since you only need one copy of the run-time DLL on a user's system and only one copy in memory at any one time, the use of p-code instead of generating a true executable does have a few advantages. (Having both options, of course, would be best.)

Tip: Visual Basic comes with a Setup Wizard that makes the process of distributing a finished application easier.

(See Chapter 30 of the *Programmer's Guide* for more on distribution issues and how to use the Setup Wizard.)

Creating an Executable

You start the process of creating an executable by choosing File | Make EXE File. This opens a dialog box that looks like this:

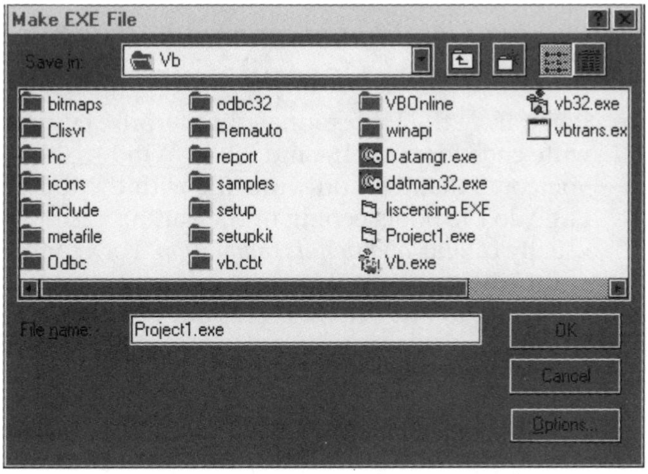

Most of the options in this dialog box are straightforward. For example, use the File Name text box for the filename for the executable file. (The default is the project filename with a .EXE extension.) Use the Directories and Drive list boxes to specify where you want to store the executable. When you are happy with the choices, you can just click on the OK button to create the executable. However, it is probably best if you click on the Options button in order to bring up the EXE Options dialog box shown here:

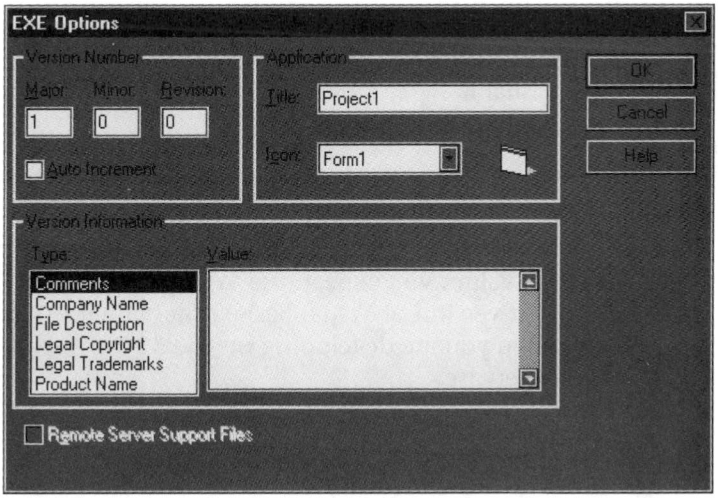

As you can see from this dialog box, you can actually set the title and icon for your application; major and minor versioning information; and copyright, trademark, company name, and product name information. First, set the options you want, and then click on the OK button in order to go back to the Make Exe dialog box to actually create the executable.

Conditional Compilation

If you have the Professional or Enterprise edition of Visual Basic, you can write code for both 16- and 32-bit Windows. It would obviously be nice if you could maintain only one file with the source code and have Visual Basic do the bookkeeping in the various cases. The key to this is what is usually called *conditional compilation*. For example, suppose you get to a point where you need to write different code for Window 3.*x* than for Windows 95 or Windows NT. Your code needs to include a block like the following at that point.

```
#If Win16 Then
   ' Place statements that will work only under
    '16-bit Windows statements here.
    '
#ElseIf Win32 Then
   'Place statements that will work only under
   '32-bit Windows here.
#Else
   'Place other platform statements here.
#End If
```

(Notice the similarity to an ordinary If-Then-Else.)

Note: The Option Compare statement doesn't affect the tests in a #If. Visual Basic always uses case-insensitive (Option Compare Text) comparisons.

In the example above, Win16 and Win32 are built-in *compiler constants* They have the values you expect: the Win16 constant is True when you are using the 16-bit version of Visual Basic, otherwise it is False. The Win32 constant is True when you are developing on the 32-bit version of Visual Basic but is False otherwise.

You can define your own compiler constants at any point you would define an ordinary constant. Here's an example:

```
#Const DebugVersion = True
```

Notice that you use the # to define a conditional compiler constant. Conditional compiler constants defined in code belong to the form or module in which they appear—they cannot be global (public) in scope. Notice as well that a constant like this would be very useful when adding debugging code (see Chapter 8) to your project while it is under development. This is because code that is excluded using conditional compilation is omitted from the final executable file. In particular, it has no size or performance effect.

Note: If you need to define conditional compiler constants that affect the whole project, choose Tools | Options and then fill in the appropriate line of the Project dialog page. (You separate multiple constants by colons.)

The GoTo

Like most programming languages, Visual Basic retains the unconditional jump, or GoTo. To paraphrase the old joke about split infinitives—modern programmers may be divided into three groups: those who neither know nor care about when they should use the GoTo, those who do not know but seem to care very much, and those who know *when* to use it.

Obviously, routine use of the GoTo leads to spaghetti code: code that is hard to read and harder to debug. On the other hand, there are times when using the GoTo actually makes your code cleaner and easier to understand. In Visual Basic this situation typically comes up when you are deep inside a nested loop and some condition forces you to leave all the loops simultaneously. You can't use the various forms of the Exit command because all that does is get you out of the loop you are currently in.

To use a GoTo in Visual Basic, you must label a line. Labels must begin with a letter and end with a colon. They must also start in the *first* column. Obviously you should use as descriptive a label as possible. Here's an example:

```
BadInput:
  'Code we want to process can GoTo here
```

For example, suppose we are using a nested For loop to input data and want to leave the loop if the user enters a 'ZZZ'.

```
For i = 1 to 10
    For j = 1 to 100
    GetData := InputBox("Data Input", "Enter data, ZZZ to end",
"")
    If GetData =  "ZZZ" then
        GoTo BadInput
    Else
       'Process data
    End If;
Exit Sub
BadInput:
  MsgBox("Data entry ended at user request");
```

Notice how using an **Exit For** keyword would be cumbersome here. For example, it would require extra code in order to break completely out of the nested loop. Also notice the exit **Sub** keyword then prevents us from "falling into" the labeled code.

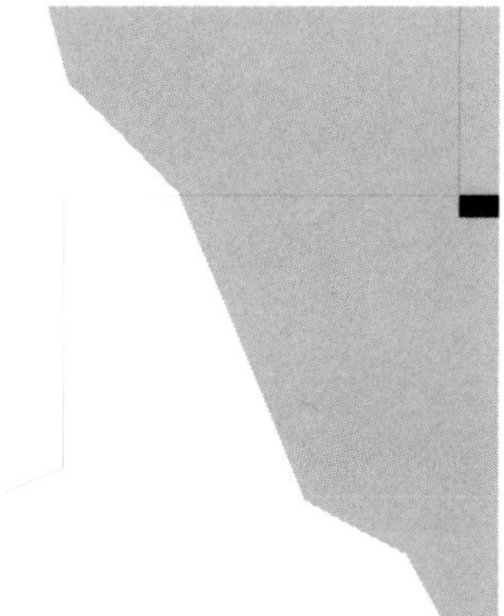

Chapter 6

Objects

At this point, you are probably pretty comfortable with the basic techniques for manipulating Visual Basic's built-in objects. To go further with Visual Basic, you will want to know how to create new objects. In particular, Visual Basic 4 is the first version of Visual Basic that gives you access to some of the power and so some of the advantages of *object-oriented programming*. Object-oriented programming (OOP) seems to be the dominant programming paradigm these days, having replaced the "structured" programming techniques that were developed in the early '70s. If you haven't worked with OOP before, you are probably wondering what all the hoopla is about. This chapter is also designed to show you (or at least to give you a glimpse). Since there's a fair amount of terminology needed to make sense of OOP, you'll start by learning some concepts and definitions. After this, you'll see how Visual Basic implements the part of OOP that it supports. Then you will get started on ways to create your own objects.

Getting Started

Let's start with a question that, on the surface, seems to have nothing to do with programming: how did Gateway 2000 become a billion-dollar company faster than any other company in American history? Most people would probably say they made good computers and sold them at rock-bottom prices. But go further—how did they do *that*? Well, a big part of the answer is that they farmed out a lot of the work. They bought components from reputable vendors and then assembled them. They didn't invest any money in designing and building power supplies, disk drives, motherboards, and so on. This made it possible for them to have a good product at a low price.

Ask yourself for a second how this could work. The obvious—and to a large extent correct—answer is that what they were buying was "prepackaged functionality." For example, when they bought a power supply, they were buying something with certain properties (size, shape, and so on) and a certain functionality (smooth power output, amount of power available, and so on.) Object-oriented programming springs from the same idea. Your program is made up of objects with certain properties and functions. You depend on the objects to not interact in undocumented ways with other objects or the code in your project. Whether you build the object or buy it might depend on the state of your wallet or how much time you have free. In either case, as long as the objects satisfy your specifications, you don't much care how the functionality was implemented. In OOP, the jargon says that what you care about is what the objects *expose*.

So, just as Gateway doesn't care about the internals of a power supply as long as it does what they want, most programmers don't need to care how command buttons are implemented in Visual Basic as long as they do what *they* want. And, as you certainly know by now, on the whole, Visual Basic's objects do what you would expect them to!

The key to being most productive in object-oriented programming is to make your objects as complete as possible and, *as much as possible,* have the other objects and parts of your program tell the objects what to do. OOP jargon describes this by saying that in object-oriented programming you *have clients send messages to objects*. By designing your objects to handle all appropriate messages and manipulate their data internally, you maximize reusability and minimize debugging time.

By this point you have seen pretty clear evidence that Visual Basic's built-in objects fit this paradigm well. They are extremely rich in functionality.

Unfortunately, Visual Basic misses implementing one of the key features of OOP here. Ideally, if you do have to write your own objects, another tenet of OOP would make this easier as well: objects can be built on other objects.

When you do this, the new object starts out by inheriting all the properties and functions of its parent—you can pick and choose whether you want to keep or modify any property or function of the parent. Visual Basic 4 simply doesn't allow this. You cannot modify the controls supplied with it.

The Vocabulary of OOP

Traditional structured programming consists of manipulating data. This is one reason why computer programming used to be called *data processing*. You manipulated the data in specific ways—usually called *algorithms*—that are theoretically sure to terminate. Now, for our next bit of terminology, *data structures* means the arrangements used in your program for the data. All this explains in part why one of the most important computer scientists (he designed Pascal, for example), a Swiss professor named Niklaus Wirth, called his famous book on programming *Algorithms + Data Structures = Programs* (Prentice-Hall, 1976). Notice that in Wirth's title the algorithms came first and the data structures after. This mimicked the way programmers worked at that time. First, you decided how to manipulate the data, and then you decided what structure to impose on the data in order to make the manipulations easier.

OOP puts both algorithms and data structures on the same level. With OOP you work with packages consisting of both data and the functions that manipulate them. The rest of this section explains the basic terminology of OOP. There's a fair amount of it, but it is worth learning for two reasons. The first is that you will need it to understand the discussions in this chapter; the second is that knowing it is useful if you move on to a fully OOP language like C++ or Delphi in order to extend Visual Basic.

Classes

A *class* is usually described as the template or blueprint from which the object is actually made. The standard way of thinking about classes is as the cookie cutter, with the actual object being the cookie. The "dough" in the form of memory will sometimes need to be allocated as well. Visual Basic is pretty good about hiding this "dough preparation" step from you. You rarely have to worry about creating memory for an object or releasing memory when a program ends under Visual Basic.

When you create an object from a class, you are said to have *created an instance* of the class. For example, all forms in Visual Basic are instances of the Form class and an individual form in your application is actually a class you can use to create new forms. (See the section on the **New** keyword below.) On the other hand, the controls on the toolbox represent individual classes, but an individual control on a form does not.

Encapsulation

This is the key concept in working with objects. Formally, *encapsulation* is nothing more than combining the data and behavior in one package.

Note: The data in an object is usually called its instance variables or fields, and the functions and procedures are its methods.

A key rule in making encapsulation work is that programs should never (well, almost never) access the instance variables (fields) in an object directly. Programs should interact with this data only through the object's methods. (Properties in Visual Basic are designed to give you a way to interact with the instance variables without violating encapsulation.) Encapsulation is the way to give an object its "black box"-like behavior, which is the key to reuse and debugging efficiency.

Note: Visual Basic fully supports encapsulation.

Inheritance

Inheritance is the ability to make classes that descend from other classes. The purpose of inheritance is to make it easier to build code for specialized tasks. The instance variables and methods of the descendant classes (sometimes called the *subclasses*) start out being the same.

Note: Visual Basic does not support inheritance for creating new subclasses.

Subclasses will usually use (inherit) the same methods as the parent class. OOP (but not Visual Basic) allows you to define a new method in a subclass but give it the same name. This is called *overriding* or ad-hoc polymorphism. A true object-oriented language like C++ (but not, alas, Visual Basic) allows you to go beyond simply overriding a method into what is usually called *polymorphism.* The idea behind polymorphism is that while the message may be the same, the *object* determines how to respond. Polymorphism can apply to any method that is inherited from a base class.

Note: Visual Basic does not support polymorphism except in the form of name overloading for the objects you create. We can only hope that the next version of Visual Basic will support true polymorphism. Microsoft has made no announcement on this, and your guess is as good as mine.

Manipulating Objects Built Into Visual Basic

The key to working with objects in Visual Basic are variables of the special *object* type. For example, when you use the **Me** keyword to refer to the current object you are using an object variable.

In general, you declare an object variable with the same **Dim**, **Private**, **Public**, **Static**, and so on keywords that you've already seen. Thus, you can have local, form level, or public (global) object variables. Here are some examples:

```
Dim FormVariable As Form
Dim InfoBox As TextBox
Public AButton As CommandButton
Private MyBar As ScrollBar
```

In general, the name used for an object variable of a given control type is the name given in the help file for that control.

The Set Keyword

When you want to make an object variable refer to a specific object of that type in your project, use the **Set** keyword. For example, if your project had a command button named Command1, your code would look like this:


```
Set AButton = Command1
```

Tip: The **Set** command can also be used to simplify lengthy control references.

Here's an example:

```
Set Foo = frmHelp.txtHelp
```

Now you can write

```
Foo.BackColor
```

instead of

```
frmhelp.txtHelp.BackColor
```

Note: It is important to note that the **Set** command does not make a copy of the object, as a variable assignment would. Instead, the **Set** command points the object variable to the other object.

In particular, you cannot use an assignment statement to make an object variable equal to, say, a text box. Code like this:

```
Dim Foo As TextBox
Foo = Text1
```

will give you an error message.

The fact that all **Set** does is point your variable to an object can occasionally lead to problems. For example, if you change a property of an object variable that is **Set** to another object, the property of the original object changes as well.

There are a few general types of object variables for use in situations where you need to refer to objects of many different types. For example:

```
Dim objFoo As Control
```

gives you a way to refer to any control. Similarly,

```
Dim objGeneral As Object
```

lets you *Set* the variable named *objGeneral* to *any* Visual Basic object.

You should always use the most specific object variable you can.

For example, code with this statement

```
Dim txtFoo As TextBox
Set Foo = Text1
```

will always run faster than

```
Dim Foo As Control
Set Foo = Text1
```

which in turn will always run faster than

```
Dim Foo As Object
Set Foo = Text1
```

Note: You can use variant variables as the type instead of object variables, but this will slow your program down and make it harder to debug.

You use the **Is** keyword to test if two object variables refer to (have been **Set** to) the same object. Suppose AControl and BControl are two control object variables. A line of code like

```
If AControl Is BControl Then
```

lets you test whether they refer to the same object. (It is a wise precaution to find out if changing the properties of one variable will also change the properties of the other!)

The New Keyword

One case where you can create a new instance of a Visual Basic object at run time is when you use an existing form as the class. The syntax for this is a little different. Assume you have a form named Form1 in your project already. Then the statement

```
Dim AForm As New Form1
```


creates a new instance of Form1. This new instance has the same properties as the original Form1 at the time the code is executed. Use the **New** keyword only when you want Visual Basic to create a new instance of the original object. For example,

```
Dim AForm As New Form1
Dim BForm As New Form1
AForm.Show
BForm.Show
AForm.Move Left - 199, Top + 100
BForm.Move Left - 399, Top + 200
```

shows two copies of the original Form1. The locations are determined by the value of the Left and Top properties of the original Form1. (We needed to change them to prevent them from stacking one on another because instances inherit all the properties of their parent.)

Note: You cannot use the **New** keyword to create new controls. Only Forms in Visual Basic 4 are classes (templates for new objects).

(To see the method for creating new controls at run time in Visual Basic, see the section on "Control Arrays" given below.)

The Nothing Keyword

Once you use the **Set** keyword to assign an object to an object variable, you need to release the memory used for the object. This is done by setting the object variable to the keyword **Nothing**. For example:

```
Dim objFrm As New Form1
  ' code to manipulate the new instance of Form1 would go here
  Set objForm = Nothing
```

Note: Since object variables merely point to the object, it is possible for several object variables to refer to the same object. When several object variables refer to the same object, then you must set all of them to **Nothing** in order to release the memory and system resources associated with the object.

Memory may be released automatically: this happens, for example, after the last object variable referring to the object goes out of scope. However, relying on this is sloppy. For example, if you set a local object variable inside a procedure, set it to **Nothing** before the Sub is exited; don't rely on Visual Basic to clean up after you!

Control Arrays

It would be logical if you could also use the **New** keyword to create controls at run time; unfortunately, that isn't the way it works. Visual Basic 4 still uses the older (and somewhat clumsier) method of *control arrays* to create new controls of a specific type. (You may have discovered control arrays inadvertently if you gave two controls of the same type the same control name or tried to copy a control using the Edit menu. If you did, then you saw a dialog box that looks like the one shown in the folowing illustration:

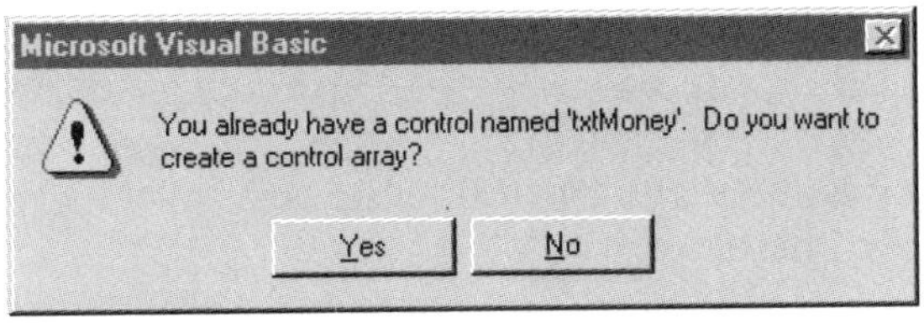

Any time you use the same control name more than once while designing a Visual Basic application, Visual Basic asks you whether you really want to create a control array. Click the Yes button (or press ENTER), and you now can add more controls of the same type while the application is running. Each new control in a control array is called an *element* of the control array.

Since both controls now have the same name, Visual Basic needs a way to distinguish them. You do this with the Index property. When you ask Visual Basic to create a control array, Visual Basic gives the first control an Index property of 0 and the second control an Index property of 1. Like any properties of Visual Basic objects, you can change them at design time using the Properties window. In fact, if you assign any number to the Index property of a control at design time, Visual Basic automatically creates a control array. This lets you create a control array without having to use two controls at design time.

Note: Create the control array first before writing any event procedures for its first element.

Suppose you want to work with the Change procedure for an element of the text box control array created as in the previous illustration. When you move to the Code window by, say, double-clicking one of these text boxes from the control array, your code event template looks like this:

```
Private Sub txtMoney_Change(Index As Integer)

End Sub
```

Notice how instead of having no parameters, as the Change procedure ordinarily does, this event procedure now uses a new parameter, Index As Integer. This index parameter is the key to the smooth functioning of control arrays. If you want to use the Change procedure for any element of the control array, call it with the appropriate index parameter:

```
txtMoney_Change(0)          'applies to the original text box
txtMoney_Change(1)          'applies to the second text box
```

For example, add the following code to the event procedure template shown here:

```
Private Sub txtMoney_Change (Index As Integer)
  If Index = 0 Then
    MsgBox ("You typed in text box 0")
  Else
    MsgBox ("You typed in text box 1)
  End If
End Sub
```

Now, when you type in one of the text boxes, Visual Basic calls this event procedure and passes the index parameter to the procedure. In this way, the event procedure can use the index to determine what to do.

If you inadvertently added a control to a control array at design time, you can remove it by changing the control name or deleting the control. However, once Visual Basic creates a control array, you must change all the control names or delete all the controls that were in the array in order to eliminate the control array. At that point, you can reuse the name.

Adding and Removing Controls in a Control Array

Once you've created a control array at design time, you can add controls while the application is running. To do this, you use a variation of the Load command that you already used to load a new form in an application with multiple forms. For example, suppose you want to add four new text boxes to the Money text box control array created in the previous section. To do this when the startup form loads, you only need to add the following code to the Form_Load event procedure for the startup form:

```
Private Sub Form_Load()
  Dim I As Integer

  For I = 2 To 5
    Load txtMoney(I)
    txtMoney(I).Text = "Text box #" + Str$(I)
  Next I
End Sub
```

Note: Whenever Visual Basic loads a new element of a control array, the object is invisible—the visible property is set to False. All other properties (except the Tab Index and Control Array Index) are copied from the object that has the lowest index in the array.

This means that newly created controls in a control array default to being stacked one on top of the other. Because of this, you'll often find yourself applying the Move method to controls in a control array after you tell Visual Basic to load them.

You can use the Unload statement to remove any element of a control array that you added at run time. You cannot use the Unload statement to remove the original elements of the control array that you created at design time. For example, if you add the

```
Private Sub Form_Click()
  Static I As Integer

  If I < 4 Then
    Unload txtMoney(I+2)
    I = I + 1
  Else
    Exit Sub
  End If
End Sub
```

each click on an empty place in the form removes the next control in the control array, but this routine will not remove the initial element in the control array.

You must be careful, of course; you can only load or unload an element of a control array once. If you try to load or unload a control array element twice in succession, Visual Basic gives a run-time error you can trap (Err = 360).

Manipulating Object Variables via Code

It is quite common to need a general procedure that manipulates properties of forms or controls or even the forms and controls themselves. This requires new techniques that we explain in this section.

First, *properties* of forms and controls can only be passed by value. For example, consider the following simple Sub procedure:

```
Sub ChangeText (ByVal X As String, Y As String)
  Y = X
End Sub
```

If you call it using the following code,

```
Call ChangeText(Form1.Caption, Y$)
```

then the current value of Y$ is the caption for Form1.

Tip: If you set the Tag property of the form or control to contain information otherwise not available at run time, you can write a general procedure using this technique to analyze the Tag property in order to find information about the control that would otherwise not be available at run time.

On the other hand, you will often want to affect the properties of a form or control by using a general procedure. For this, you have to pass the form or control as a parameter by reference. To do this, declare the argument to the procedure to be of one of the object types. (You could use variants too, of course, but this should be avoided unless absolutely necessary because it is slower and creates harder-to-debug code.)

For example, if you often find yourself writing code to center a form on the screen, why not use the following general procedure?

```
Public Sub CenterForm(X As Form)
    X.Move (Screen.Width - X.Width)/2, _
(Screen.Height - X.Height)/2
End Sub
```

Then whenever you are in a procedure attached to a specific form, you can simply say

```
CenterForm Me
```

to center the form on the screen.

Similarly, you can have a Sub or Function procedure that affects a property of a control. For example, a first approximation to a general procedure to change the caption on a control might look like this:

```
Sub ChangeCaption (X As Control, Y As String)
  X.Caption = Y
End Sub
```

Notice that this procedure used the general Control type. However, suppose you tried to use this procedure in the form of

```
Call ChangeCaption(Text1, "New text")
```

where Text1 was the name of a text box. Then Visual Basic would give you a run-time error because text boxes do not have a Caption property.

The solution for this is to use a variant on the If-Then-Else loop in Visual Basic that allows you to determine what type of control is being manipulated. This takes the following form:

```
If TypeOf Control Is ControlType Then
  .
 .Else
  . .
End If
```

where the ControlType parameter is the same as that used in declaring an object variable (Form, Label, TextBox).

For example, if all you wanted to do was work with both Text boxes, and all the other controls you wanted to change *did* have caption properties, you could use

```
Sub ChangeCaptionOrText (X As Control, Y As String)
  If TypeOf X Is TextBox Then
    X.Text = Y
   Else
    X.Caption = Y
   End If
End Sub
```


You cannot use the keyword **Not** in this type of control structure, so you will often find yourself using an empty If clause. For example, if you wanted to play it safer:

```
Sub ChangeCaption (X As Control, Y As String)
  If TypeOf X Is TextBox Then
    '  Do Nothing
```

```
  Else
    X.Caption = Y
  End If
End Sub
```

Since there is also no version of the Select Case for controls, you may need the If-Then-ElseIf version of this control structure:

```
If TypeOf X Is...Then
 . .
ElseIf TypeOf X Is...Then
.
ElseIf TypeOf X Is...Then
.
Else
.. .
End If
```

Collections

A Collection object is an object whose parts can be referred to individually as needed, *and* you still can refer to the object as a whole when necessary. Visual Basic has built-in collections that give you information about all the forms loaded in a project, the controls on a specific form, or the printers that are installed. They are called Forms, Controls, and Printers. The Count property of a collection tells you how many items are in the collection. For example, Forms.Count is the number of forms you have loaded.

You can access individual forms or controls by saying, for example, Forms(0), Forms(1), and so on. Unfortunately, although the count starts at 0, Forms(0) is not necessarily the startup form. The order of the Forms, Controls, or Printers collection is unpredictable. (Since the Count property starts at 0, we go to one less than Forms.Count – 1.)

Although using a For-Next loop to iterate through a collection works fine, most programmers would use a slightly different structure called the For Each for iterating through a collection. The For Each structure makes your code a bit clearer when you need to iterate through all the elements in a collection. A framework for this structure takes the following form:

```
For Each Element In TheCollection

Next
```

as shown in the following program to print the captions of all the loaded forms in a project.

```
Dim objForm As Form
For Each objForm In Forms
  Debug.Print objForm.Caption
Next
```

Building Your Own Collections

Occasionally it is useful to build your own collections. The items in a collection (usually called its *members,* or *elements)* can be of any type, and you can mix types in a collection if you need to.

Since a collection is an object, you must create it as an instance of a built-in class in Visual Basic. The class you need is called, naturally enough, the Collection class. For example,

```
Dim X As New Collection
```

creates a new collection as an instance of the Collection class.

Just as with the Forms, Controls, or Printers collection, the Count property of each collection you create tells you the number of items in a collection. (Collections start out with no elements, of course, so the Count is 0.) Each element in a collection can be referred to by its index—just as you saw in the Forms and Controls collections. This means that the following gives you one way of dealing with all the elements in a collection

```
For I = 1 To NameOfCollection.Count
  'work with NameOfCollection(I)
Next I
```


However, it is usually a bit clearer to use the For Each structure.

Caution: Collections you create start with an index of 1 and go up to the count of the collection. The built-in collections (Forms, Controls, and Printers) start at 0 and go up to the Count –1.

The Item Method

The Item method is the default method for a collection; it is how you refer to (or return) a specific element of a collection. Its syntax is

CollectionObject.Item(*index*)

The index parameter specifies the position of a member of the collection. It is a long integer (you can have *lots* of elements in a collection) and goes to the number of items in the collection. For example,

```
NyCollection.Item(1)
```

is the first item in the collection.

In general, Visual Basic lets you use a key to access the elements in a collection. This key is set up at the time you add the element to the collection. Using a key rather than an index is often more useful: you can easily associate a useful mnemonic as the key.

Note: The Item method is the default method for a collection.

For example, this means a statement like

```
Debug.Print Forms(1).Caption
```

is actually the same as

```
Debug.Print Forms.Item(1).Caption
```

The Add Method

Once you create the collection by using the **New** keyword, you use the Add method to add items to it. The trick in using the Add method is to remember you have to first set up a variant variable to hold the information before you use the Add method. For example,

```
Dim Versions As New Collection
Dim Foo As Variant
Foo = ("Visual Basic 3.0")
Versions.Add(Foo)
Foo = ("Visual Basic 4.0")
Versions.Add(Foo)
```

In general, the Add method has the following syntax (it supports named arguments, by the way):

CollectionObject.Add *item* As Variant [, *key* As string][, *before* As Long] [, *after* As Long]

Here are short descriptions of the parts of the Add method.

CollectionObject This is any object or object variable that refers to a collection.

item This is required. Since the information will be held in a variant variable, it can be an expression of any type. (As mentioned previously, you can mix types in a collection.)

key The key parameter is optional. It must be a string expression, and within the collection it must be unique or you'll get a run-time error. For example,

```
Dim Presidents As New Collection
Dim Foo As Variant
Foo = "George Washington"
Presidents.Add Foo, "Didn't lie"
Foo = "John Adams"
Presidents.Add item := Foo, key:= "Proper Bostonian"
```

Now you can access George by

```
Presidents.Item("Didn't lie")
```

Caution: The match to the string in the key must be perfect.

For example:

```
Presidents.Item("didn't lie")
```

doesn't work.

before, after These optional parameters are usually numeric expressions that evaluate to a (long) integer. The new member is placed right before (right after) the member identified by the before (after) argument. If you use a string expression, then it must correspond to one of the keys that was used to add elements to the collection. You can specify before or after positions, but not both.

The Remove Method

When you need to remove items from a collection, you use the Remove method. It, too, supports named arguments, and its syntax is

CollectionObject.Remove *index*

where, as you might expect, the index parameter is used to specify the element you want removed. If the index is a numeric expression, then it must be a number between 1 and the collection's Count property. If it's a string expression, it must exactly match a key to an element in the collection.

The Object Browser

To this point you have seen how to use the Object Browser to look at the built-in constants in Visual Basic and to navigate among the procedures you have written. The Object Browser can do far more. In particular, it gives you complete access to the classes, objects, and their methods and properties that you can use in your Visual Basic projects. More precisely, objects that are usable in Visual Basic are usually collected into *object libraries*. For example, there's Visual Basic's object library, the Visual Basic for Applications' object library, Excel's object library, and so on. An object library contains the information that Visual Basic needs to build instances of its objects, as well as information on the methods and properties of the object in the library. One of the purposes of the Object Browser is to help you understand the object libraries in your project better.

In general, you use the Libraries/Projects drop-down list box to choose from the available object libraries, including the ones in the current Visual Basic project. Once you choose a library, other parts of the Object Browser will let you look at the classes, modules, procedures, methods, and properties of that library.

Note: When you use Tools|References to add another object to Visual Basic, you will add information about its object library to the Object Browser. The name of the libtrary gets added automatically to the Libraries/Projects drop-down list box.

Creating an Object in Visual Basic

You can build objects in two ways in Visual Basic. One is by adding custom properties to an existing form and then using that form as a class (template) for new instances of the form. Each new instance of the form will have the new properties. The second is by using a special type of module called a Class module. Class modules have the advantage that they can be compiled separately (see Chapter 10) and used by other Windows applications. The disadvantage is that, at present, they can't be visual. Classes created out of a form, on the other hand, are obviously visual, but they cannot be compiled separately for use in some other projects. (They would have to be added at the design stage whenever they were used.)

Still, in both cases, you use the same ideas for adding properties to these classes (templates). Once you think about it the right way, the terminology used actually makes sense—but at first it can be confusing. First off, what are the most basic things you will want to be able to do with a new property?

- You want to get its current value.
- You want to assign a new value to it.

For the first situation, you use a special type of procedure called a *Property Get* procedure. For the second, you use a *Property Let* procedure. (One way to remember the distinction between these two types of property procedures is that a Let statement is the way you make assignments in BASIC.)

For example, suppose you want to add a custom property to a form that will tell you whether a form named frmNeedsToBeCentered is centered. This property will also center the form if you set it to be True. Here's what you need to do:

Set up a Private variable in the declarations section of the form. (It's a Private variable to enforce encapsulation.)

```
Private IsCentered As Boolean
```


then add the following procedures to the form:

```
Public Property Let Center(X As Boolean)
  IsCentered = X 'used for the current state of the property
  If X then
    Me.Move (Screen.Width - Me.Width)/2, _
Screen.Height - Me.Height)/2
  End If
End Sub
```

The first line of code uses the Private variable to store the current value of the property. Now you can use a line of code like

```
Me.Center = True
```

to center the form (or any instance of it). From another form or code module, you can use a line of code like

```
frmNeedsToBeCentered.Center = True
```

to center the form named frmNeedsToBeCentered.

Of course, it might also be useful to know if a form is centered. For this we need to use a Property Get procedure that returns a Boolean:

```
Public Property Get Center() As Boolean
 Center = IsCentered
End Sub
```

The one line of code in this procedure uses the current value of the IsCentered (Private) variable that we are using to hold the information about the current value of the property and assigns it as the value of the Property Get procedure. (Property Get procedures are similar to Function procedures in that you asssign a value to them inside the body of the procedure.)

Note: You may be wondering: why all this bother? You can certainly use a Public function with an object variable parameter to determine if a form is centered or not. The point is that the designers of Visual Basic 4 are trying to give objects as much "black box" behavior as they can. Using a Public function to determine if a form is centered or not would partially defeat this. All this being said, in the authors' opinion, given the current limited object orientation of Visual Basic, all Property procedures in a form are really doing is setting the stage for what will be in later versions of Visual Basic!

General Property Procedures

Property Let and Property Get procedures work in tandem. The value returned by the Property Get procedure is of the same type as the one used in the assignment for the Property Let. In general, the number of arguments for a Property Get is also one less than that of the corresponding Property Let. (The last argument being the one that will be changed.) A Property Get procedure that you write without a corresponding Property Let procedure gives you a read-only property—since you have no way to change it.

The full syntax for a Property Let procedure template looks like this:

```
[Public | Private][Static] Property Let name [(arglist)]
    [statements]
```

```
    [name = expression]
    [Exit Property] ' if need be
End Property
```

Use **Public** to make the Property Let procedure accessible to every procedure in every module. Use **Private** to make Property Let procedure accessible only to other procedures in the module where it is declared.

The other keywords work as they would in any procedure. Use the **Static** keyword if you need the Property Let procedure's local variables preserved between uses. The **Exit Property** keywords give you a way to immediately exit from a Property Let procedure, and so on. The name of the Property Let procedure must follow standard variable naming conventions, except that the name can (and will most often) be the same as a Property Get or Property Set procedure in the same module.

The full syntax for a Property Get procedure template looks like this:

```
[Public | Private][Static] Property Get name [(arglist)][As type]
    [statements]
    [name = expression]
    [Exit Property] ' if need be
End Property
```

Note: The name and type of each argument in a Property Get procedure must be the same as the corresponding arguments in the corresponding Property Let procedure—if it exists. The type of the value returned by a Property Get procedure must be the same data type as the last argument in the corresponding Property Let procedure if it exists.

The last type of Property procedure is the Property Set Statement. This is used when you need to set a reference to an object instead of just setting a value (for example, when you want to set a printer different than the current one). Its syntax is

```
[Public | Private][Static] Property Set name [(arglist)]
    [statements]
    [Exit Property]
    [statements]
End Property
```

Building Your Own Classes

Although you can add custom properties to a form and then use them as templates for new objects, the most common way to build a new class (template) for new objects in Visual Basic is to use a special type of code module called a Class Module. A Class Module object contains the code for the custom properties (via Property procedures) and methods that objects defined from it will have.

You can then create new instances of the class from any other module or form in your project. (You can even compile class modules for use by other applications as In Process OLE servers—see Chapter 10 for more on this important concept.) Class Modules cannot have a visible interface of their own. Each Class Module you create gives you, naturally enough, a single class (template) for building new instances of that class. However, you can have as many Class Modules in a project as you like (subject only to operating system constraints, of course).

As you might expect, once you have a Class Module, you use the **New** keyword to create new instances of it—for example, if FirstClass is the name of a class module in your project:

```
Dim AnInstance As New FirstClass
```

You use Property procedures to define the properties of your class and use **Public** Sub and Function procedures for its methods.

You create a new Class Module at design time by choosing Insert|Class Module. Each class module can respond to only two events: Initialize and Terminate. They are triggered when someone creates an instance of your class or terminates it. As you might expect, the Terminate event for a Class module is triggered when the class created via the **New** keyword is **Set** to **Nothing**. *It does not occur if the application stops because of the End statement.*

There are three properties for a class module that you set at design time via the Properties window. As you might expect, the Name property determines the name of the class. The other two properties are described next.

Public The **Public** property determines if other applications can write code to invoke the properties and methods of your class. This property can only be set to True in the Professional or Enterprise editions of Visual Basic.

Instancing If you set the Instancing property to True, then other applications outside your project can declare new instances of your class. (This is mostly used when using a Class Module in OLE—see Chapter 10.) You must have the Public property set to True to be able to set the Instancing property to True.

An Example: A Deck of Cards Class Module

Let's start by imagining we want to provide a toolkit for the designers of computer-generated card games. We obviously need an object that takes the place of a deck of cards. Since class modules in Visual Basic can't be visual, we just need to be concerned about the data and methods this deck of cards object needs to support.

Let's call this class module CardDecks. Suppose this object needs to expose individual cards and have methods for shuffling the deck and dealing the cards. (The Initialize event is used to build up the deck of cards.)

The code for creating this nonvisual object might look like this. First, you start with the private variables used for the data:

```
Private Deck(0 To 51) As Integer
Private TheCard As String
Private Position As Integer 'position in the deck
```

The Deck array would be used to hold the integers that are the internal representation of the cards. The Private TheCard variable is for the Property procedures that encapsulate the card. (This would make it easy to change the names of the cards for a different country, for example.)

The Initialize procedure simply fills the array with 52 consecutive integers.

```
Private Sub Class_Initialize()
Dim I As Integer
For I = 0 To 51
  Deck(I) = I
Next I
End Sub
```


Now it's on to the methods. First, there's got to be a Shuffle method for shuffling the deck. It might look like this:

```
Public Sub Shuffle()
 Dim X As Integer, I As Integer
 Dim Temp As Integer, Place As Integer
 Randomize
  For I = 0 To 519 '10 times through the deck should be enough
    Place = I Mod 52
    X = Int(52 * Rnd)
    Temp = Deck(Place)
    Deck(Place) = Deck(X)
    Deck(X) = Temp
  Next I
```

```
Position = 0 'reset pointer to start of deck
End Sub
```

(Of course, you could easily add an argument to this procedure to control how many "shuffles" were made.)

Next the Read-Only property that tells you the current card is given. It simply looks up the current value of the Private TheCard variable after using the private CalculateCard function.

```
Public Property Get CurrentCard() As String
  TheCard =  Calculate Card(Deck(Position))
  CurrentCard = TheCard
End Property
```

The method that deals the card will also need to call a private procedure that converts the integer in the Deck array to a card. Assuming that function is called CalculateCard, then the DealCard method might look like this:

```
Public Function DealCard() As String
  If Position > 51 Then Err.Raise Number :=vbObjectError + 32144,_
Description := "Only 52 cards in deck!" 'see Chapter 7 for errors
  TheCard = CalculateCard(Deck(Position))
  DealCard = TheCard
  Position = Position + 1
End Function
```

Finally, here's the private procedure for converting a number in the card array to a string describing the card.

```
Private Function CalculateCard(X As Integer) As String
  Dim Suit As Integer, CardValue As Integer
  Suit = X \ 13
  Select Case Suit
   Case 0
     TheCard = "Clubs"
   Case 1
     TheCard = "Diamonds"
   Case 2
     TheCard = "Hearts"
   Case 3
     TheCard = "Spades"
   End Select

  CardValue = X Mod 13
  Select Case CardValue
   Case 0
    TheCard = "Ace of " + TheCard
```

```
    Case 1 To 9
     TheCard = Str$(CardValue + 1) + " of " + TheCard
    Case 10
      TheCard = "Jack of " + TheCard
    Case 11
      TheCard = "Queen of " + TheCard
    Case 12
      TheCard = "King of " + TheCard
    End Select
CalculateCard = TheCard
End Function
```

Finally, to use this class module all you need to do is have a line like

```
Dim MyDeck As New CardDeck
```

before you start working with it. For example, you could test it with the following code.

```
Private Sub Form_Load()
Dim MyDeck As New CardDeck, I As Integer
  MyDeck.Shuffle
  For I = 1 To 53
    MyDeck.DealCard
    MsgBox MyDeck.CurrentCard
  Next I
End Sub
```

Chapter 7

Error Handling

Regardless of how carefully you debug your own program, it's impossible to anticipate all the crazy things an inexperienced user may do. If you want your program to "degrade gracefully" and not just roll over, you'll want to prevent fatal errors. This chapter shows you the tools that Visual Basic provides for handling errors. The command that activates (*enables*) error trapping within a given procedure is

```
On Error GoTo...
```

where the three dots stand for the label (line number) that defines the error trap. The labeled code must be in the current procedure. You cannot jump out of a procedure using an On Error GoTo command. On the other hand, the code for the error trap will often use other Sub or Function procedures.

Since you don't want Visual Basic to inadvertently "fall" into the error-trapping code, it is a good idea to have an Exit (Sub or Function) on the line immediately preceding the label for the error trap.

The On Error GoTo command can occur anywhere in an event, Sub, or Function procedure. Usually, the error-trapping code is inside that procedure. The only exception to this is when one procedure has been called by another. In this case, Visual Basic will look to see if an error trap was enabled in the earlier procedure if one does not exist in the second procedure.

Once you start error trapping with the On Error GoTo command, a run-time error will no longer bomb the program. (Operating system errors cannot be helped, of course; Windows 95 will have fewer of them than Windows 3.*x* had.) In any case, the On Error GoTo command should transfer control to a piece of code that identifies the problem and, if possible, fixes it.

If the error can be corrected, the Resume statement takes you back to the statement that caused the error in the first place. However, you can't correct an error if you don't know why it happened. You identify the problem by means of the Err Object. Err.Number is the default property and it gives you a Long integer that you can assign to a variable. For example, if you write

```
ErrorNumber = Err.Number
```

the value of the variable ErrorNumber can help you pick up the type of error. Visual Basic can identify many run-time errors. The Trappable Errors item available from the Contents menu in the online help gives you the current list of errors, and you can even jump to short explanations of what might have caused any specific error. This table gives some examples:

Error Code	Explanation
57	Device I/O error (for example, trying to print when the printer is offline)
68	Device unavailable (the device may not exist or is currently unavailable)

The way you use this information is simple. Suppose an event procedure will be using the printer. Somewhere in the procedure, before the error can occur, place a statement such as this:

```
On Error GoTo PrinterCheck
```

Now, before the End Sub, add code that looks like this:

```
Exit Sub
PrinterCheck:
  ErrorNumber = Err.Number
  Beep
```

```
  Select Case ErrorNumber
    Case  25
      MsgBox "Your printer may be off-line."
    Case 27
      MsgBox "Is there a printer available?"
    Case Else
      M$ = "Please tell the operator (= program author?) that"
      M$ = M$ & vbCrLf '=  Chr$(10) + Chr$(13) New Line
      M$ = M$ & "error number"+ Str$(ErrorNumber) + " occurred."
      MsgBox M$
      End
  End Select

M$ = "If the error has been corrected click on OK."
M$ = M$ & vbCrLf
M$ = M$ & "Otherwise click on Cancel."
Continue = MsgBox(M$, vbOKCancel)
If Continue = vbOK Then Resume Else End
```

The idea of this error trap is simple, and the Select Case statement is ideal. Each case tries to give some indication of where the problem is and, if possible, how to correct it. If you reach the Case Else, the error number has to be reported. In any case, the final block gives you the option of continuing or not by using a message box with two buttons. You might want to get into the habit of writing a general procedure that analyzes the error code. The error trap inside a procedure just sends control to the general procedure. If you do this, you can reuse the general procedure in many different projects.

Error trapping isn't a cure-all. Obviously, very little can be done about a hard disk crash or running out of paper.

A variant on the Resume command lets you bypass the statement that may have caused the problem. If you use

```
Resume Next
```


Visual Basic begins processing at the statement following the one that caused the error. You can also resume execution at any line of code that has been previously identified with a label. For this, use

```
Resume Label
```

It is unusual to have labels in Visual Basic except in connection with error trapping. Nonetheless, for compatibility with older BASICs, Visual Basic does let you use the unconditional GoTo (see Chapter 5) or GoSub to transfer to the line of code following the label, but there is rarely any reason to use an unconditional GoTo, and GoSubs are far less flexible than procedures.

Both the Resume and Resume Next commands behave differently if Visual Basic has to move backward to find the error trap in another procedure. Recall that this happens when one procedure is invoked by a previous procedure and the current procedure doesn't have an error trap. In both cases, the statement executed by Visual Basic will not be in the procedure where the error occurred. For the Resume command, Visual Basic will call the original procedure again. For the Resume Next command, Visual Basic will execute the statement after the call to the original procedure. You will never get back to the original procedure.

Suppose the chain of procedural calls goes back even further: Procedure1 calls Procedure2, which calls Function3. Now an error occurs in Function3, but the only error handler is in Procedure1. If there is a Resume command in the error handler in Procedure1, Visual Basic actually goes to the statement that called Procedure2.

Because this is unwieldy and so prone to problems, it is probably better to rely only on error handlers that occur in a specific procedure. If one procedure calls another, turn off the error handler in the calling routine.

Occasionally, when debugging a program, it's helpful to know what the error message for the last error was (for example, to place it in a message box). The command that does this is

```
ErrorMessage$ = Error$
```

You can also use

```
ErrorMessage$ = Error$(ErrorNumber)
```

to give the error message corresponding to a specific error number. Of course, Visual Basic gives the current error number as the value of Err.Number.

There's one other error-handling function, Erl (Error Line). If you get really desperate and need to find the line that caused the error and Visual Basic isn't stopping the program at that line, you can do the following:

1. Add line numbers before every statement in the procedure.
2. Add a Debug.Print Erl statement inside the error trap.

When developing a program, you may want to test how your error handler works. Visual Basic includes the statement

```
Error(errorcode number)
```

which, when processed, makes Visual Basic behave as if the error described by the given error number had actually occurred. This makes it easier to develop the trap.

If you are confident that you will no longer need an error trap, you can disable error trapping with the statement

```
On Error GoTo 0
```

(although strictly speaking the 0 is not needed). Similarly, you can change which error trap is in effect by using another On Error GoTo statement. Be sure to have an Exit command between the error traps. Visual Basic uses the last processed On Error GoTo statement to decide where to go.

More on the Err Object

The Err object has several properties and methods you can use to get information on run-time errors. The Err object's properties are set in three possible ways: Visual Basic, the Visual Basic developer, or as an OLE object. When a run-time error occurs, the Err object's properties are set with information specific only to the error and you can use the error information to handle the error. You can also Raise errors at run time in your code. Below are some of the Err object's properties and methods:

Err.Number

The Number property is a Long integer value specifically identifying an error.

Err.Source

The Source property is a String containing the name of the Visual Basic project.

Err.Description

The Description property is a String containing the error message, if one exists.

Err.LastDLLError

The LastDLLError property is only available on 32-bit operating systems. LastDLLError is a Long that contains the system error code for the last call into a DLL (if the DLL supports returning an error).

Err.Clear

The Clear method resets the Err object.

Err.Raise

The Raise method triggers a run-time error in your code.

Chapter 8

Tools and Techniques for Testing and Debugging

Once a program becomes in any way complicated, no matter how carefully you outline or plan it, it probably won't do what you expect—at first. This is one lesson programmers are forced to painfully relearn over and over again. So after you write a program, you will need to test it for *bugs*. Once the testing process convinces you that there are bugs lurking, you need to find and eradicate them. Visual Basic has many tools to assist with this task, and this chapter will show you how to use them.

Finally, this chapter gives you techniques for speeding up your programs that do the job but are unlikely to introduce new bugs (trying to overoptimize code is one of the most common sources of programming bugs). You will also find some information on good programming style.

Note: The Enterprise edition of Visual Basic comes with a tool called Source Safe that is designed to make Visual Basic easier to use in multigroup projects. This tool is not covered here.

The Debugging Tools and What They Do

You use the Run and Tools menus to gain access to the tools needed for debugging; most can be found on the toolbar as well. Usually, the debugging tools are used when the program is temporarily suspended (in break mode). The following table lists the debugging tools you can use in the order they are in the toolbar.

Tool	Keyboard Equivalent	Function
Run/Restart	ALT R, S (F5/SHIFT+F5)	Starts the program anew
Break	CTRL+BREAK	Interrupts the program
End		Ends the program
Breakpoint	ALT R, B (F9)	Stops the program immediately before the line is executed
Instant Watch	ALT T, W (SHIFT+F9)	Checks the value of the expression while the program is in break mode
Calls	ALT T, S (CTRL+L)	Shows how the procedure calls interrelate
Step Into	ALT R, T (F8)	Moves through the program one statement at a time
Step Over	ALT R, O (SHIFT+F8)	Performs like the single-step tool except procedure and function calls are treated as one step

The first three tools provide the most common way of switching from project design, or design mode, to break mode—where you'll be doing most of your debugging. You can always tell what mode you're in by looking at the title bar. For example, when you stop a program by switching to break mode, the title bar switches to

```
Visual Basic [break]
```

Testing Programs

Testing programs is the first step in debugging because you cannot correct errors until you determine that errors exist. Some people's idea of testing a program consists of running the program a few times to see what happens, each time using slightly different input. This process can succeed when you have a short program, but it's not effective—or convincing—for a long program or even a short program that is in any way subtle. In any case, even for the simplest programs, the choice of test data (sometimes dignified with the fancy term *the testing suite*) is all-important.

The key to testing lies in the word *reasonable,* and the following story explains how subtle this concept can be. A utility company had a complicated but, they thought, carefully checked program to send out bills, follow up bills, and finally, automatically cut off service if no response to a bill was received. One day, the story goes, someone went on vacation and shut off the electricity. The computer sent out a bill for $0.00, which, understandably, wasn't paid. After the requisite number of follow-up requests, the computer finally issued a termination notice saying that if this unfortunate person didn't pay $0.00 by Thursday, his electricity would be cut off.

A frantic call might have succeeded in stopping the shut-off; the story doesn't say. If this story is true, the programmer forgot to test what the program would do if the bill was $0.00. To the programmer, this wasn't a "reasonable" possibility. However, all the programmer had to do was change a >= to a > somewhere in the program.

One moral of this story is that you must always test your programs using the boundary values—the extreme values that mark the limits of the problem, like the $0.00 that the programmer in the story forgot. For example, for sorting routines, a completely ordered or reverse-ordered list is a good test case. In programs that require input, the empty string (or 0) is always a good test case.

Since errors are often caused by bugs, error trapping can help you isolate what portion of a procedure caused the bug. For example, you can add line numbers to your program and then use the Erl statement to find out which half of the program caused the error. Continue this bisection process until you isolate the line that caused the bug. (Of course, Visual Basic ordinarily stops a program at the line that causes an error, but you will often need to insert line numbers to debug a program with an error trap.)

Tip: Having an active error trap (On Error Goto) can prevent your tests from doing their job. You often will need to temporarily disable any active error traps before starting the testing process. For more information on error traps, see Chapter 7.

Note: Professionals might want to consider buying Microsoft's Test program. This comes with a language related to Visual Basic and lots of tools to make a professional testing procedure go smoother.

Designing Programs to Make Testing Easier

Long and complicated programs are never easy to test, but writing the programs in certain ways will make your job easier. These methods also make programming in general easier. By breaking the program into manageable pieces (giving the program *modularity,* in the jargon), each of which ideally does one task alone, you can make testing your programs much easier. After you finish each procedure or function, you can test it thoroughly to see whether it can handle all possible parameters that may be passed to it.

Next, combine all the procedures you've checked and test everything again. In some cases, a procedure or function may need results from a piece not yet written in order to run. In this case, the best technique, often called *stub programming,* substitutes constants, where necessary, for the results of as-yet-unwritten procedures or functions. Define the Sub procedure or Function procedure, but fill it with constants instead of having it do anything. The procedure calls will still work the same, but they receive only the constants from the stubs. You can then change the constants to vary the tests.

There are essentially two kinds of bugs: grammatical and logical. An example of a grammatical error is a misspelled variable name, which leads to a default value that ruins the program. Surprisingly enough, they are often the most difficult kind of bug to detect. Probably the best way to avoid such bugs in Visual Basic is to prevent them in the first place by using the Option Explicit command (see Chapter 5), which forces you to declare all variables. Logical bugs are a vast family that encompasses all errors resulting from a misunderstanding of how a program works. This includes procedures that don't communicate properly and internal logic errors inside code.

Another useful tool for understanding how variables are used in your programs is a programmer's tool called a cross-reference (or XREF) program. This program works through the source code of a program and then lists the names of all variables and where they occur. A cross-referencing program is especially useful for detecting the common error of an incorrect variable in an assignment statement. Although using meaningful variable names can help to a certain extent, the mistake of using the variable *ThisWeeksSales* when you really meant the variable *ThisMonthsSales* is still easy to make.

(The Option Explicit command doesn't help if the wrong variable was already dimensioned.).

Note: Both MicroHelp and Crescent Software should have excellent XREF programs available for Visual Basic 4 by the time this book is printed.

Logical Bugs

To get rid of subtle logical bugs, you have to isolate them—that is, find the part of the program that's causing the problem. If you've followed the modular approach, your task is a lot easier. The pieces are more manageable, so finding the bug means the haystack isn't *too* big.

If you've been testing the program as you develop it, then you should already know in what procedure or function the problem lies. Pinpointing the problematic procedure or function is usually easier if you developed the program, mostly because you start off with a good idea of the logic of the program. If the program is not yours or you've waited until the program is "finished," you can use the following techniques to check the pieces one at a time.

Assume that you've chosen a faulty procedure or function to test. There are only three possibilities:

- What's going in is wrong—what you've fed to the procedure or function is confusing it.
- What's going out is wrong—the procedure or function is sending incorrect information to other parts of the program (for example, it may be causing unplanned side effects).
- Something inside the procedure or function is wrong (for example, it's performing an operation too many times, or it's not clearing the screen at the right time).

In the first two cases, the fault can be traced to any or all of the following: the parameters you send to the procedure or function, what you've assigned to the parameters, or the form-level or global variables modified within the function or procedure.

How do you decide which situation you're dealing with? First, it's hard to imagine a correctly written short procedure or function that you can't analyze on a piece of paper to determine what should happen in most cases. Work through the procedure or function by hand, "playing computer." This means don't make any assumptions other than what the computer would know at that point; don't assume variables have certain values unless you can convince yourself that they do. You now need to check that the functions and procedures are doing what they are supposed to.

The Debug Window

Most versions of BASIC have a way to test program statements, procedures, and functions, and Visual Basic is no exception. Visual Basic uses the Debug window, shown in Figure 8-1.

The Debug window pops up when you run a program and is available for testing when you press CTRL+BREAK (or choose the Break option from the Run menu or toolbar) to interrupt a program or choose the Debug Window option from the View menu.

To bring the Debug window to the foreground, use the View menu or click any part of the Debug window that is visible. The Debug window is moveable or resizable by the ordinary Windows technique. As in QuickBASIC, you can use the Debug window to test statements or to perform quick calculations when you are in break mode. If you type **Print 2 + 2** in the Debug window and press ENTER, Visual Basic quickly responds with a **4**. You can use the ordinary Microsoft Window editing commands to modify the contents of a line in the Debug window. You can also cut and paste between lines. Remember, though, that the moment you press ENTER, Visual Basic attempts to process the line.

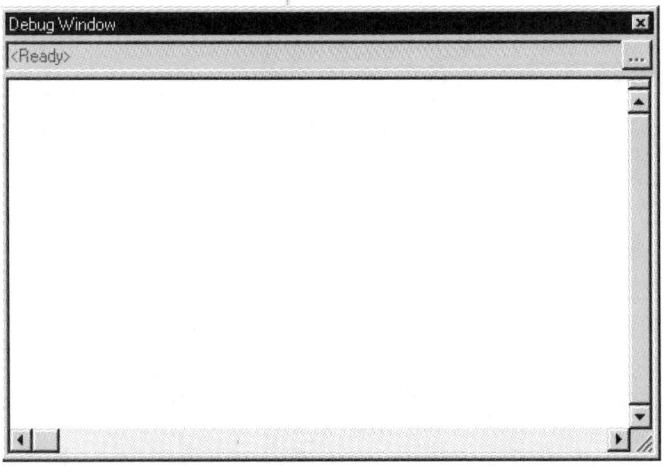

The Debug window
Figure 8-1.

Keep in mind that you can always reexecute any lines that currently appear in the Debug window by moving the cursor anywhere in the line and pressing ENTER. (Use the arrow keys or mouse to move around the Debug window.)

More on Debugging in the Debug Window

When you stop a program, the Debug window displays the title all the time. Also, the active form is highlighted in the Project list box, the title bar of the Debug window, as shown in Figure 8-2. It displays the name of the active form and the name of the procedure (if any) that Visual Basic was processing at the moment program execution was stopped—in this case, the Load procedure for Form1. It also shows the line about to be processed, in a box (which, incidentally, is drawn right on top of any embedded underscores, making them invisible).

The Debug window makes it easy to test an isolated procedure or function for its effects on certain values (for example, to see whether the results match with your hand calculations). You can test only procedures and functions that are attached to the form or module shown in the title bar of the Debug window.

Most debugging techniques use the Debug window to examine the current value of variables, but the only variables you can view from the Debug window are

- Variables local to the procedure listed in the title bar
- Form-level variables for the form listed in the title bar
- Global variables

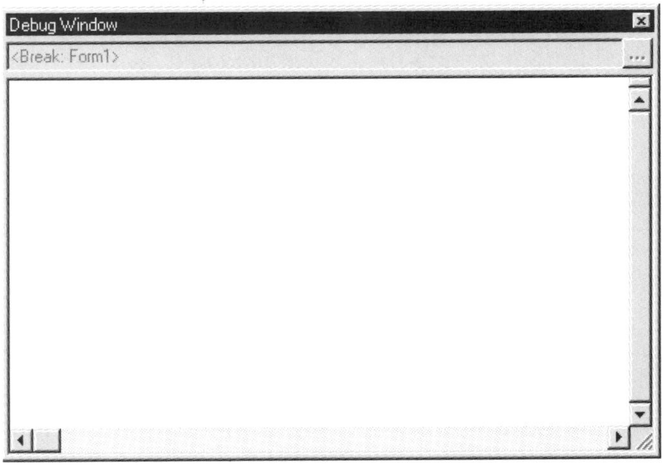

The Debug window in break mode
Figure 8-2.

To look at the value of a variable that fits one of these categories, use a simple Print statement inside the Debug window:

Print *NameOfVariable*

You can also add lines of code to your program that print values directly to the Debug window. For this, you use a predefined Visual Basic object called Debug:

Debug.Print *NameOfVariable*

Whenever Visual Basic encounters a Debug.Print statement, it sends the requested information to the Debug window. It does not stop the program. You can then examine it at your leisure.

When you are through debugging your program, you'll want to remove all the Debug.Print statements, although theoretically you can leave them in a compiled .EXE file without the user noticing.

Single-Stepping or Step Into

Often, when you have worked through a program by hand, you will want to have the computer walk through the same example one line of code at a time. Visual Basic lets you execute one statement in your program at a time—single-stepping—by repeatedly pressing F8 or the Step Into tool on the toolbar. (Of course, if Visual Basic is waiting for an event to happen, there won't be any statements to execute.)

When single-stepping is first used, the first executable statement of the program is boxed in the Code window. Each subsequent press of F8 or the single-step tool executes the boxed statement and boxes the next statement to be executed. As you can imagine, single-stepping through a program is ideal for tracing the logical flow of a program through decision structures and procedures.

Another possibility is to use the Debug window to check the values of constants, variables, or conditions by using Print statements. You also might consider having the Debug window and Code window simultaneously on the screen. You can do this by resizing and relocating them as needed.

Whenever a procedure is called during single-stepping, the procedure code fills the Code window. After its statements have been highlighted and executed (one at a time), the routine that called it reappears in the Code window.

Besides the F8 key or single-step tool from the toolbar, you can also use SHIFT+F8 (or Step Over tool) to single-step through a program. With this tool, each procedure is processed as if it were a single statement. In many cases, this is preferable to single-stepping through a complex function that you already know works.

Single-stepping through a program will probably take you to the place where you know a problem lurks. Now you want to place a break at that point before continuing the debugging process. This can be done with the Stop statement or, more commonly, by using a *breakpoint,* one of the tools available from the Run menu or toolbar (see the next section).

Stopping Programs Temporarily

Debug.Print statements help you debug your program by printing values *dynamically*—while the program is running. More often than not, though, you'll need to stop your program temporarily and look at a snapshot of the values of many of the variables. For example, suppose you want to know why a variable seems not to have the value you want. You need to pinpoint the location where the value starts behaving strangely. Just printing the values to the Debug window may not be enough. There are two ways to stop a program temporarily. The least flexible is to use the Stop statement within your code. This method was inherited from GW-BASIC. Stop statements remain in your code until you remove them by hand.

Breakpoints, on the other hand, are toggled off or on by pressing F9 or using the Hand-Up tool from the toolbar. (You can also select Toggle Breakpoint from the Run menu by pressing ALT R, B.) Breakpoints are usually shown in red in your code. When you run the program and Visual Basic encounters a breakpoint, Visual Basic stops the code just before the statement where the breakpoint is executed and enters break mode.

You can set multiple breakpoints. To remove a breakpoint, position the cursor on the breakpoint and press ALT R, B (or press F9). To clear all breakpoints from a program, press ALT R, A (or choose the Clear All Breakpoints option on the Run menu).

Using Breakpoints to Test Programs

Now suppose you want to test a procedure. Put a breakpoint right before the call to the procedure or function you want to test. Once the program stops at the breakpoint, open the Debug window, if necessary, and write a driver program. A *driver* is a program fragment that calls a function or procedure with specific values. For example, suppose you know that with the parameter 8

```
Variable1 = 10
```

and the parameter

```
Variable2 = 20
```

the result of a procedure of two parameters (a form-level variable named, say, FormLevel1) has the value 97. When you want to test how this procedure or function behaves at a particular place in a program, add the breakpoint at the appropriate point and use the Debug window to enter

```
WhateverYouAreTesting 10, 20
Print "The value of the variable FormLevel1 is: "; FormLevel1
```

See what happens. If the value of the variable *FormLevel1* isn't right, something inside this procedure is probably wrong. To confirm your suspicions, you'll need to check that no other form-level variable is causing the problem. You can add Print statements inside the Debug window to check this. (Another possibility is to use Watch variables—see the section on these that follows.) Examine the values of the relevant variables, the variables whose values affect the value of the variable *FormLevel1*. This check may quickly tell you whether something is wrong inside the procedure or function. If the value of the variable *FormLevel1* is correct, then determine, again by hand, what happens for some other values. Always remember to try the boundary values—the strange values, like the $0.00 that the programmer in the story forgot. If the values always match your expectations, there's probably nothing wrong with the procedure or function.

Of course, in practice, you have to make sure your driver fragment sends all the information needed by the procedure or function—and that's not likely to be only the values of two variables. Before calling the procedure, you can make all the necessary assignments in the Debug window while the program is stopped.

Assume that you've tested the procedure and know that the problem seems to be coming from outside it. Check each procedure that calls this procedure or function. Apply the same techniques to them: check what goes in and out of these procedures or functions.

Tip: Use SHIFT+F8 or the Step Over tool on the toolbar to treat a call to a Sub procedure or Function procedure as a single step. This way, you don't have to step through all the lines in all the functions and procedures in your program when you don't need to. Combine this with the Calls option on the Tools menu to see which procedure called the one you are in or to look at the entire chain of procedure calls if need be.

Instant Watch

In every case, you eventually wind your way down to a procedure or function that just doesn't work. You now know that you have an error internal to a procedure or function. Although the Debug window can be used to examine the values of expressions while single-stepping through a program, using Visual Basic's *Instant Watch* provides a more efficient mechanism.

The Instant Watch item (SHIFT+F9) on the Tools menu lets you look at the value of any variable or expression. For example, you can look at the truth or falsity of an expression (see Figure 8-3). It complements Visual Basic's feature that lets you use the Debug window to look at the value of any variables inside a procedure when a program is stopped within the procedure. To use Instant Watch,

1. Select the variable or expression you want to watch by moving the cursor to the item or highlighting the expression using SHIFT+ARROW key combinations.
2. Choose Instant Watch from the Tools menu (ALT T, W or SHIFT+F9).

A dialog box like the one in Figure 8-3 appears.

If the value isn't currently available, Visual Basic will tell you. At this point, you can close the box with the ESC key or choose to add this variable as a Watch item.

Watch Items

Watch items are variables, expressions, or conditions that are displayed in a special part of the Debug window (see Figure 8-4). Notice that the Debug window has split into two parts: the *Watch Pane* (where the Watch items are shown) and the *Immediate Pane* (which you use for displaying information or checking code).

You can choose the Watch items you want to examine either before you start the program or while the program is running and you have temporarily stopped it. Any variable, expression, or condition can be entered into the dialog box that pops up when you choose Add Watch from the Tools menu.

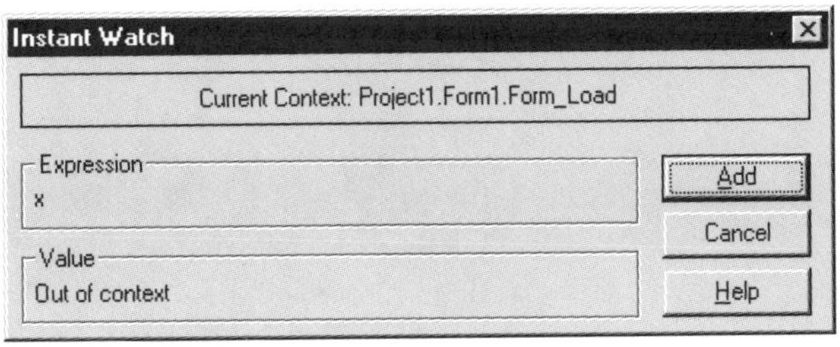

Instant Watch dialog box
Figure 8-3.

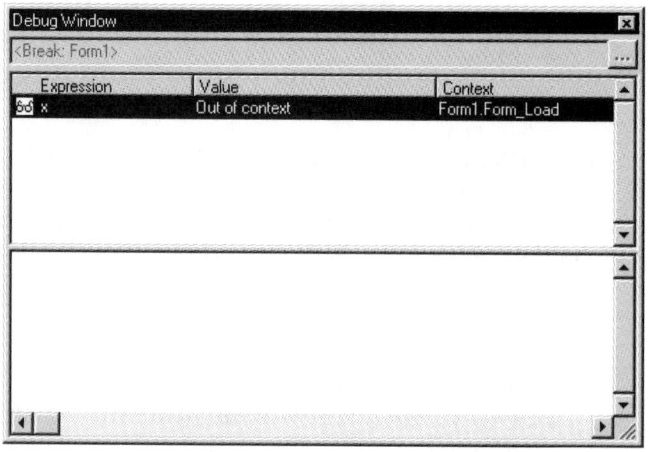

Debug window with Watch items
Figure 8-4.

However, you can watch only global variables or variables attached to the current form or module. When you press ENTER, the item will appear in the Watch Pane of the Debug window with a little pair of eyeglasses as the icon at the far left (see Figure 8-4). As Visual Basic executes the program, the values of the Watch items will be updated in the Watch Pane of the Debug window.

To create a Watch item, press ALT T, A (the Add Watch option on the Tools menu). A dialog box will appear as shown in Figure 8-5. The expression box initially uses whatever expression you highlighted. The context option buttons are used to set the scope of the variables in the expression. You can restrict the scope to procedure-level, form-level, module, or global variables. The last option buttons offer two other ways of watching your program, covered in the next section.

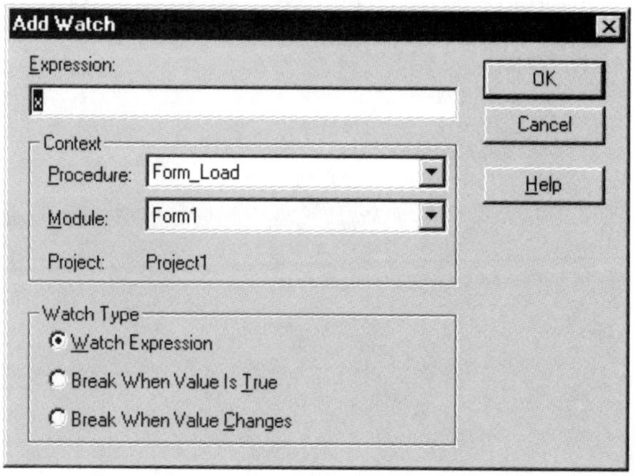

Add Watch dialog box
Figure 8-5.

To remove an item from the Debug window, press ALT T, E (Edit Watch). This opens a dialog box.

Use the DOWN ARROW key to highlight the item and then click the appropriate command button. To remove all Watch items, click Delete All. To remove a specific item, highlight it and click Delete.

Tip: If you have to watch a string variable, use an expression like

"{" + *NameOfStringVariable* + "}"

Then you can quickly detect whether the string is the empty string; if it is, all you'll see in the Debug window is the brackets with nothing between them.

Watchpoints

As mentioned above, sometimes the problem with a program appears to be tied to a variable or expression whose value falls outside some anticipated range, yet it is unclear in which line this occurs. In this case, setting a breakpoint at a specific line is not appropriate, and watching the variable and single-stepping may be too time-consuming. What is needed instead is the ability to suspend the program at the line that causes the variable or expression to reach or exceed some value. In Visual Basic, this debugging procedure is referred to as setting a watchpoint and is done from the Add Watch dialog box.

If you choose the Break When Value Is True option button, Visual Basic stops the program as soon as the watched value is True, and it highlights the line after the one that caused the expression to become True. The other option button lets you stop execution when a value has changed. The icons for these watch items in the Watch pane are a raised hand with an equal sign and a raised hand with a triangle.

Setting the Next Statement

Set Next Statement on the Run menu lets you bypass part of a program while you are stepping through it. Sometimes (especially when using the stub programming technique described earlier) you'll want to start a program other than at the beginning of a procedure or function, or you may, while single-stepping, want to skip to another place in the program. To use this option, you need to be in a running program (usually one you are stepping through). To set this option, while in the Code window, move the cursor to the line where you want to restart execution. Press ALT R, N. When you tell

Visual Basic to continue, Visual Basic starts executing at the line you just set. You can move both backward and forward within the procedure.

Final Remarks on Debugging

Feeding a procedure or function specific numbers and using the debugging techniques described here are not cure-alls. No technique can help unless you have a good grip on what the procedure or function should do. If you are using an If-Then statement, are you testing for the right quantity? Should a >= be a >? Use Watch items to check the value (True or False) of any Boolean relations that seem to be off (it is perfectly legal to enter X=19 as a Watch value). Check any loops in the routine; loops are a common source of problems. Are counters initialized correctly (is there an off-by-one error)? Are you testing your indeterminate loops at the top when you should be testing them at the bottom?

Event-Driven Bugs and Problems

When you debug an event-driven program, you have to be aware of certain problems that could never come up in older programming languages. "Event cascades" are perhaps the most common. These are bugs caused by an infinite sequence of one event procedure calling itself or another event procedure, with no way to break the chain. The most likely time such bugs are introduced is when you make a change in the Change event procedure for a control. The Change procedure is called again, which in turn is called again, and so on—theoretically forever, but in practice you'll get an "Out of Stack Space" error message.

Other special problems occur when you stop a program during a MouseDown or KeyDown event procedure. In both situations, during the debugging process you'll naturally release the mouse button or lift the key that invoked the event procedure. However, when Visual Basic resumes the program, it assumes the mouse button or the key is still down, and so the relevant MouseUp and KeyUp procedures will never be called. The usual solution is to call the MouseUp or KeyUp procedure from the Debug window as needed.

Documentation and Program Style

Although you can remember the logic of a complicated program for a while, you can't remember it forever. Good documentation is the key that can open the lock. Some people include the pseudocode or outline for the program as multiple remark statements. Along with meaningful variable names, this is obviously the best form of documentation. Set up conventions for global, form, or local variables and stick to them. Try to avoid tricky code; if you need to do something extraordinarily clever, make sure it's extensively commented. (Most of the time, you'll find that the clever piece of code wasn't really needed.) Nothing is harder to change six months down the line than "cute" code. Cute code often comes from a misplaced attempt to get a program to run more quickly. While this is sometimes necessary, versions of Visual Basic after 1.0 are usually fast enough for most situations.

Finally, if a procedure or function works well, remember to save it for reuse in other programs. Complicated programs will often have many procedures and functions. These procedures and functions may often have come up before in a slightly different context. This means that after you design the interface, sometimes all you have to do is modify and connect parts of a thoroughly debugged library of subprograms and functions to the event procedures for the interface. This is one reason why commercial toolkits for Visual Basic are so useful. The time saved is worth the small cost.

Chapter 9

Working with Files

This chapter shows you how to handle disks and disk files within Visual Basic. The first section explains the commands in Visual Basic that let you rename files, change the logged drive, or switch directories. Then you'll see the commands that make handling disk files easier. For example, you can copy files from within a Visual Basic program with a single command. Next you'll see how to use the file system controls on the toolbox. Finally, there's an extensive introduction to file handling in Visual Basic.

The File Commands

Visual Basic has six commands that under Windows 3.1 interacted directly with the underlying operating system, mimicking the usual operating system commands that handle files and drives on your machine. The following table summarizes these commands.

Command	Function
ChDrive	Changes the logged drive for the underlying operating system
ChDir	Changes the default directory
MkDir	Makes a new directory
RmDir	Removes a directory
Name	Changes the name of a file or moves a file from one directory to another
Kill	Deletes a file from a disk

The commands that handle files also accept the normal file-handling wildcards. For example,

```
Kill "*.*"
```

deletes all the files in the current directory (not to be done casually!). As the preceding table indicates, the Name command can actually do a bit more than the old DOS REN command; it can copy files from one directory in the current drive to another. To do this, give the full path name. For example,

```
Name "C:\VB\TEST.BAS" As "C:\EXAMPLES\TEST.BAS"
```

moves the TEST.BAS file from the VB directory to one named EXAMPLES.

As with any function that uses disk drives, you can generate a run-time error if the underlying operating system cannot perform the function asked. See the section "Making a File Program Robust: Error Trapping" later in this chapter for more information on dealing with these types of errors.

The Shell Function

Although a few file-handling utility programs are built into Visual Basic commands—usually with slightly different names, such as Kill for Del—most are not. Experienced users can move to the Windows 95 desktop and use the Explorer or the Start button to format disks, copy multiple files, or run another program. On the other hand, inexperienced users might not be comfortable doing this. For this reason you may want to build in the ability to start other programs from within your Visual Basic programs.

You can use the Shell function to run any .COM, .EXE, .BAT, or PIF file from within a Visual Basic program. For example, you can call the FORMAT.COM program under Windows 95 by a line like this:

```
X = Shell "C:\WINDOWS\COMMAND\FORMAT.COM A:"
```

(The value returned by the Shell function is now only useful under the 16-bit version of Visual Basic under Windows 3.*x*.)

In general, Windows 95 must know where the file you are running is located. It can know this if the file you are shelling to is located in a directory in the path or in the current directory. If you give the full path name of the application, then you can use files not in these directories.

When Visual Basic shells to a program, it generates a new iconized window and gives it the focus. In many situations this is not ideal. For example, the user has to actually press ENTER for formatting to occur. You can change this behavior with the general form of the Shell function, as follows:

Shell(*PathName,* WindowStyle)

where *PathName* contains the full path name of the stand-alone program that you want to execute along with any information needed by the program, and WindowStyle sets the type of window the program runs in. The possible values for WindowStyle are as follows:

Symbolic Constant	Value	Type of Window
vbHide	0	Window is hidden but has the focus
vbNormalFocus	1	Normal with the focus
vbMinimzedFocus	2	Iconized with the focus
vbMaximizedFocus	3	Maximized with the focus
VbNormalNoFocus	4	Normal without the focus
vbMinimzedNoFocus	6	Iconized without the focus

Note: The Shell function takes named arguments by the way.

The integer returned by the Shell function identifies the task identification number of the started program (or 0 if the program wasn't successfully started). This information was extremely useful in earlier versions of Visual Basic—it is less useful now. Previously you could use this value along with the Windows 3.1 GetModuleUsage API call in order to make sure the program you have shelled to finishes before the next Visual Basic statement executes. This no longer works under Windows NT or the 32-bit version of Visual Basic.

Tip: There is still a way to do this, but you need to use the CreateProcess( ) function to begin the program instead of the Shell( ) function. The CreateProcess( ) function returns the process handle of the shelled process via one of its passed parameters, then passes that handle to the WaitForSingleObject( ) function. This causes your Visual Basic application to suspend execution until the shelled process terminates—see the Win32 API help files for more information.

Command-Line Information

Most professional programs allow (or require) you to type in additional information when you invoke the program. This extra information is usually called *command-line information.* For example, when you write

```
COPY A:*.* B:
```

the command-line information is the string "A:*.* B:".

Visual Basic makes it easy to read command-line information. When you run any program from the Run box on the Start button and use the line

FileExeName *info1 info2 info3...*

then the value of the reserved variant variable Command is the string whose value is "*info1 info2 info3...*". Obviously, you need a way to create sample pieces of command-line information while developing the program; otherwise, you wouldn't have any test data with which to debug the program. Choose Tools|Options and then go to the Advanced Page on the Options dialog box. In the command-line arguments box, enter the string that you want to be used in the Command command within the program.

The File-Handling Functions

Certain tasks are so common that the designers of Visual Basic decided to add them to the language itself rather than make you use Windows API calls or shell to one of the utility programs. There are four of these functions.

The FileCopy Function The FileCopy function copies a file from the source path to another path. It does not use SHELL to activate the underlying operating system copy routine or call the File Manager. This function takes named arguments, and its syntax is

FileCopy *source, destination*

The FileCopy function does not allow wildcards. (Use SHELL "COPY..." if you need wildcards.)

The FileDateTime Function The FileDateTime function returns the date and time a file was created or last modified. The syntax is

FileDateTime (*PathName*)

The GetAttr Function The GetAttr function returns an integer. Using masking techniques to get at the individual bits, you can determine how the various attributes are set. The syntax for this function is

GetAttr (*PathName*) As Integer

Table 9-1 summarizes these values as symbolic constants.

For example, if

GetAttrib(*FileName*) = vbReadOnly + vbHidden 'or just 3

then the file is hidden and read-only.

Tip: You can use this masking technique with the Dir function to find files that match both a file specification and a file attribute. The syntax for this version is

Dir(*PathName, attributes*)

where you add together the various symbolic constants (or their values) in order to specify the types of files to be looked for.

The SetAttr Function The SetAttr function sets attribute information for files. Using the same bit values given in the preceding table, you can change the various attributes. The syntax for this function is

SetAttr *PathName, attributes*

Attribute Constants
Table 9-1.

Attribute	Constant	Value
Normal	vbNormal	0
Read Only	vbReadonly	1
Hidden	vbHidden	2
System	vbSystem	4
Volume	vbVolume	8
Directory	vbDirectory	16
Archive	vbArchive	32

You can use the same symbolic constants as shown in Table 9-1 for the GetAttr function. For example,

SetAttr *FileName$,* vbHidden+ vbReadOnly

would hide the file and set it as read-only.

The File System Controls

The file system controls in Visual Basic allow users to select a new drive, see the hierarchical directory structure of a disk, or see the names of the files in a given directory. As with all Visual Basic controls, you need to write code to take full advantage of the power of the file system controls. In addition, if you want to tell the underlying operating system to change drives or directories as the result of a mouse click by a user, you need to write code using the commands listed in the first section in this chapter. The file system controls complement the common dialog boxes you will see in Chapter 12. The illustration shown here displays the toolbox with the file system controls marked. The file system controls are designed to work together. Your code checks what the user has done to the drive list box and passes this information on to the directory list box. The changes in the directory list box are passed on to the file list box. (See the section "Tying All the File Controls Together" a little later in this chapter.)

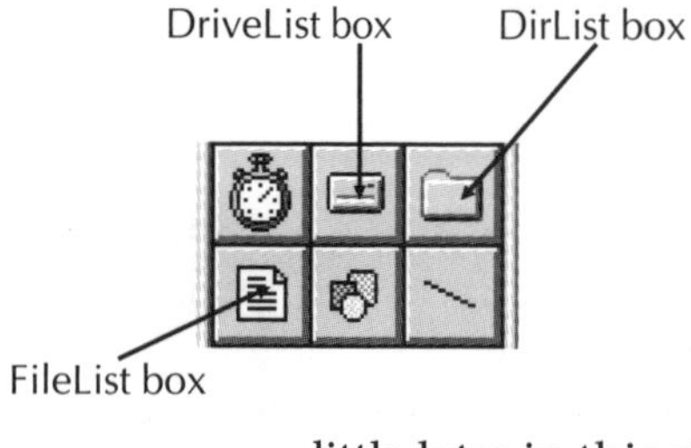

File List Boxes

A file list box defaults to displaying the files in the current directory. (Microsoft's suggested prefix for the Name property is *fil.*) As with any list box, you can control the position, size, color, and font characteristics at design time or via code. Most of the properties, events, and methods of a file list box are identical to those of ordinary list boxes. For example, as with all list boxes, when the number of items can't fit the current size of the control, Visual Basic automatically adds vertical scroll bars. This lets the user move through the list of files using the scroll bars. One point is worth remembering, though: the Windows convention is that double-clicking a file, not single-clicking, chooses the file. This is especially important when using a file list box, because using an arrow key to move through a file list box would call any Click procedure that you have written. (Recall that arrow movements are functionally equivalent to a single mouse click for a list box.)

It is quite common to use the List, ListCount, and ListIndex properties rather than the Dir command to analyze the information contained in a file list box. For example, suppose the file list box has the default name of File1 and you have already set up a string array for the information contained in the box. Then a fragment like

```
For I% = 0 To File1.ListCount -1
  FileNames$(I%) = File1.List(I%)
Next I%
```

fills a string array with the information contained in the file list box named File1. If you need to find out the name of the file that a user selects, you can use File1.List(ListIndex) or the FileName property which, when read, has the same function.

There are five Boolean properties (True, False) that control what type of files are shown in a file list box: Archive, Hidden, Normal, ReadOnly, and System. The default setting is True for Archive, Normal, and ReadOnly and False for Hidden and System.

Pattern and Path

The most important new properties for file list boxes are Pattern and Path. The Pattern property determines which files are displayed in the file list box. The Pattern property accepts the ordinary file wildcards—the * (match any) and the ? (match a single character). The default pattern is set to *.* to display all files. (Of course, the Pattern property works with the attribute properties discussed earlier before Visual Basic displays the files.) When you change the Pattern property, Visual Basic looks to see if you have written a PatternChange event procedure for the file list box and, if so, activates it.

The Path property sets or returns the current path for the file list box, but not for the underlying operating system. To tell the underlying operating system to change the current path from within Visual Basic, you need the ChDir command. When you change the Path property, Visual Basic looks to see if you have written a PathChange event procedure for the file list box and, if so, activates it.

Changing the FileName property activates the PathChange event or the PatternChange event (or both), depending on how you change the FileName property. For example, suppose you are in the C:\ root directory. Setting

```
File1.FileName ="C:\WINDOWS\COMMAND\*.COM"
```

activates both the PathChange and PatternChange events.

Directory List Boxes

A directory list box displays the directory structure of the current drive. (Microsoft's naming convention is to use a *dir* prefix for the Name property.) The current directory shows up as an open file folder. Subdirectories of the current directory are shown as closed folders, and directories above the current directory are shown as nonshaded open folders.

Note: When you click on an item or move through the list, that item is highlighted. When you double-click, Visual Basic automatically updates the directory list box.

The List property for a directory list box works a little differently than it does for file list boxes. While subdirectories of the current directory are numbered from zero to ListCount–1, Visual Basic uses negative indexes for the current directory and its parent and grandparent directories. For example, –1 is the index for the current directory, –2 for its parent directory, and so on. Unfortunately, you cannot use the LBound function to determine the number of directories above a given directory; you must either count the number of backslashes in the Path property or move backward through the items in the directory list box.

As an example of how powerful the file system controls can be when they begin to work together, put a directory list box and a file list box together on a new project. Now suppose you want a change by the user in a directory list box named dirBox to tell Visual Basic to update the file list box immediately. All you have to do is enter one line of code in the Change event procedure:

```
Sub dirBox_Change()
  File1.Path = dirBox.Path
End Sub
```

To activate this event procedure, you simply double-click on a new directory in the Dir1 list box.

Note: Directory list boxes do not recognize the DoubleClick event; instead, they call the Change procedure in response to a double-click and reassign the Path property.

Again, Visual Basic cannot use a single click to activate the Change event because then users could not use the arrow keys to move through the list box. If you want pressing ENTER to update the file list box as well, use the directory list boxes KeyPress event procedure as follows:

```
Sub dirBox_KeyPress(KeyAscii As Integer)
  If KeyAscii = 13 Then     'Or vbKeyReturn
    dirBox.Path = dirBox.List(dirBox.ListIndex)
  End If
End Sub
```

You can also write a procedure that calls the previous event procedure when the user presses ENTER.

Again, this procedure didn't change the Path property directly because doing so is superfluous. Visual Basic calls the Change event procedure for a directory list box whenever you change the value of the Path property.

Finally, it's important to keep in mind that while the meaning of the Path property for file list boxes and directory lists boxes is similar, they are not identical. For directory list boxes, the Path property specifies which directory was selected; for file list boxes, it specifies where to look for files to display.

Drive List Boxes

Unlike file and directory list boxes, drive list boxes are pull-down boxes. (Microsoft's naming convention suggests *drv* as the prefix for the Name property.) Drive list boxes begin by displaying the current drive, and then when the user clicks on the arrow, Visual Basic pulls down a list of all valid drives.

The key property for a drive list box is the Drive property, which can be used to return or reset the current drive. For example, to synchronize a drive list box with a directory list box, all you need is code that looks like this:

```
Sub drvBox_Change()
  dirBox.Path = drvBox.Drive
End Sub
```

Tying All the File Controls Together

When you have all three file system controls on a form, you have to communicate the changes among the controls in order to have Visual Basic show what the user wants to see. For example, if the user selects a new drive, Visual Basic activates the Change event procedure for the drive box. Then the following occurs:

1. The Change event procedure for the drive box assigns the Drive property to the directory box's Path property.
2. This changes the display in the directory list box by triggering the Change event procedure for the directory list box.
3. Inside the Change event procedure, you assign the Path property to the file list box's Path property. This updates the File list box.

Sequential Files

Sequential files are analogous in Visual Basic to recording information on a cassette tape. The analogy is a particularly useful one to keep in mind. For example, the operations on sequential files that are analogous to easy tasks for a cassette recorder, such as recording an album on a blank tape, will be easy. Those analogous to more difficult tasks, such as splicing tapes together or making a change within a tape, will be more difficult.

To avoid unnecessary work, use a sequential file only when you know that you will

- Rarely make changes within the file
- Massage (process) the information the file contains from start to finish, without needing to constantly jump around
- Add to the file at the end of the file

It's not that you can't make changes within the file, jump around when processing information, or add to the file other than at the end; it's just that these procedures are a bit painful.

Here's a table of some common operations on a cassette tape and the analogous operations on a sequential text file called TEST in the currently active directory:

Operation	Visual Basic Equivalent
Rewind the tape, put the machine in playback mode, and pause.	Open "TEST" for input as #1
Rewind the tape, put the machine in record mode, and pause.	Open "TEST" for output as #1
Push Stop.	Close #1

Each time Visual Basic sees the Open command, it gets ready to send information into or take information out of the file. (The jargon is that it "sets up a channel" to communicate with the file.) What follows the Open command is the name of the file you are working with. The filename must be a string variable or enclosed in quotation marks, and unless it is in the current directory, you need to provide enough information to identify its path. (The value of a string variable must be a legal filename.) Under Windows 95, of course, what constitutes a legal filename is much improved over the earlier versions of Windows. You can use up to 255 characters, and spaces are allowed. (You still can't use a \, ?, :, *, < , >, or |, however.)

On the other hand, if you want your files to be completely compatible with machines not running Windows 95 or Windows NT, you should follow the rules for filenames that DOS imposes.

Note: Only the 32-bit version of Visual Basic supports long filenames.

In any case, you also need a file identifier. This is a number between 1 and 255 preceded by the # sign that you will use to identify the file. Although you can't change this number until you close the file, the next time you need the file you can open it with a different ID number. The number of possible files you can have open at once is limited to the limit set files= statement in your CONFIG.SYS file. The easiest way to find an unused file identifier is with the command FreeFile. The value of FreeFile is always the next unused file ID number. Therefore, you merely have to have a statement like

```
FileNumber% = FreeFile
```

(to pick up the next free file number).

When Visual Basic processes an Open command, it also reserves a file buffer in the computer's memory. The Close command usually empties the buffer and tells the underlying operating system to update the FAT (file allocation table). But because of Windows' own buffering techniques this may not happen precisely when Visual Basic processes the Close command.

Tip: The Reset command, unlike the Close command, seems to force the underlying operating system to flush the buffers. Use this command in critical situations to make it more likely that the underlying operating system file buffer is flushed.

The Print command sends information to a form. A slight modification, Print #, provides one way to send information to a file. Here is an example of a fragment that sends one piece of information to a file named TEST:

```
' Writing to a file
Open "TEST" For Output As #1
Print #1, "TESTING, 1 2 3"
Close #1
```

Caution: If a file in the current directory already exists with the name TEST, it is erased by this statement. Opening a file for output starts a new file; the contents of a previous file with the same name are lost.

The Print# statement sends the information to the file. The comma is necessary, but what follows the comma can be anything that might occur in an ordinary Print statement. And what appears in the file is the exact image of what would have occurred on the screen. In our case the file will contain the word "TESTING," followed by (in order) a comma, a space, the numeral 1, another space, the numeral 2, another space, the numeral 3, and finally the characters that define a carriage return/line feed combination.

Visual Basic uses the Write # statement to send items to a file separated by commas and with quotes around strings. For example,

```
Write #3, "Testing 1,2,3"
```

sends everything (including the quotes and the commas) to the output (or append) file with ID #3.

The LOF command

Instead of using FileLen, once a file is open you can use the Visual Basic command LOF( ) (Length Of File) to learn how large the file is. To use this command, place the appropriate file identifier number within the parentheses. To see this command at work (and to confirm what was said earlier about the sizes of the TEST file), try the following Click procedure in a new project:

```
Private Sub Form_Click()
' demonstrates the 'exact' image property of Print #
  Open "Test1" For Output As #1
  Open "Test2" For Output As #2
  Open "Test3" For Output As #3
  Print #1,"TESTING, 1,2,3"
  Print #2,"TESTING, 1,2,3";
  Print #3,"TESTING",1,2,3
  Print LOF(1)
  Print LOF(2)
  Print LOF(3)
  Close
End Sub
```

Reading Back Information from a File

To read information back from a file, you must open the file for Input using its name (again, the full path name if it's not in the currently active directory) and give it a file identifier that is not currently being used within the program. (It doesn't have to be the same identifier that it was set up with originally.) The easiest way to read information up to a carriage return/line feed combination is with the LineInput command, as in the following example:

```
Open "TEST1" For Input As #1
Line Input #1, A$
Close #1
```

To pick up individual items when you know their nature, use the Input command, as in the following example:

```
Open "TEST1" For Input As #1
Input #1, A$, B, C, D
Close #1
```

This recovers the numbers as numbers (values of numeric variables) rather than as strings of numerals (part of a larger string). (You can use variants, of course, if you don't know the nature of the information stored in the file.)

Adding to an Existing File

To add information to the end of an already existing file, use the statement

Open *FileName* For Append As *File#*

This causes three things to occur at once:

- Visual Basic opens the file (if the file doesn't exist, it creates it) and sets up the appropriate buffer.
- Visual Basic locates the end of the file on the disk.
- Visual Basic prepares to output to the file at its end.

Caution: Recall that if you open an existing file for Output, you erase it. Only by using the Append command can you add to an existing file.

Reading Back General Sequential Files

Although For-Next loops are a convenient way to read back information contained in a file, there are times when they are not practical—you simply don't know what limits to use. You obviously need a way to test when you're at the end of a file. The statement in Visual Basic that lets you do this is mnemonic: it's called EOF( ) (End Of File), where the parentheses hold the file ID number. A quite general fragment to read back the information contained in a file set up with Print # statements looks like this:

```
FileNum = FreeFile
Open FileName$ For Input As #FileNum
Do Until EOF(FileNum)
   Line Input #FileNum, A$
Loop
Close #FileNum
```

One common use of the EOF statement is to read back the information contained in a file character by character. The command that picks individual characters from the keyboard is Input$. In Visual Basic, you pick up individual characters from a file with the statement

Input$(*NumberOfChars, File Id*)

where the first entry holds the number of characters and the second holds the file ID.

Note: Sequential file techniques in Visual Basic stop reading a file when they encounter a CTRL+Z combination (CHR$(26)), the traditional end-of-file character. This means you cannot use sequential file input to read files created by many programs. To do so, use the binary techniques described later in this chapter.

The RichTextBox Control and File Handling

If you are working with Windows 95 and have the Professional or Enterprise edition of Visual Basic, you can use some properties of the RichTextBox control to make it easy to send its contents to a file (or conversely, to display the contents of a file inside of one.) Here are short descriptions of the properties and methods of the RichTextControl that can be used in file handling.

LoadFile Method This loads an .RTF file or text file into a RichTextBox control at one gulp. The syntax is

NameOfRichTextBox.LoadFile*(PathName, FileType)*

where the *PathName* is a string expression defining the path and filename of the file you want to load into the control. The optional *FileType* parameter controls whether the file is loaded as an RTF file (the default is that it is, but you can use a value of 0 or the symbolic constant rtfRTF). Use the value 1, or the constant rtfText, to load a text file.

Note: The LoadFile method replaces whatever was in the control with the contents of the file.

SaveFile Method The SaveFile method saves the contents of a RichTextBox control to a file in one swoop. The syntax is similar to that of LoadFile:

NameOfRichTextBox.SaveFile(*PathName, FileType*)

Note: You can, of course, use ordinary file-handling techniques for working with a rich text box control. For example,

```
Open "FOO.RTF" For Input As 1
RichTextBox1.TextRTF = Input$(LOF(1), 1)
```

Making a File Program Robust: Error Trapping

Table 9-2 gives the error codes most common to file-handling programs and their likely causes.

Code	Message
52	Bad file name or number (Remember to use FreeFile correctly.)
53	File not found (probably a typo)
54	Bad file mode (The code uses two types of file handling—without closing the file in between.)
55	File already open (You obviously can't open a file that is already opened unless you use a different identification number.)
57	Device I/O error (Big problems! Your hardware is acting up. I/O stands for Input/Output, but check the disk drive anyway.)
58	File already exists
59	Bad record length
61	Disk full (not enough room to do what you want)
62	Input past end of file (You put the test for EOF in the wrong place.)
63	Bad record number
67	Too many files at the same time
68	Device unavailable
70	Permission denied (The disk you're writing to has the write-protect notch covered or the file is write-protected.)
71	Disk not ready (The door is open, or where's the floppy?)
74	Can't rename files across different drives
75	Path/File access error
76	Path not found (Probably a typo—you asked to open a file that doesn't exist.)

Common error codes
Table 9-2.

Now add code to your event procedure as in the fragment given here:

```
DiskErrorHandler:
Select Case Err.Number
    Case 53
     M$ = "Your file was not found. Please check on the "
     M$ = M$ + "spelling or call your operator for assistance."
    Case 57
     M$ = "Possibly big problems on your hardware. You should "
     M$ = M$ + "call your operator for assistance."
    Case 61
     M$ = "The disk is full. Please replace with a slightly less "
     M$ = M$ + "used model." 'could Shell to FORMAT.COM here
    Case 71
     M$ = "I think the drive door is open - please check."
    Case Else
     M$ = "Please tell the operator (= program author?) that"
     M$ = M$ & " error number " & Err.Number & " occurred. "
  End Select
  M$ = M$ + vbCrLf + vbCrLf + "If the error has been corrected click on"
  M$ = M$ + " retry, otherwise click on cancel."
  WhatToDo% = MsgBox(M$, vbRetryCancel)     'retry/cancel message box
  If WhatToDo% = vbRetry Then Resume Else End
```

Random-Access Files

With random-access files you gain instant access to individual pieces of information, but only at some cost. You must standardize the packets of information involved, which means that some things may not fit or that space is not efficiently used; and if the file grows too big—with too many pieces of information—you'll have to set up another file to index the first.

A *random-access file* is a special disk file arranged by records. This lets you immediately move to the 15th record without having to pass through the 14th before it, which saves a considerable amount of time. When you first set up a random-access file, you specify the maximum length for each record. When you enter data for an individual record, you can, of course, put in less information than this preset limit, but you can never put in more.

The command that sets up a random-access file is analogous to the one for opening a sequential file. For example,

```
Open "SAMPLE.RND" As #5 Len = 100
```

opens a random-access file called SAMPLE.RND on the current directory with a file ID of 5, and each record can hold 100 characters. Note that, unlike the situation for sequential files, you don't have to specify whether you're opening the file for input, output, or appending. You can have any mixture of random access and sequential files open at the same time. The only restrictions are set by the underlying operating system (the FILES command in your CONFIG.SYS file). To prevent confusion between file types, many programmers use an extension like .RND for all random-access files, as in the preceding example.

Similarly, you close a file opened for random access by using the Close command followed by the file ID number. As before, the Close command alone closes all open files, regardless of whether they were opened for sequential or random access.

Suppose you want to write a random-access file that would keep track of someone's library. You start by designing the form. You decide on five categories—AUTHOR, TITLE, SUBJECT, PUBLISHER, and MISCELLANEOUS—and after looking over your library, you decide on the following limits for the categories:

Category	Size
AUTHOR	20
TITLE	30
SUBJECT	15
PUBLISHER	20
MISCELLANEOUS	13

Therefore, the total for each record is 98. A random-access file to fit this form is set up (via FileNum = FreeFile, as always):

```
Open "MYLIB.RND" As FileNum Len = 98
```

Each record within a random-access file has a record number. A single random-access file can hold from 1 to 16,777,216 records. Moreover, you don't have to fill the records in order. As you'll see, you can place information in the 15th record without ever having touched the first 14. The disadvantage of doing this, however, is that Visual Basic would automatically set aside enough space for the first 14 records on the disk, even if nothing was in them.

To work with a random-access file, first set up a type corresponding to the record. For example:

```
Type Bookinfo
  Author As String*20
```

```
  Title As String*30
  Subject As String*15
  Publisher As String*20
  Miscellaneous As String*13
End Type
```

Note: You must use fixed-length strings in order to work within the limitations of a random-access file because of the record length.

Next, suppose ExampleOfBook had been previously dimensioned as being of type Bookinfo. Then the command

```
Get #FileNum, 10, ExampleOfBook
```

(the general syntax is Get *#FileNumber, RecordNumber, Variable*) would transfer the contents of the 10th record from the random-access file into the record variable *ExampleOfBook*, automatically filling in the correct components of *ExampleOfBook*.

The command

```
Put #FileNum, 37, ExampleOfBook
```

would send the components of *ExampleOfBook* to the 37th record of file *#FileNum*. The general syntax for the Put command is, as you would expect:

Put *#FileNumber, RecordNumber, Variable*

Binary Files

Binary files are not a new type of file but a new way of manipulating any kind of file. Binary file techniques let you read or change any byte of a file. Among other features, binary file techniques do not care about any embedded EOFs (CTRL+Z = Chr$(26)) that the file may have.

Visual Basic 3 Tip: Binary file-handling techniques have changed for Visual Basic 3; be sure to read the next few sections carefully. Depending on what you are doing, you may have to change your code in order to make it work with the 32-bit version of Visual Basic.

The command

Open *FileName* For Binary As # *FileNum*

sets up a file to be read with these new techniques. And, just as with random-access files, you can now both read and write to the file.

Now, as long as you are reading back information you are sure was stored as strings, the easiest way to pick up the information from a text file open in binary file mode is with the Input$ function you saw earlier. Because of the automatic conversions the 32-bit versions of Visual Basic makes between Unicode and ANSI strings, this will work transparently for you. (Visual Basic automatically converts ANSI strings to Unicode when data is read back to your application and back to ANSI when strings are written back to a file.)

The first slot of the Input$ function still holds the number of characters and the second the file ID number. For example, the following listing gives a module that prints the contents of any file, regardless of any embedded control characters:

```
Sub PrintAFile(A$)
' example of binary input
Dim I As Integer, FileNum As Integer, Char$
FileNum = FreeFile           ' get free file i.d.
Open A$ For Binary As #FileNum

For I = 1 To LOF(FileNum)
 Char$ = Input$(1,#FileNum)
 Print Char$;
Next I
Close #FileNum
End Sub
```

Using Binary Access in More General (Nontext) Situations

The big change (and one that will break a lot of previous code, unfortunately!) is

In the 32-bit version of Visual Basic you cannot use the Input$(,) for picking up individual bytes from a file.

Instead, you must use the Get statement with an array of bytes. (Arrays of bytes will also work in the 16-bit version of Visual Basic, so you might as well use it all the time.) The problem is that because of Unicode a character no longer takes up a single byte. Thus, because of Unicode, the procedure is a lot more cumbersome then it was in earlier versions of Visual Basic. (In general, in a Unicode 2-byte encoding for an ordinary ANSI string, the first byte will be the ANSI code, while the second is used only for the language.)

The first step is easy. Get the bytes out of the file into a byte array using the Get function. The syntax is

Get *file#, position,* ByteArray

The number of characters this statement picks up is equal to the size of the byte array given as the last parameter. The second parameter is needed because Visual Basic maintains a file pointer within a file opened for binary access. Each time you pick up a byte, the file pointer moves one position farther within the file.

Here's an example of how to use Get for a small enough binary file to fit in memory:

```
Sub BinaryPickUp (A$)
  Dim FileNum As Integer, I As Integer
' Example Of Binary Input for a general file!
  FileNum = Freefile                    ' get free file i.d.
  Open A$ For Binary As #FileNum
  Redim ArrayOfBytes(1 To LOF(FileNum)) As Byte
  Get #FileNum,1, ArrayOfBytes
End Sub
```

(Theoretically this would let you store up to 2^31 characters—but memory constraints would probably prevent this in most machines.)

Once you have the bytes in memory you will have to decide how you want to manipulate the raw byte information. One possibility is that you can leave them in the array of bytes and then work with them using ordinary array-handling techniques. Another possibility is to

- Assign the byte array to a string. (This will not do any translations.)
- Use the appropriate "B" character function from those given in the following table to work with the byte string. (B character functions work similarly to their ordinary namesakes that you saw in Chapter 5—except that they work with byte strings.)

Function	Purpose
AscB	Returns the value given by the first byte in a string of binary data

Function	Purpose
InStrB	Finds the first occurrence of a byte in a binary string
MidB	Returns the specified number of bytes from a binary string
LeftB, RightB	Takes the specified number of bytes from the left or right end of a binary string
ChrB	Takes a byte and returns a binary string with that byte

The Seek Command

The Seek command is a combined fast-forward and rewind command. More precisely,

Seek *FileNum, position number*

moves the file pointer for the file with *FileNum* directly to the byte in that position. Any Input$ would start picking up characters from this location.

Seek has another use. Seek(*FileNum*) tells you the position number for the last byte read for either a binary or sequential file. You can also use the Seek function with random-access files. Now it will return the record number of the next record.

The Put Command

To place information within a file opened for binary access, use a modification of the Put command. For example,

```
Put #1, 100, ByteArray()
```

would place the contents of the byte array directly into the file with file ID #1 starting at the 100th byte. The number of characters sent to this file is, of course, given by the size of the byte array. The Put command overwrites whatever was there. If you leave a space for the byte position but don't specify it in the Put command, like this:

```
Put #1, , ByteArray()
```

then the information is placed wherever the file pointer is currently located.

Note: You can also use Put with string variables by replacing the ByteArray with a string variable. However, to avoid problems that come from mixing bytes and strings in the same file when doing binary access, you are best off doing this only for text files.

Sharing Files

As more files are available only off networks, it becomes more important to prevent someone from inadvertently working with a file while you are working with it. Visual Basic's file-handling functions can easily be adapted to a networking environment by using the keywords described in the following table.

Keyword	Function
Lock	Prevents access to all or part of an open file
Unlock	Allows access to a file previously locked

You can use these functions after you have opened the file, in which case the syntax takes the form:

Lock [#]*FileNumber*[, *WhatToLock*]

for the Lock command and

Unlock [#]*FileNumber*[, *WhatToUnlock*]

for the Unlock command. Both commands use the file number with which the program opened the file. The WhatToLock (WhatToUnlock) parameter specifies what portion of the file to lock or unlock. You use it in giving the Start and End values where they denote the first record (for random-access files) or first byte (for binary access).

For example, the following code:

```
Open "Foo" For Binary As #1
Lock #1, 1 To 100
```

would lock the first 100 bytes of the file foo.

(For sequential files, Lock and Unlock affect the entire file, regardless of the range specified.)

Caution: You must use the Lock and Unlock statements in pairs: the arguments must match exactly. (If you leave off the optional To parameter in the Lock statement, then Lock locks the whole file.)
Be sure to remove all locks with the corresponding Unlock statement before closing a file or quitting your program. Not doing this may foul up the files from that point on!

The General Form of the Open Command

You can also control file sharing at the time you open the file using the most general form of the Open statement. Its full syntax looks like this:

> Open *PathName* [For *mode*] [Access access] [lock] As [#] FileNumber [Len=reclength]

Here are short descriptions of the syntax elements:

PathName This is a string expression that specifies the *FileName*. It may include both directory and drive information.

mode This keyword specifies the file modes you have already seen: Append, Binary, Input, Output, or Random.

access This specifies what operations are permitted on the open file. There are three: Read, Write, or Read Write. You use it as in the following example:

```
Open Filename For Binary Access Read As #1
```

This will let you read the file but not make any changes to it.

lock This parameter specifies the operations permitted on the open file by other processes (unlike the Access parameter, which controls how your program can access the file). There are four possibilities: Shared, Lock Read, Lock Write, and Lock Read Write, as described in the following table:

Keyword	Description
Shared	Other processes can both read and write to the file even while your program is working with it.
Lock Read	No other program can open the file to read it while your program is working with it.
Lock Write	No other program can open the file to write it while your program is working with it.
Lock Read Write	Prevents other programs from working with the file at all while you are working with it.

For example:

```
Open Filename For Binary Access Read Lock Read As #1
```

would let you read the file but nobody else.

FileNumber A valid file number must be in the range 1 to 511, inclusive. (As you have seen, it's best to use the FreeFile function to find the next available file number.)

reclength This is an integer from 1 to 32,767. For files opened for random access, this number gives the record length. For sequential files, this value is the number of characters buffered by the operating system.

Note: In Binary, Input, and Random file modes, you can open a file using a different file number without first closing the file. For sequential Append and Output, you must close a file before you can use it.

Chapter 10

Communicating with Other Windows Applications

The various versions of Microsoft Windows can *multitask,* or run several applications at once. (How effective this will be depends on how the applications were written: for example 16-bit applications must cooperate by releasing the CPU for multitasking to work.) As you'll soon see, Visual Basic lets you take advantage of Windows multitasking powers by writing code that activates any Windows application or that send commands directly to the active application from within a Visual Basic project. Multitasking becomes even more powerful if the various applications can work with each other. Suppose you could write a Visual Basic program that monitors what a spreadsheet like Excel or Lotus 1-2-3 for Windows is doing. This would make it possible to use Visual Basic to add a feature that isn't built into the spreadsheet. For example, you might want to notify the user if a crucial quantity has changed or reached a target. Perhaps you want to write a program that analyzes a document being written in a Windows word processor like Word for Windows in real time, notifying the user when he or she has written a certain number of words. All this and more are possible through *dynamic data exchange* (DDE for short) and *object linking and embedding* (OLE for short), both of which are surveyed in this chapter.

DDE may seem mysterious at first, but if you think of it as automated use of the Windows clipboard, the mystery should disappear. The first section of this chapter covers the clipboard. If you haven't spent much time using the clipboard, you'll see that it is much more than a passive place to store objects for cutting and pasting. Essentially, what your Visual Basic program does in DDE is tell the other application what to put into or take out of the clipboard.

Note: Although you must use a registered clipboard format, DDE doesn't use the clipboard the way an ordinary cut-and-paste operation does. Any data already there doesn't get overwritten, and you can have multiple simultaneous DDE conversations.

OLE is potentially an even more powerful way to have Windows applications communicate. OLE lets you build your own integrated Windows applications using Visual Basic as the "glue" to bind disparate Windows applications.

Note: While OLE 2.0 support may one day be very common in Windows applications, right now very few applications support it fully. (Even Microsoft Office only gives you access to part of OLE's power.) Nonetheless, OLE is an essential part of a product receiving Windows 95 certification, and so more and more Windows 95 applications will work with OLE.

Finally, because of the currently limited availability of fully OLE-compliant applications, the section on OLE 2 in this chapter is more a survey of what you will be able to do with it someday than what you can do with it now. In particular, this book gives only the simplest example of OLE automation, which is the ability of one application to actually program another application. Using Visual Basic to build OLE servers is also just briefly surveyed here.

The Clipboard

The Windows clipboard lets you exchange both graphics and text between Windows applications and is often used for cut-and-paste operations inside a specific Windows application. In particular, Visual Basic uses the clipboard for its cut-and-paste editing feature, and you can use the clipboard together with the properties given in the section "Selecting Text in Visual Basic" to implement similar features into your projects.

The clipboard can hold only one piece of the same kind of data at a time. If you send new information of the same format to the clipboard, you wipe out what was there before. Sometimes, however, you will want to make sure that the clipboard is completely free before working with it. To do this, add a line of code inside your project that looks like this:

```
Clipboard.Clear
```

As you might expect, this applies the Clear method to the predefined Clipboard object. If you need to send text to and from the Clipboard, use the two additional methods described next.

Clipboard.SetText The SetText method is normally used in the following form:

```
Clipboard.SetText StringData
```

This sends the string information contained in the variable or string expression *StringData* to the clipboard, wiping out whatever text was there.

Clipboard.GetText The Clipboard.GetText method takes a copy of the text currently stored in the clipboard. Because the text contents of the clipboard remain intact until you explicitly clear the clipboard or send new text to it, you can do multiple pasting operations.

You use this method like a function. The general form is

Destination = Clipboard.GetText( )

Selecting Text in Visual Basic

When you use a text box or a combo box on a Visual Basic form, users can select text following the usual Windows convention: press SHIFT and use an arrow key, PGUP, or PGDN. Sending selected text to other Windows applications is quite common. Moreover, you will often want to add to your project cut-and-paste editing functions that work with selected text, especially for multiline text boxes. To do this within Visual Basic, you refer to selected text by three properties, two of which have long integer values and the third of which is a string.

SelStart The SelStart long integer gives you the place where the selected text starts. If the value is 0, the user has started selecting text from the beginning of the text or combo box. If the value is equal to the length of the text string—Len(Text1.Text), for example—the user wants the code to start working after all the text that's currently in the box. You can specify where selected text starts (for example, in a demonstration program) by setting the value of this property from code. For example, for a text box named Text1, a line of code like

```
Text1.SelStart = Len(Text1.Text)/2
```

starts the selected text in midstream.

SelLength SelLength gives you the number of characters the user has selected. If SelLength equals 0, no text was selected. If SelLength is equal to the length of the text string, all the characters in the control were selected. To highlight the first half of the contents of a text box, you would use code like this:

```
Text1.SelStart = 0
Text1.SelLength = Len(Text1.Text)/2
```

SelText SelText is the actual string the user has selected. If the user hasn't selected any text, this is the empty (null) string. If you add the following line of code to the fragment just given,

```
FirstHalfOfText$ = Text1.SelText
```

then the value of the string variable FirstHalfOfText$ is the selected string.

If you assign a new string value to the SelText property, Visual Basic replaces the selected string with the new value. To allow users to copy selected text, combine these properties with the SetText method. For a menu item named Copy and a text box named Text1, all you need to do is use

```
Sub Copy_Click()
  Clipboard.SetText Text1.SelText
End Sub
```

To change this to a procedure that cuts out the selected text, use the following code:

```
Sub Cut_Click()
  Clipboard.SetText Text1.SelText
  Text1.SelText = ""
End Sub
```

By adding the line that resets the value of SelText to the empty string, you have cut the selected text out of the text box.

For example, to implement a Paste_Click procedure at the place where the user has set the insertion point inside a text box named Text1, use the following code:

```
Sub Paste_Click()
  Text1.Text = Clipboard.GetText()
End Sub
```

Notice that if the user hasn't selected any text, this acts as an insertion method. Otherwise, it replaces the selected text.

Note: You can also use the selected text properties when working with RichText Box controls (see the online help for more details.)

Clipboard Formats and Graphics Transfers

To retrieve graphics images from the clipboard, Visual Basic must know what type of image is stored there. Similarly, to transfer images to the clipboard, the program must tell the clipboard what type of graphics it is sending. The following table summarizes this information. The last column of the table gives the name of the predefined constants.

Symbolic Constant	Value	Format
vbCFLink	&HBF00	DDE conversation information
vbCFText	1	Text (.TXT)
vbCFBitmap	2	Ordinary bitmap (.BMP)
vbCFMetafile	3	Windows metafile (.WMF)
vbCFDIB	8	Device-independent bitmap (.DIB)
vbCFPalette	9	Color palette

You ask the clipboard what type of image it is currently storing by using the GetFormat method. The syntax for this method is

Clipboard.GetFormat(*Format%*)

where *Format%* is one of the values given in the previous table. This method returns True if the image in the clipboard has the right format, for example:

```
If Clipboard.GetFormat(2) Then MsgBox "Clipboard has a bitmap"
```

To retrieve an image from the clipboard, you use the GetData method. The syntax for this method looks like this:

Clipboard.GetData(*Format%*)

where *Format%* has the value 2, 3, or 8, as in the preceding table. (Remember, you use the GetText method to retrieve text data from the clipboard.)

Activating Windows Applications

Not all Windows applications can engage in dynamic data exchange (DDE). However, you can always send to the active Windows applications any keystrokes you want via Visual Basic. You can even have a Visual Basic project send keystrokes to itself—the obvious key to a self-running demo.

The AppActivate statement moves the focus to another project currently running on the Windows desktop; it does not start a program, nor does it change whether the application is minimized or maximized. The syntax for this statement (it takes named arguments) is

AppActivate *title*[, *wait*]

The *title* argument is a string expression that matches the one in the title bar of the application you want to activate. It is not case sensitive. The wait parameter is either True or False. Usually you will leave it at the default value of False. (If you set it to True, then whichever application is doing the calling waits until it has the focus before it activates the new application.)

If the *title* parameter doesn't make a match with the whole title bar of an active application, Windows looks for any application whose title string begins with that title and activates it—you cannot control which one gets activated in this case. For example, AppActivate "Exploring" will usually start an instance of the Windows Explorer even though its title bar might be something weird, like "Exploring - HardDisk1_(C:)"

Sending Keystrokes to an Application

Once you've activated another Windows application by using AppActivate, you use the SendKeys statement to send keystrokes to the active window. SendKeys cannot send keystrokes to a non-Windows application that happens to be running under Windows in a virtual DOS window. If no other window is active, the keystrokes go to the Visual Basic project itself. (This is useful in testing programs and self-running demos.) The syntax for this statement (it takes named arguments) is

SendKeys *string*[, *wait*]

If the *wait* Boolean expression is True (nonzero), Visual Basic will not continue processing code until the other application processes the keystrokes contained in *string*. If the expression is False (0, the default), Visual Basic continues with the procedure immediately after it sends the keystrokes to the other application. The *wait* parameter matters only when you are sending keystrokes to applications other than your Visual Basic application itself. If you send keystrokes to your Visual Basic application and you need to wait for those keys to be processed, use the DoEvents function (see Chapter 5).

The value of the *string* parameter is the keystrokes you want to send. For keyboard characters, use the characters. For example,

```
SendKeys "Foo is not Bar", False
```

sends the keystrokes "F", "o", "o", and so on, to the active application, exactly as if the user had typed them on the screen. Since the *wait* parameter is False, Visual Basic does not wait for these keystrokes to be processed by the active application.

The only exceptions to sending keystrokes are the plus sign (+), caret (^), percent sign (%), brackets ([ ]), tilde (~), parentheses (( )), and braces ({ }). As you'll soon see, these have special uses in the SendKeys statement. If you need to send these keys, enclose them in braces. For example, to send "2+2" to the active application, use this:

```
SendKeys "2{+}2"
```

You'll often need to send control key combinations, function keys, and so on, in addition to the ordinary alphanumeric keys (A to Z, 0 to 9). To send a function key, use F1 for the first function key, F2 for the second, and so on. For other keys, such as BACKSPACE, use the following codes:

Key	Code
BACKSPACE	{BACKSPACE} or {BS} or {BKSP}
BREAK	{BREAK}
CAPS LOCK	{CAPSLOCK}
CLEAR	{CLEAR}
DEL	{DELETE} or {DEL}
DOWN ARROW	{DOWN}
END	{END}
ENTER	{ENTER} or ~
ESC	{ESCAPE} or {ESC}
HELP	{HELP}
HOME	{HOME}
INS	{INSERT}
LEFT ARROW	{LEFT}
NUM LOCK	{NUMLOCK}
PGDN	{PGDN}
PGUP	{PGUP}
PRTSCRN	{PRTSC}
RIGHT ARROW	{RIGHT}
SCROLL LOCK	{SCROLLOCK}
TAB	{TAB}
UP ARROW	{UP}

For combinations of the SHIFT, CTRL, and ALT keys, use the codes just given, but place one or more of these codes first:

Key	Code
SHIFT	+
CTRL	^
ALT	%

To indicate that one (or all) of the SHIFT, CTRL, and ALT keys should be used with a key combination, enclose the keys in parentheses. For example, to hold down CTRL while pressing A and then B (that is, what this book would symbolize as CTRL A,B), use "^(AB)". The string "^AB" would give you the three keystrokes individually.

You can also send repeated keys more easily by using the string in the form *Keystrokes$ Number%*. There must be a space between the keystrokes and the number. For example, SendKeys "UP 10" sends ten presses of the UP ARROW to the active application.

As an example of putting all this together, the following fragment activates the Windows Explorer and maximizes the window in which it is running by sending the keystrokes needed to open the control box and then choosing the Maximize item on its control box menu:

```
AppActivate "Exploring"
SendKeys "% {Down 4}{Enter}", -1
```

The SendKeys statement sends the ALT key followed by a press of the SPACEBAR (because the quotes enclose a space). These keystrokes open the control menu. The next strokes move you to the Maximize menu item and choose that item.

Note: This technique (using cursor keys instead of the accelerator letters) also works in the international version of Visual Basic where the words on a menu may differ.

Dynamic Data Exchange (DDE)

The way DDE works is that one Windows application (called the *client*) tells another Windows application (called the *server*) that it wants information. (Technically, a DDE conversation is between two *windows*, and from the point of view of Microsoft Windows it turns out that most controls are windows—as, of course, are forms themselves.)

This is called setting up a DDE conversation or DDE link. For Visual Basic, only forms can be DDE servers; but text boxes, picture boxes, or labels can be DDE clients. Although technically only forms can be servers, the controls on the form will probably be providing the information via their properties, so this isn't usually much of a problem. Information generally flows from the server to the client, although the client can, if necessary, send information back to the server.

Windows allows an application to engage in many DDE conversations at the same time. An application can even play the role of server and client simultaneously. For example, your Visual Basic project can send information to Word for Windows while receiving it from Excel. However, only one piece of information may be sent at any one time.

You must know the name of the application you want to talk to. If an application supports DDE, the DDE name will be given in the documentation. For example, as far as DDE is concerned, the name for Word for Windows is "WinWord." The DDE name for Excel is still "Excel." The DDE name for any Visual Basic form acting as a DDE server is the name you chose when you made it into an executable file. If you are running the project within the Visual Basic development environment, the DDE name is the name of the project without any extension.

Next, you need to know the *topic* of the DDE conversation. Usually this is a specific filename. For example, Excel recognizes a full filename (a path name) ending in .XLS or .XLC as a suitable topic. Finally, you need to know what you are currently talking about. This is called the *item* of the DDE conversation. For example, if Excel is the DDE server, the item for a DDE conversation could be a cell or range of cells. If Visual Basic is the DDE server, the control name of a picture box, text box, or label can be the item for a DDE conversation.

Note: The one exception to this rule is the System topic. This allows a program to find out information about the application as a whole (for instance, what data formats it supports, what the other valid topics are, and so on). The System topic also allows you access to DDE Execute commands, which typically run macros (or, in the case of Visual Basic, become parameters to subroutines).

You can have three kinds of DDE conversations (links). A *hot link* means that the server sends the data contained in the item specified for the DDE conversation whenever it changes in the server application. Hot links occur in real time. A *cold link* means that the client must explicitly request updates. A *notification link* is one where the server tells the client that data has changed, but the destination is only changed after a LinkRequest method is processed (see below for this event).

Creating DDE Links at Design Time

This section uses Microsoft Excel for the examples. If you do not have Excel, you should still be able to follow the discussion. All you need to know is that spreadsheets like Excel are organized into rows and columns and that Excel, like Visual Basic, has a Copy menu on its main menu bar with similar items.

For the following discussion, start a new project and add a text box and label to it. Next, start Excel (or imagine that you are starting it). To set up a client link with Excel as the DDE server and the contents of the first row and column as the item for this DDE conversation, do the following:

1. Move to the Excel window and highlight (select) the contents of the cell in the first row and first column.
2. From the Edit menu in Excel, choose the Copy command.
3. Move to the Visual Basic window and select the text box by moving the mouse and clicking.
4. From the Edit menu in Visual Basic, choose Paste Link. (If you followed steps 1 through 3, this should be enabled.)

Now you can test whether the link was successfully made. For this, move back to the Excel window and type something in the cell in the first row and first column. Whatever you type should instantaneously appear in the text box in the Visual Basic window, because links made at design time are hot links. In addition, every time the DDE server updates the information for a Visual Basic control acting as the DDE client, Visual Basic generates the Change event. This lets you act on the information in real time as well.

Note: Excel 5.0 fully supports OLE, and you would actually be more likely to use OLE Automation than DDE for dealing with Excel 5.0. (See the following pages for some examples of using OLE with Excel.)

When you switch from designing a Visual Basic project to running it within the development environment, Visual Basic must break the DDE link. Many applications will automatically attempt to reestablish the DDE link, but you may find that server links, especially, need to be established by code.

This link is permanent. If you save the project, Visual Basic preserves the information about the link as the value of certain properties. You'll see these properties in the next section. In particular, try the following for the DDE link set up previously:

1. Close Excel and save the Visual Basic project.
2. Start a new project temporarily.
3. Open the Visual Basic project with the DDE link.

As you will see, Visual Basic will always attempt to start the application that was the server for a DDE conversation set up at design time.

You can also make a Visual Basic form the server at design time (although ultimately the contents of a control provide the data) by essentially interchanging the roles of Visual Basic and Excel in the previous outline. For example, to have the contents of a text box sent automatically to the cell in the first row and first column of an Excel spreadsheet, follow these steps:

1. In the Visual Basic project, select the text box.
2. From the Edit menu in Visual Basic, choose the Copy command.
3. Move to the Excel window and select the cell in the first column and first row.
4. From the Edit menu in Excel, choose Paste Link.

As before, this link is permanent, but this time Excel will tell Windows to try to start the Visual Basic project when you load this spreadsheet into Excel.

DDE Properties

As you might expect, DDE conversations—at least as far as Visual Basic is concerned—are determined by the value of certain properties. Manipulating the values of these properties via code will make your DDE conversations far more flexible than DDE links made at design time can ever be.

LinkTopic The value of the LinkTopic property always takes the form

ServerName|Topic

The name of the application is separated from the topic by the pipe symbol (|, found above the backslash on most keyboards, or ASCII code 124). For example, for the default Excel worksheet SHEET1.XLS found in the \EXCEL directory, this property takes the form

```
Excel|C:\EXCEL\SHEET1.XLS
```

You can set the value of this property for any text box, picture box, or label.

If a Visual Basic form is acting as the server, the LinkTopic property for the form determines which DDE requests the form will respond to. For example, suppose the name of the Visual Basic project is IaServer and you set the LinkTopic property of a form in that project to AskForInfo. Then any DDE client application that asks for a conversation named

IaServer|AskForInfo

will link up with the project named IaServer. Moreover, if this project were made into an .EXE file that Windows had access to, then Windows would try to start it up. Any controls on the form whose link property was AskForInfo could be items for this DDE link.

If you change the LinkTopic property at design time or run time, all conversations on that topic are ended. This lets client applications switch topics.

LinkItem The LinkItem property identifies what data is actually going to be passed from server to client. For example, if Excel was the server, the item can be R1C1—the contents of the cell in the first row and first column. The syntax for this property is

[*FormName*.]*ControlName*.*LinkItem* = *Item$*

You only set the *LinkItem* for the client control, so *ControlName* in the previous syntax statement must identify a text box, picture box, or label. *Item$* is the string expression that identifies the item the server should send, such as R1C1.

If the DDE server determines what kind of item to send, the value of the LinkItem property is set to the string "DDE_LINK" for the first link, "DDE_LINK2" for the second, and so on. These generic LinkItems are used if the application doesn't have a way to name items systematically, as Excel does by rows and columns. Visual Basic uses the control name of the control for the DDE item.

LinkMode Setting the LinkTopic and LinkItem properties is not enough to activate a DDE link; you must also change the LinkMode property to Hot (a value of 1) or Cold (a value of 2). The default value of this property is None (0). Once you change the LinkMode property to a nonzero value, Visual Basic tries to establish the link using whatever topic you specified as the value of the LinkTopic properties.

Any time you change the value of LinkMode, Visual Basic ends the link. The standard programming practice is to set LinkMode to 0 (None) before you fiddle with the LinkTopic or LinkItem properties.

LinkTimeOut The LinkTimeOut property specifies how long Visual Basic will try to establish the link. The default value is five seconds. However, the LinkTimeOut property uses tenths of seconds; so to double the time to ten seconds, for example, change the value of this property to 100 (instead of the default value of 50). (Some applications are slower to respond than others.)

The DDE Events

There are four link events. Like any Visual Basic events, you can write code to respond to these events as you see fit. The four events are described here.

LinkOpen Visual Basic generates the LinkOpen event when a DDE link succeeds. One common use of this event procedure is to generate a message telling the user that the link is open, for example:

```
Sub Picture1_LinkOpen(Cancel As Integer)
  M$ = "DDE link made with" + Picture1.LinkTopic
  M$ = M$ + " concerning "+ Picture1.LinkItem
  MsgBox M$
End Sub
```

If you change the value of the Cancel parameter to a nonzero value (True) in the course of a LinkOpen event procedure, Visual Basic will not immediately cancel the link.

LinkClose The template for the LinkClose event procedure starts out like

Sub *FormName*_LinkClose( )

for forms, or

Sub *ControlName*_LinkClose([Index As Integer])

for controls. As always, the optional index parameter identifies an element of a control array. Visual Basic calls this event procedure when the DDE link ends.

LinkExecute The LinkExecute event procedure is used only when the DDE client wants the DDE server to do something. This event is generated when the DDE client sends a command to the server (see the upcoming section, "The DDE Methods"). The template for this event procedure starts out like this:

Sub Form_LinkExecute(*CommandString As String, Cancel As Integer*)

The syntax for the command string depends completely on the application you are talking to. You must consult the documentation provided with that application to see what to say.

LinkError Visual Basic calls the LinkError event procedure whenever something goes wrong in a DDE conversation. The syntax for this event procedure template starts out like this for forms:

Sub Form_LinkError(LinkErr As Integer)

and like this for controls:

Sub *ControlName*_LinkError(LinkErr As Integer)

There are 12 possible error codes. Visual Basic will supply these as the value of the LinkErr parameter. The following table gives these codes:

LinkErr Value	Reason
1	The other application requested data in the wrong format.
2	The other application tried to get data before a link was established.
3	The other application tried to send data before a link was established.
4	The other application tried to change an item before establishing a link.
5	The other application tried to poke data (see the LinkPoke method in the next section) before a link was established.
6	After you cut links by changing LinkMode to 0 (None), the other application tried to continue the conversation.
7	Too many DDE links for Windows to handle.
8	Text too long to send via DDE.
9	Client specified wrong control array index.
10	Unexpected DDE message.
11	Too little memory for DDE.
12	The server tried to switch roles and become the client.

The LinkError event is not generated for ordinary run-time errors, such as your project accepting a value of 0 from a server and then trying to divide by 0. You handle these errors by using an ordinary error trap (see Chapter 8). Roughly speaking, Visual Basic generates the LinkError event only when no code is running—for example, when a client tries unsuccessfully to send data automatically because of a previously established hot link.

LinkNotify This event occurs only when the LinkMode property is set to 3 (Notify). This is used when the server has changed the source and needs to tell the client that. Use the LinkRequest method to actually get the new data.

The DDE Methods

There are four DDE methods you can use with Visual Basic controls that are acting as clients for a DDE link.

LinkExecute Use the LinkExecute method to send a command to the DDE server. The syntax for this method is

ControlName.LinkExecute *CommandString$*

where, as with the LinkExecute event procedure, the form of the command string depends on what the server application will accept.

LinkPoke The LinkPoke method is the only way for a DDE client to send data to the server. You can use this method to transfer the contents of any DDE client control on your Visual Basic project to the server. The syntax for this method takes the form

ControlName.LinkPoke

If the client control is a text box, Visual Basic sends the string that is the value of the Text property. For a label, it's the value of the Caption property. For a picture box, it's the value of the Picture property.

LinkRequest You use the LinkRequest method to request the DDE server to send information to the control. This method is needed only if you've set the value of LinkMode to 2 (Cold). (Recall that for hot links, the server sends updates automatically.) The syntax for this method takes the form

ControlName.LinkRequest

LinkSend The LinkSend method is used when you have a form acting as a DDE server and want to send the contents of a picture box. Although hot links normally work automatically, the designers of Visual Basic felt that resending the contents of a picture box every time even one pixel is changed would cut down performance too much. For this reason, you must use the LinkSend method to tell the DDE client that the contents of a picture box have changed. (For example, you could use this method after you make a significant change to the image stored in a picture box.) The syntax for this method takes the form

PictureBoxControlName.LinkSend

The picture box must be a control on the form that is the DDE server.

OLE 2

OLE, which originally stood for *object linking and embedding,* is a technology that complements and extends dynamic data exchange. (Now it's just another one of those acronyms that has passed into simply meaning—itself.) OLE goes beyond DDE in that, instead of information being merely transferred, information passed with OLE is presented in the same way it would appear in the originating application. Spreadsheets appear as spreadsheets, word-processed documents as they would in the word processor, and so on. When you add an OLE Container control to your Visual Basic project, you give the user a bridge to another Windows application, and what they see *will look to them like that other application.*

When working with OLE, first and foremost come the *objects*. This is the data supplied by the Windows applications that support OLE—for example, an Excel worksheet (or, more likely, part of an Excel worksheet). You use Object variables (Chapter 6) for dealing with OLE objects, and you normally use the Variant data type when communicating information to these objects.

To understand *linking,* imagine that you are part of the group working on this book. Besides the author, there are a technical editor, a copyeditor, a proofreader, and others involved. The most efficient method for your group to work would be to maintain a single copy of the document and have each person involved be able to link to it and make changes. *There should still be only one copy of the document* (on a central server) *involved*; that way your group doesn't have to worry about important changes being missed. (In the jargon, it allows work in a parallel rather than a serial way.) With a linked object, the data stays in the application that created it. Think of linking as attaching a chain to preexisting data—like any chained objects, you can effect changes by jerking on the chain. Technically, linking inserts a placeholder into the Visual Basic application, and an image of the data is stored in the OLE 2 control.

The idea of the *embedding* part of OLE is that you create documents that integrate various Windows applications under one roof. Embedding in OLE 2 allows the custom control to maintain the data in the object inside itself. When Visual Basic activates the OLE 2 control, control switches back to the application that created the data, and you can use that application's power to modify the data in place.

One of the main ideas behind the introduction of OLE was that Microsoft wanted to get users away from thinking of applications as being paramount. Instead you think of the document itself as central. For example, suppose you are preparing a complicated report that uses spreadsheet data and a graphics package. You want parts of the document to be under the control of the word processor and parts to be under the control of the spreadsheet. In OLE 2, the other application temporarily takes over to work with the data embedded in the control. When you embed an object in an OLE client control, then no other application can access the data (as opposed to linking it where they can). Moreover, the application that created the embedded data is automatically started up whenever the user works with the embedded data.

You can also use the newest part of OLE called *OLE automation.* OLE automation allows you to take control of other applications. For example, from within Visual Basic you can control Excel by using *its* version of Visual

Basic or you can control Word using *its* WordBasic. In fact, your own Visual Basic applications can be controlled by other applications. (Although we don't spend much time on it here, Visual Basic can create OLE servers, which in turn can be driven by applications that support OLE Automation.)

Using OLE

When you add an OLE 2 client control to your Visual Basic projects, you create what Microsoft calls an *OLE compound document.* (In fact, the moment you add a client control, Visual Basic pops up a dialog box asking you for the name of the application it should hook into. See the next section for more on this dialog box.) The OLE client control comes with all versions of Visual Basic—it is one of the three custom controls supplied with the standard edition of Visual Basic. The icon is usually at the bottom of the toolbox and has a grid and an "OLE 2" in a box inside of it.

As with DDE, your Visual Basic project can be the *client* (or *container*) application that receives the information or the *server* (*source*) application that sends it out. In most cases with OLE, your Visual Basic project receives the information and serves as the client. In any case, the OLE control supplied with Visual Basic is an OLE client control and does not allow a Visual Basic application to become an OLE server (although Visual Basic 4, unlike early versions of Visual Basic, does allow this: you just need to use code or a custom control in order to create an OLE server).

Some important terminology for dealing with OLE is explained in the following sections.

OLE Objects As mentioned earlier, this is any data the OLE control can work with. It can be a single graph, a range of cells in a spreadsheet, a whole spreadsheet, or part or all of a word-processed document. An application that supports OLE will have an *object library* that it can *expose.* (Expose is jargon for "here are the things you can work with. You can work with them in the following ways.") Before we move on with OLE, there is one phrase that will frequently recur, that is, the *OLE Class*. This is the application that produces the OLE object. Any application that supports OLE has a unique OLE class name. For example, "WordDocument" or "ExcelWorksheet." (Class names can be case sensitive.) You can get a list of the class names available by clicking on the ellipses for the Class property in the Property window.

Creating OLE Objects

There are four ways you can create OLE objects, described in the sections that follow. The simplest is to embed or link the object within an OLE container control. This enables you to change objects on the form at run time and create linked objects.

Descriptions of the more sophisticated methods follow.

Creating OLE Objects via the Toolbox

To add an OLE object to the toolbox:

Choose Tools|Custom Controls

Check off the box in the dialog box that pops up.

For example, you can add an Excel Worksheet object to the toolbox by filling in the dialog box as shown here:

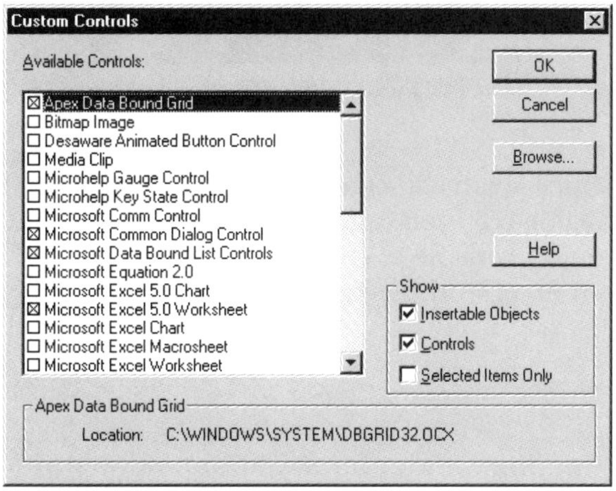

Now, when you use this tool to draw the object directly on a form, you automatically embed the object in your application. Figure 10-1 is a picture of what your form looks like if you embed an Excel object this way. (Notice the Excel object in the toolbox in Figure 10-1.)

Objects via the Tools | References Item

The most modern OLE-compliant applications are available from the dialog box that pops up when you choose Tools|References. These object libraries are particularly nice because they contain definitions of all the objects, methods, and properties the object supplies. Moreover, help is usually available for the syntax of the needed commands from the Object Browser. For example, if you add the Excel object library to Visual Basic this way and then use the Object Browser to study this library, you can see at a glance what the syntax is. Figure 10-2 is an example of this.

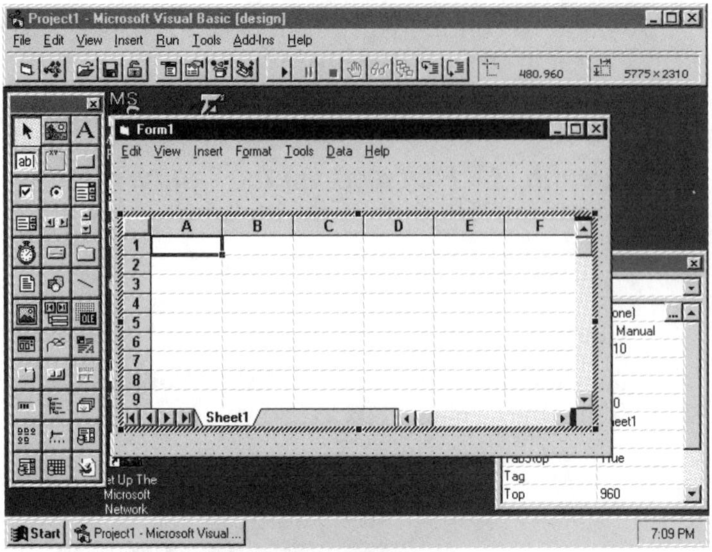

An Excel embedded object
Figure 10-1.

Once you have set a reference to the Object library via the Tools|References dialog box, you can use the CreateObject function with a previously declared object variable to create the object in code. Here's an example of the code for an Excel worksheet:

```
Dim objExcel As Object
Set objExcel = CreateObject("EXCEL.SHEET")
```

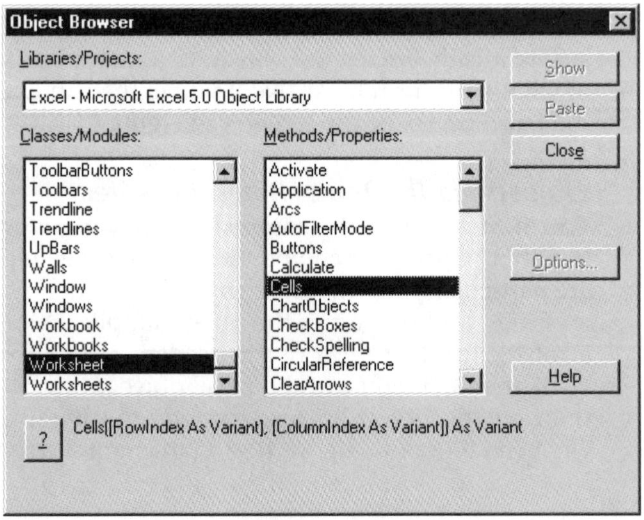

Object Browsing for the Excel object library
Figure 10-2.

These two lines of code created an object variable (named objExcel in this case). This object variable can be used to control Excel. (See the section on OLE automation, later in this chapter.)

Caution: Always set the object variable to Nothing when you have finished with it. (Otherwise the memory and resources it takes up will not be freed.)

Creating Objects When the Object Does Not Supply an Object Library

This is the situation for objects like Word 6.0, which, although they are OLE-aware, do not yet have all the behavior the user would like. In particular, applications that do not expose an object library make you dig out their objects, methods, and properties from their documentation (or in some cases, from a cry on the Internet). For this situation you first use the CreateObject function to refer to the object. Here's an example:

```
Dim objWordBasic As Object
Set objWordBasic = CreateObject("Word.Basic")
```

(Remember to set the object variables to Nothing in this case as well.)

Using OLE 2 at Design Time

Compared to OLE 1.0, creating links or embeddings at design time is easy. Essentially, you need only work with the dialog boxes that will be described in this section.

If you have added an OLE 2 client control to a form, you immediately got a dialog box like Figure 10-3. (The more applications you have, the more items will appear.) This gives you the names of all the Windows applications you can hook into. As Figure 10-3 indicates, you can have the object show up as an icon or with the data visible in the OLE 2 control. The two radio buttons on the far left determine whether you will work with an existing file created by the application (a linked object) or want the other application to create one anew (an embedded object). If you choose to link the control by choosing the Create from File option, the dialog box changes to Figure 10-3. You can click on the Browse button to open a dialog box that lets you pick the file. When you have done that, check the Link box in Figure 10-4.

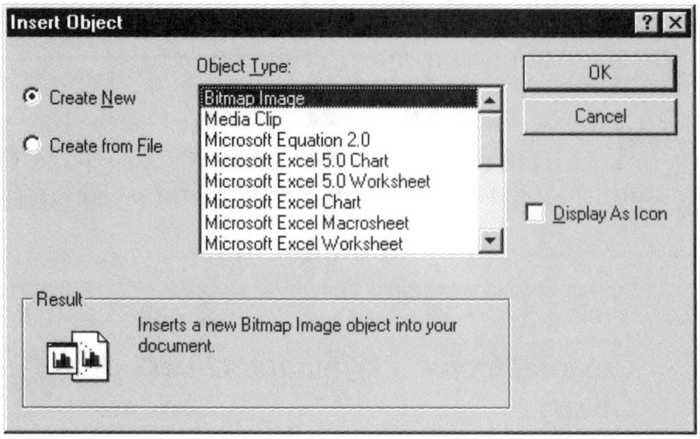

The Insert Object dialog box
Figure 10-3.

Note: You can click on Cancel if you want to set the OLE properties via code. You do not need to use this dialog box in order to work with OLE. In fact, if you create an executable file with an OLE connection made at design time, the file will be much larger than if you create the connection at run time with code.

Paste Special

Sometimes you want to create linked or embedded objects by using information stored in the Windows clipboard to determine the SourceDoc

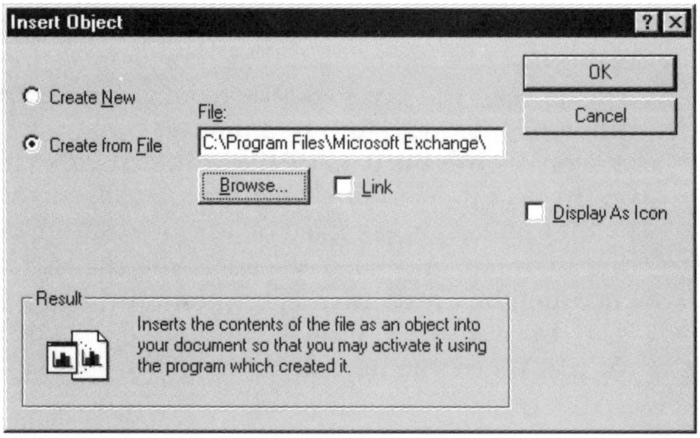

Insert dialog
Figure 10-4.

and SourceItem properties. To do this, you first need to copy the data from the application to the clipboard by using the Copy command in the application. You then need to use the Paste Special dialog box, which is available at design time by clicking the right mouse button when the focus is in the OLE control and choosing Paste Special from the pop-up menu that results. This dialog box automatically examines the contents of the clipboard to determine the needed OLE properties.

The OLE Properties

As you might expect, the dialog box only makes it simpler to set the properties of the OLE control. You can always change them via the Property window or code (and of course you will have to do this to enable OLE at run time).

For example, the Icon/Display Data choice in Figure 10-3 actually sets the DisplayType property. The SizeMode property allows you to change how the control looks at run time. If the value is 0 (vbOLESizeClip), then the control clips the data displayed at run time. If you want to stretch the image to fit the current size of the OLE control, set the value of this property to be 1 (vbOLESizeStretch). Finally, you can have the control automatically resize itself by setting the property to a value of 2 (vbOLESizeAutoSize).

The dialog box that pops up is also setting the crucial *Class* property, which specifies the application containing the data. The *OLETypeAction* property determines what type of object you have created. Is it linked, embedded, or either? The *SourceDoc* property gives the name of the linked object or the file to be used as a template for an embedded object. The *SourceItem* property is used for linked objects to specify what portion of the linked document the Visual Basic application can work with. (For example, a spreadsheet range might be indicated by setting this property to "R1C1:R1C10.")

Common OLE Container Methods

Finally, there are the very important methods that apply to the OLE Container control, which specifies exactly what should be done to the OLE object. Do you want to update the object, create it, delete it, save the information in the object to a file, retrieve it from a file, and so on? The syntax is always

OLEControlName.CreateEmbed

What follows is a short discussion of the methods.

CreateEmbed This creates an embedded OLE object. To do this, you must first set (via the OLE dialog box or code) both the Class and OleTypeAllowed properties. Recall that the OleTypeAllowed property is 1 for Embedded or 2 for either, and the Class property determines the type of OLE object. (Class names are available from the OLE dialog box or the Property window.) When you create a new embedded OLE object, the application must either be active (use AppActivate) or in the system's path.

CreateLink This creates a linked OLE object from an existing file. To do this, first set the OleTypeAllowed and SourceDoc properties. In this case, the OleTypeAllowed is 0 (Linked) or 2 (Either).

The SourceDoc property gives the name of the file for the linked object. If you want to restrict yourself to working with a portion of the linked object, set the SourceItem property as well.

Just as with embedding a document, the application must either be active or in the path.

Copy This sends all the data and linking properties of the object to the Windows clipboard. Both embedded and linked information can be copied to the clipboard.

Paste This copies data from the clipboard to an OLE control. You'll need to check the PasteOK property of the control.

Update This is a very important action because it pulls the current data from the application and gives you a view of it in the OLE control.

DoVerb This activates an OLE object. To use this action, you will need to set the Verb parameter of this method, which specifies what operation you want performed.

Note: If you set the AutoActivate property of the control to double-click (value = 2), the OLE control will automatically activate the current object when the user double-clicks in the control. If the application supports "In Place Activation," then you can arrange it so that the application is activated whenever the OLE control gets the focus (set AutoActivate to 1).

Close This is used only for embedded objects, since it closes the OLE object and cancels the connection with the application that controlled the object.

Delete Use this if you want to delete the object. OLE objects are automatically deleted when a form is closed.

SaveToFile If the OLE object is embedded, then this method is vital. The reason is because the data in the OLE control is maintained by the OLE control and will be lost unless you save it. You save it by tying together the necessary code with setting the SaveToFile method.

ReadFromFile If you used the SaveToFile method discussed previously, this Method reloads an OLE object from the data file created using the SaveToFile method. The code needed for this action is similar to that for saving data, except, of course, this time you'll be reading the data back.

InsertObjDlg This pops up the same Insert Object dialog box that Visual Basic uses when you put an OLE control on a form. At run time, use this method to allow the user a friendly way to create a linked or embedded object.

PasteSpecialDlg This displays the Paste Special dialog box. At run time, you display this dialog to allow the user to paste an object from the clipboard.

FetchVerbs This gets the list of verbs supported by the application.

SaveToOLE1File Use this if you need backward compatibility with the earlier version of OLE.

OLE Automation

Visual Basic is extendable—that's one of its greatest strengths. However, you may not want to spend your time creating custom controls or DLLs that duplicate functionality found in other applications like Excel or Word. The key to tapping other (OLE-compliant) applications is OLE Automation. You can use Visual Basic to write programs that let you manipulate the data and the objects in these applications.

Some objects that support OLE Automation also support linking and embedding. If an object in an OLE container control supports OLE Automation, then you can access its properties and methods using the Object property. If you draw the object directly on a form or create it in code, you can directly access the properties and methods of the object. A full discussion of OLE Automation is beyond the scope of this section. If what we show you here about OLE Automation whets your appetite, refer to your Visual Basic manuals for more information.

Using OLE Automation

As you have seen earlier, you can create a reference to objects in code if you can set a reference to the object with the **New** keyword, **CreateObject**, or **GetObject** from outside the OLE server that created it. Microsoft Excel's and Word's Application objects are examples of these types of objects. Some subsidiary objects, such as a cell in Microsoft Excel, can only be accessed by a method of a higher level object.

For example, go to Tools|References and then select the Excel object library in order to make Visual Basic aware of Excel's objects. Now add a text box to a form. Then use the following OLE automation code to fill a bunch of cells in the second column of an Excel worksheet with consecutive values, sum them, and then place the sum into a text box in Visual Basic:

```
Private Sub Form_Click()
  Dim objExcel As Object
  Set objExcel = CreateObject("EXCEL.SHEET")
  objExcel.Application.Visible = True
  For I = 1 To 10
    objExcel.Cells(I, 2).Value = I
  Next I
  objExcel.Cells(11, 2).Formula = "=sum(B1:B10)"
  Text1.Text = objExcel.Cells(11, 2)
  objExcel.Application.Quit
  Set objExcel = Nothing
End Sub
```

A couple of points worth noting:

- OLE automation requires being familiar with the object you want to program. The syntax is always going to be tricky.
- Even on a Pentium 90 with 16 megabytes of RAM (the fastest machine available to the authors), this simple code took a bit of time (roughly .6 of a second).
- Point 2 shows that although OLE may be a great technology, incredibly fast it ain't.

You should think long and hard before using OLE Automation in an application that is destined to run on anything less than state-of-the-art machinery. (You can use Windows API calls to detect the kind of hardware a user has. The amount of RAM seems to be even more important than the speed of the CPU. Don't try to use OLE automation with 4 megabytes of RAM, think hard before using it when you have 8. OLE will start getting usable when you have 16 megs of RAM, but 32 megs (!) seems to work best.

OLE Servers

The ability to create OLE servers is a new feature in the 32-bit versions of both the Professional and Enterprise editions of Visual Basic 4.0. As you have seen in the above sections, OLE servers are applications that expose their object's properties and methods to other applications. There are two types of OLE servers you can create. The first is usually called an *Out-of-Process OLE server*. This is an executable file that runs in its own process and therefore has its own memory space reserved for it by the operating system. An *In-Process OLE server* is a DLL file that runs in the space of the OLE Client that calls it (and therefore the operating system allocates memory in the calling process's memory space). The basics of In-Process OLE servers are given in the section that follows. To create an Out-of-Process OLE server, you follow steps similar to those used to create any Visual Basic executable application, except that you choose the OLE server option on the Project page in the Tools|Options dialog box.

Creating an Out-of-Process OLE Server

Here are the steps needed to create an out-of-process OLE server

1. Add a code module and create a Sub Main().
2. Add a class module for the class you want to define.
3. Create **Public** properties and methods for the class.
4. Add code to the class's Initialize and Terminate event procedures.

Now you need to set the Project Options for your OLE server in order to ensure that your OLE server functions properly.

Choose Tools|Options and then select the Project page.

1. Set the Startup Form to Sub Main. (Using a Sub Main will allow your application to run and not have to display a visible interface.)
2. Set the Project Name edit field. The Project Name is part of the fully qualified class name used to create objects exposed by your application.
3. Set StartMode to the OLE Server option. (Normally OLE servers stop running when no applications are requesting their objects. This means if you do not have StartMode set to OLE Server, your application would start and immediately stop. The StartMode option takes care of this problem by keeping your application running until you can test the application.)

The last important setting you need to work with on this page is the Application description. This edit field identifies your OLE server in the References dialog box of other applications that will use your server.

Note: The StartMode property is used at design-time-only—its purpose is to help you debug your OLE server. StartMode has no effect when you make an executable file.

To actually create the code:

1. Insert a code module and create a Sub Main procedure.
2. Place any initialization code, if needed, in this procedure.
3. Insert a class module, and in the Properties window set the Name property.
4. Set the Public property to True to expose the class to other applications.
5. Set the property Instancing to Creatable MultiUse. (This allows an OLE client to create multiple instances of your class.)

Now that you have exposed an object, you need to give your OLE clients something to use. The Public variables and Property procedures in the class will be the properties that your OLE clients see. To expose methods, you must create Public Sub and Public Function procedures. For example, the following line in a class module's declarations section

```
Public Name As String
```

exposes the variable *Name* as a property that another application can read and write. Creating a read-only property requires a Property Get procedure.

```
Private Name As String
Property Get NameOfClass () As String
  NameOfClass = Name
End Property
```

The Property NameOfClass will now be read-only to other applications.

The following code exposes a method called SquareIt in our OLE server:

```
Public Sub SquareIt (Foo as Long)
  Foo = Foo * Foo
End Sub
```

The last step in creating an OLE server is to place any needed startup or cleanup code in the Initialize and Terminate events.

Of course, you will want to test your OLE server, and Visual Basic 4.0 makes this easy by actually allowing you to run multiple instances of Visual Basic. The first instance of Visual Basic will contain your OLE server in run mode, and a second instance can contain an application that will test your OLE server. Once the second instance of Visual Basic with your test application is loaded, use the Tools|References to add a reference to the new OLE server. Now you are ready to add code in your test form's code module to call the properties and methods of the object you exposed in the OLE server's class module.

Once your OLE server is fully tested, you are ready to make the final executable and register the OLE server. An OLE server executable is created the same way as any Visual Basic executable, by choosing the Make EXE File choice from the File menu. Registering the OLE server on your machine is done automatically by Visual Basic. To register the OLE server on another machine, simply execute the OLE server with the command-line parameter of **/REGSERVER**. The **/REGSERVER** command-line parameter will automatically register the OLE server on that machine and then immediately terminate the OLE Server. It is advisable to use the Visual Basic SetupWizard to distribute your OLE server. The SetupWizard creates disk images or the files needed for a network installation that automatically handles many of the complicated configuration needs for a Visual Basic 4 application.

Creating an In-Process OLE Server

To create an In-Process OLE server, you follow most of the steps you used to create an Out-of-Process OLE server. One difference is that instead of creating an executable, you create a DLL file. There are some special programming considerations, since an In-Process OLE server runs in the same process as the calling OLE client. Please see the chapter "In-Process OLE Servers" in the Visual Basic Professional edition manual. To create an In-Process OLE server, choose the Make OLE DLL File from the File menu.

Note: Visual Basic Enterprise edition also allows you to create Remote OLE Automation servers. This moves the OLE server off the workstations and onto the network servers.

Chapter 11

An Introduction to Graphics

This chapter introduces you to the techniques needed for building graphics into your Visual Basic applications. A review and more detailed explanation of the Scale method introduced in Chapter 3 begins the chapter. This is followed by more information on how the important AutoRedraw method works. Next are the Line and Shape controls. These let you easily draw lines and various shapes such as circles and rectangles on your form. (They work best if you have relatively few things to draw.) Then it's on to the graphical methods built into Visual Basic. Using the graphical methods can require writing a fair amount of code, but in return, these methods allow you to control every dot that appears on your screen or prints on your printer. Because Microsoft Windows is a graphics-based environment, the graphics powers of Visual Basic can be astonishing.

You should be aware that in traditional programming languages, graphics are usually distinguished from text. This distinction is much less important with Windows and, therefore, with Visual Basic. With the exception of text boxes and labels, Visual Basic considers essentially everything placed on a form to be graphical. This is why forms can display text with such varied fonts and why you are able to use the CurrentX and CurrentY properties to position text accurately on the screen. Nonetheless, the graphics methods themselves work only on forms, picture boxes, and the printer. Since the Z-Order layer for controls (in particular, picture boxes and text boxes) is above that of the form, you can often get dramatic special effects by combining the two.

Tip: If you need to make graphs and charts, and all you have is the Standard edition of Visual Basic, you may want to upgrade to the Professional edition rather than reprogram all the tools yourself. The Graph custom control supplied with the Professional and Enterprise editions makes it amazingly simple to build the most complex graphs–it's much easier than reprogramming all the tools yourself.

Fundamentals of Graphics

To draw on the screen, Visual Basic tells Windows what to display. Windows in turn tells the display adapter how to display the image. What this means is that what you can do with Visual Basic's graphics statements depends on the driver programs that Windows uses to control the screen and printer. However, using these driver programs is automatic. You do not have to worry about all the possible hardware combinations a user may have. This is different from what MS-DOS programmers are used to. When graphics are programmed under DOS, part of the program must check to see what kind of graphics board (if any) is installed, and the program must be adjusted accordingly.

However, nothing comes for free. Windows has to do a lot to manage a graphics environment, and this forces trade-offs. For example, unless you set the AutoRedraw property to True so that Visual Basic saves a copy of the object in memory, you will have to manage the redrawing of graphics yourself. (The jargon says that AutoRedraw controls whether graphics are *persistent* or not.)

Note: Images deriving from setting the Picture property of a control or those coming from the Line and Shape controls are always persistent.

There are slight differences between how the AutoRedraw property being set to True works for forms and picture boxes:

- For a resizeable form, Visual Basic saves a copy of the entire screen. Thus, when you enlarge the form, no graphics information is lost. This option can use much more memory than leaving AutoRedraw at False since Visual Basic needs to reserve enough memory for a bit-by-bit description of the whole form. However, if your graphics do not currently fit on a form but will when the form is enlarged, choose this option.
- For a picture box, Visual Basic saves an image only as large as the current size of the box. Nothing new will appear even if the box is enlarged later.

Thus, drawing to picture boxes requires less memory than drawing to the form, even if the picture box fills up the form.

A Feature of the AutoRedraw Property

There is one other interesting feature of AutoRedraw: Suppose you change AutoRedraw to False while a program is running. Then you clear the object by using the Cls method. Whatever you drew before you changed the Auto-Redraw property will remain, but everything that was drawn after the switch will disappear. This feature can be very useful. To see how it works, start a new project and try the following demonstration program (recall that text is treated as graphics output on a form). For the Form_Load procedure, write

```
Private Sub Form_Load ()
  AutoRedraw = True
  Print "Please click to see a demonstration of AutoRedraw."
  Print "These two lines will stay on the screen after you double
click."
End Sub
```

Now, for the Click procedure, add

```
Private Sub Form_Click ()
  AutoRedraw = False           'keeps old stuff
  Cls
  Print: Print: Print      'third line
```

```
  Print "But this line will disappear after you double click."
End Sub
```

Finally, the Double_Click procedure is simply

```
Private Sub Form_DblClick ()
  Cls                    'Clears line from Click() procedure
End Sub
```

The ClipControls Property and the Paint Event

Visual Basic activates the Paint event each time a part of the form is newly exposed. What happens within the Paint event in this case depends on how the ClipControls property is set at design time. If the ClipControls property is set to True (the default) and the AutoRedraw property is False, then Visual Basic repaints the entire object. If ClipControls is set to False, Visual Basic repaints only the newly exposed areas.

Note: The ClipControls property has a few other features worth noting. Setting ClipControls to True also creates what Microsoft calls a clipping region around nongraphical controls on the object. This means Visual Basic creates an outline of the form and the controls on it in memory. Because the clipping region is created in memory, setting this property to False can reduce the time needed to paint or repaint the object. The cost is more time needed if the object is graphically complex. Clipping regions exclude the Image, Label, Line, or Shape controls.

Tip: If AutoRedraw is set to True, you can speed up your program by setting ClipControls to False.

More on the Paint Event

In any case, if AutoRedraw is False, you write the necessary code in the Paint procedure whenever you want to redraw part or all of a form or picture box. Therefore, the least memory-intensive way to handle the problem of graphics disappearing because a user covered a form or picture box is to redraw the image in the form or picture box in the Paint event procedure. Again this solution involves a trade-off between memory-intensive and CPU-intensive programming activities. Setting AutoRedraw to True uses up memory (if you have it), potentially speeding up the program. Using the Paint event procedure uses up time. You have to choose what's best for the application. At the extremes, the choice is easy: if the amount of drawing to be done is minimal, using the Paint event procedure is better. In any case, Visual Basic calls the Paint procedure for the object only if the AutoRedraw property of the object is set to False.

Caution: Be very careful about including in the Paint event procedure any commands that move or resize the object. If you include such commands, Visual Basic will just call the Paint procedure again, and you'd be stuck in an infinite regress.

The Refresh Method

You will occasionally need to use the Refresh method when working with graphics. This method applies to both forms and controls. It forces an immediate refresh of the form or control and, as mentioned previously, will let you see an image develop even when AutoRedraw is True. If you use the Refresh method, Visual Basic will also call any Paint event procedure you have written for the object. This method is commonly used in the Form_ReSize procedure to redisplay any graphics that are calculated in the Paint event procedure. Also, while Visual Basic handles refreshing the screen during idle time, occasionally you will want to control this process yourself. Whenever Visual Basic processes an *ObjectName*.Refresh statement, it will redraw the object immediately and generate the Paint event, if the object supports this feature.

Saving Pictures

Finally, Visual Basic makes it easy to save the pictures you've drawn to a form or picture box. The SavePicture statement uses the following syntax:

SavePicture *ObjectName.Image, Filename*

The operating system uses the Image property to identify the picture in the form or picture box. If you leave off *ObjectName*, then, as usual, Visual Basic uses the current form. The syntax for this version of the method is

SavePicture *Image, Filename*

If you originally loaded the picture from a file by assigning an image to the Picture property of the form or picture box, Visual Basic saves the picture in the same format as the original file. (For example, icon files stay icon files.) Otherwise, Visual Basic saves the picture as a bitmap (.BMP) file.

Screen Scales

There are six other possible scales besides the default scale, as well as a totally flexible user-defined scale that you'll see in the next section. These scales are set by changing the ScaleMode property at design or run time, as shown here:

ScaleMode (Constant)	Units
1 (vbTwips)	Twips (the default)
2 (vbPoints)	Points (72 per inch)
3 (vbPixels)	Pixels (the number of dots as reported by Windows)
4 (vbCharacters)	Characters (units default as 12 points high and 20 points wide)
5 (vbInches)	Inches
6 (vbMillimeters)	Millimeters
7 (vbCentimeters)	Centimeters

Once you set the ScaleMode property, you can read off the size of the *drawing area*, which is the area inside the form or control or the printable area on the paper. This is reported in the current units when you use the ScaleHeight and ScaleWidth properties. Since both ScaleHeight and ScaleWidth report their results using the units selected by ScaleMode, they are very convenient for resetting form-level or global variables in a ReSize event procedure. On the other hand, the Height and Width properties of an object are less useful for graphics. This is because these properties give you the area of the object including the borders and title bar, if there are any. In graphics, you usually care more about the dimensions of the drawing area.

Tip: Use form or global variables for the Height and Width properties of the Screen object and recalculate these in the Form_Resize event. Then you can use a percentage of these variables in your code in order to make it easier to have your code independent of the particular monitor and card.

Custom Scales

The screen is normally numbered with (0, 0) as the top-left corner. This is obviously inconvenient for drawing tables, charts, graphs, and other mathematical objects. In most of these situations, you want the coordinates to decrease as you move from top to bottom and increase as you move from left to right. For example, mathematics usually uses an X-Y (Cartesian) system, with X measuring distance across from a central point (the origin) and Y measuring distance up or down from the center.

The Scale method sets up new coordinates for forms and picture boxes that you can use in any of the graphics methods. For example,

```
Scale (-320, 100) - (320, -100)
```


sets up a new coordinate system with the coordinates of the top-left corner being (–320, 100) and the bottom-right corner being (320, –100). After this method, the four corners are described in a clockwise order, starting from the top left:

(–320, 100)
(320, 100)
(320, –100)
(–320, –100)

Now 0, 0 is roughly in the center of the screen. This placement occurs because whenever Visual Basic processes a Scale method that changes to a custom scale, the program automatically finds the pixel that corresponds to your coordinates (rounding if necessary).

In general, the Scale method looks like this:

Scale *(LeftX, TopY) – (RightX, BottomY)*

where *LeftX* is a single-precision real number that will represent the smallest X coordinate (leftmost), *TopY* is a single-precision number for the largest Y (top), *RightX* is the right corner, and *BottomY* the bottom edge. For example,

```
Scale (-1E38, 1E38) - (1E38, -1E38)
```

gives you the largest possible scale, which means the smallest amount of detail. Large X and Y changes are needed to light up adjacent pixels.

If you use the Scale method with no coordinates, Visual Basic will reset the coordinates back to the default scale of (0, 0) for the top left-hand corner and the units go back to being twips.

Note: Some programmers prefer using a custom scale rather than percentages of the Screen.Height and Screen.Width objects in their code.

Another Way to Set Up Custom Scales

The Scale method is the simplest way to set up a custom scale. There is one other way that occasionally may be useful. You can specify the coordinates of the top left-hand corner and how Visual Basic should measure the vertical and horizontal scales. You do all this by using combinations of the ScaleLeft, ScaleTop, ScaleWidth, and ScaleHeight properties. For example, after Visual Basic processes

Object.ScaleLeft = 1000
Object.ScaleTop = 500

the coordinates of the top left-hand corner of the object are (1000, 500). After Visual Basic processes a statement like this one, all graphics methods for drawing within the object are calculated based on these new coordinates for the top left-hand corner. For example, if you made these changes to a form, then to place an object at the top left-hand corner now requires setting its Top property to 500 and its Left property to 1000.

Similarly, if you set the ScaleWidth to 320 and the ScaleHeight to 200, the horizontal units are 1/320 of the graphics area and the vertical units are 1/200 of the height of the graphics area.

Just as with the Scale method, you can use any single-precision number to reset these four properties. If you use a negative value for ScaleWidth or ScaleHeight, the orientation changes. If ScaleHeight is negative, the coordinates of the top of the object are higher values than those of the bottom. If ScaleWidth is negative, the coordinates of the left side of the object are higher values than those of the right side.

The Line and Shape Controls

These two controls let you quickly display simple lines and shapes or print them on a printer. They are different than most other controls because they do not respond to *any* events: they are for display or printing only. They are also quite sparing of Windows resources

The Shape control can be used to display rectangles, squares, ovals, or circles. You can also use it to display rounded rectangles and rounded squares. The icon for the Shape control is three overlapping shapes. The Line control can be used to display lines of varying thickness on a form. The icon for the Line control on the toolbox is a diagonal line.

The Shape Control

The Shape control has 20 properties. Usually, you change them dynamically with code while the application is running. The most important properties for the Shape control at design time are described in the following sections.

The Shape Property This determines the type of shape you get. There are six possible settings.

Setting of Shape Property	Effect
0 (vbShapeRectangle)	Rectangle (default)
1 (vbShapeSquare)	Square
2 (vbShapeOval)	Oval
3 (vbShapeCircle)	Circle
4 (vbShapeRoundedRectangle)	Rounded rectangle
5 (vbShapeRoundedSquare)	Rounded square

For example, if you add a Shape control in the default size and shape to a form and write the following in the Form_Click procedure, you can see the shapes for yourself.

```
Private Sub Form_Click
  Static I As Integer
  Shape1.Shape = I
  I = I + 1
  I = I Mod 6 'to prevent error
End Sub
```

The BackStyle Property This property determines whether the background of the shape is transparent or not. The default value is 1, which gives you an opaque border; BackColor fills the shape and obscures what is behind it. Set it to 0 (Transparent) and you can see through the shape to what is behind it.

BorderWidth BorderWidth determines the thickness of the line. It is measured in pixels and can range from 0 to 8192 (rather too large to display on a form).

BorderStyle Unlike the case for Image controls, the BorderStyle for Shapes controls have seven possible settings, as shown in the following table. Having no border (BorderStyle = 0) prevents the control from being visible unless you modify the FillStyle and FillColor properties.

Value of BorderStyle Property	Effect
0 (vbTransparent)	No border shown
1 (vbBSSolid)	Solid (default)
2 (vbBSDash)	A dashed line
3 (vbBSDot)	A dotted line
4 (vbBSDashDot)	A dash-dot line
5 (vbBSDashDotDot)	A dash-dot-dot line
6 (vbBSInsideSolid)	Outer edge of border is the outer edge of the shape.

Note: If you set the BorderWidth property to greater than 1, then resetting the BorderStyle property has no effect.

(To see these in effect, add the line Shape1.BorderStyle = I to the previous demonstration program.)

FillColor, FillStyle The FillColor property determines the color used to fill the shape in the manner set by the FillStyle property. You can set the FillColor property in the same way as setting any color property, either directly via a hexadecimal code or by using the color palette.

The FillStyle property has eight possible settings:

Setting For FillStyle Property	Effect
0 (vbFSSolid)	Solid
1 (vbFSTransparent)	Transparent (default)
2 (vbHorizontalLine)	Horizontal line
3 (vbVerticalLine)	Vertical line
4 (vbUpwardDiagonal)	Upward diagonal
5 (vbDownwardDiagonal)	Downward diagonal
6 (vbCross)	Cross
7 (vbDiagonalCross)	Diagonal cross

The Line Control

The Line control has 15 properties. Usually, you change them dynamically with code while the application is running. The most important properties for the Line control at design time are the BorderWidth property and the

BorderStyle property. BorderWidth determines the thickness of the line. It is measured in pixels and can range from 0 to 8192 (too large to display on most forms). Like the Shape control, the BorderStyle property has six possible settings, but as before, only the last five are really useful.

The most important properties at run time for the line control are the X1, Y1, X2, and Y2 properties. These govern where the edges of the line appear. The X1 property sets (or tells you) the horizontal position of the left end of the line. The Y1 property sets (or tells you) the vertical position of the left-hand corner. The X2 and Y2 properties work similarly for the right end of the line.

Note: These properties use the underlying scale of the container for the line control.

Graphics via Code

If all you want to do is draw a few shapes on the screen, there is no need to use any of the graphical methods. On the other hand, once you master this material, you'll be able to take complete control of each dot on the screen or that prints on the printer.

Colors

The first step is to decide what colors you want. If you do not specify a color, Visual Basic uses the foreground color of the object for all the graphics methods. There are four ways to specify colors. The first way is directly from the hexadecimal coding (see Chapter 5).

The second way is to use the RGB function. The syntax for this function is

RGB(*AmountOfRed, AmountOfGreen, AmountOf Blue*)

where the amount of color is an integer between zero (do not blend in that color) and 255 (maximum amount of that color blended in). Strangely enough, this is exactly the opposite order of that used in the &HBBGGRR coding. (This is unfortunate because what this function does is return a long integer corresponding to the codes chosen, although you can still use this function in the Immediate window as another way to find the hex coding for a color.)

If you are comfortable with QuickBASIC and want to use the color scheme from there, use the fourth way, the QBColor function. The syntax for this function is

QBColor(*ColorCode*)

where *ColorCode* is an integer between 0 and 15. The colors this function gives are summarized in the following table:

0	Black	5	Magenta	10	Light green
1	Blue	6	Brown	11	Light cyan
2	Green	7	White	12	Light red
3	Cyan	8	Gray	13	Light magenta
4	Red	9	Light blue	14	Yellow
				15	High-intensity white

Pixel Control

Now you know how colors are assigned and can change the scale of your screen as you see fit. How do you turn a pixel on? The syntax for this method is

PSet(*Col, Row*) [, *ColorCode*]

(The Pset method doesn't support named methods.)

Since the color code is optional (as indicated by the square brackets), all you need to do is replace the parameters with the values you want. The value of the first entry determines the column and the second determines the row. After Visual Basic processes this statement, the pixel defined by that point lights up. Obviously, where that point is depends on what scale you've chosen. For example, in the ordinary scale, using the default size for a form, the line

```
Pset(3722, 2212)
```

would turn on the center pixel on a standard 14-inch VGA screen, but after a ScaleMode=3 command, this would cause an overflow run-time error. It is possible to use PSet outside the current limits of the form, but if you exceed the limits on the size of the screen, you'll almost certainly get an overflow run-time error. When you use PSet to turn on a point that is outside the form, Visual Basic records this information but doesn't plot any points. This is where the AutoRedraw property's being set to True can help. Suppose you ask Visual Basic to plot a point that is too large to fit the current size of the form and AutoRedraw is True for the form. Then the information isn't lost; set the WindowState property to 2 (maximized), and the point will show up.

Tip: In a situation like this where you need to know how many twips correspond to a single pixel, turn to Visual Basic's built-in TwipsPerPixelX/TwipsPerPixelY functions. (Since Windows API functions usually require pixels, these functions are often needed in using API graphics calls.)

Note: You can use the Point Method to determine the color code of any point on the screen. This returns a long integer using the &HRRGGBB& code you saw in Chapter 5. The syntax is

object.Point(*x*, *y*)

where *x*, *y* are single-precision values giving the X axis (the left/right position) and Y axis (up/down position) coordinates of the point using the ScaleMode property of the Form or PictureBox.

Lines and Boxes

Obviously, if you had to draw everything by plotting individual points, graphics programming would be too time-consuming to be practical. In addition to line and shape controls, Visual Basic comes with a rich supply of graphics tools, usually called *graphics primitives*, that allow you to plot such geometric figures as lines, boxes, circles, ellipses, and wedges with a single statement.

The statement

Line (*StartColumn, StartRow*) – (*EndCol, EndRow*), ColorCode

gives you a line connecting the two points with the given coordinates, using the color specified by ColorCode. (The Line method also doesn't support named arguments.)

For example, the following program gives you a starburst by drawing random lines in random colors from the center of the screen. This program uses a custom scale so that (0, 0) is the center of the screen. Since the number of pixels in the default-size form on a 14-inch monitor is 491 across and 268 down, (–245, 134) is the top right-hand corner and (245, –134) is the bottom right-hand corner:

```
Private Sub Form_Click()
  'random lines in random colors
  Dim I As Integer, CCode As Integer
  Dim Col As Single, Row As Single

  Randomize
  Cls
  Scale (-245, 134) - (245, -134)
  For I = 1 To 100
    Col = 245*Rnd
    If Rnd < .5 Then Col = -Col
    Row = 134*Rnd
    If Rnd < .5 Then Row = -Row
    CCode = 15*Rnd
    Line (0, 0) - (Col, Row), QBColor(CCode)
  Next I
End  Sub
```

Last Point Referenced

Visual Basic keeps track of where it stopped plotting. This location is usually called the *last point referenced (LPR)*, and the values of the CurrentX and CurrentY variables store this information. If you are continuing a line from the last point referenced, Visual Basic allows you to omit the LPR in the Line method.

When you start any graphics mode with a ScaleMode method or a custom scale, the last point referenced has the coordinates (0, 0) in that scale. For custom scales, this need not be the top left-hand corner. After a Line method, the last point referenced is the end point of the line (the second coordinate pair).

An Example Drawing Program

Suppose we wanted to have a program that would use the mouse to draw lines on the screen. To make it more powerful, we will let a click on the right mouse button start and stop drawing. Surprisingly enough, a program to do this takes one form-level variable and just a few lines of code. We use the MouseDown event to determine if the right mouse button has been clicked. If it has, we flip the global flag and reset the CurrentX and CurrentY properties. We do the actual drawing in the MouseMove event. Here's the code:

```
Dim OKDraw As Boolean ' set as a form level variable

Private Sub Form_MouseDown(Button As Integer, Shift As Integer,_
X As Single, Y As Single)
  If Button = vbRightButton Then OKDraw = Not (OKDraw)
  CurrentX = X
```

```
  CurrentY = Y
End Sub

Private Sub Form_MouseMove(Button As Integer, Shift As Integer,_
X As Single, Y As Single)
  If OKDraw Then Line -(X, Y)
End Sub
```


Relative Coordinates

Up to now you've been using *absolute coordinates*. Each point is associated with a unique row and column. It's occasionally helpful to use *relative coordinates*, where each point is defined by how far it is from the last point referenced. For example, if you write

```
PSet(12, 100)
```

which makes 12, 100 the last point referenced, then you can write

```
PSet Step(50, 10)
```

to turn on the point in column 62 (50 + 12) and row 110 (10 + 100). In general, when Visual Basic sees the statement

Step (*x*, *y*)

in a graphics method, it uses the point whose coordinates are *x* units to the right or left and *y* units up or down from the last point referenced (depending on whether *x* and *y* are positive or negative).

DrawWidth and DrawStyle

When you draw on the printer or the screen by using the PSet or Line method (and circles—see the section "Circles and Ellipses" later in this chapter), Visual Basic uses dots that are normally drawn one pixel wide. If you need to change the width of points or lines, use the DrawWidth property. The syntax for this method is

Object.DrawWidth = *Size%*

The theoretical maximum size for DrawWidth is 32,767.

If you do not want a solid line, all you need to do is change the DrawStyle property. You can see the effect of DrawStyle only when the DrawWidth is 1. There are seven possible settings when DrawWidth is 1:

Value of DrawStyle Property	Description
0 (vbSolid) (default)	Solid
1 (vbDash)	Dashes
2 (vbDot)	Dotted line
3 (vbDashDot)	Dash-dot-dash-dot pattern
4 (vbDashDotDot)	Dash-dot-dot pattern
5 (vbInvisible)	Transparent—nothing shown
6 (vbInsideSolid)	Inside solid

Boxes

A modification of the Line method lets you draw a rectangle. The statement

Line (*FirstCol, FirstRow*) – (*SecCol, SecRow*), *CCode*, B

draws a rectangle in the given color code (*CCode*) whose opposite corners are given by *FirstCol, FirstRow* and *SecCol, SecRow*. For example, the following fragment gives you nested boxes in a scale like QuickBASIC's SCREEN 2:

```
Private Sub Form_Click()
  Dim I As Integer
  Scale (0, 0) - (639, 199)

  For I = 1 To 65 Step 5
    Line (5*I, I) - (639 - 5*I, 199-I), ,B
  Next I
End Sub
```

Notice that this program leaves off the color code but still keeps the comma to separate out the B. Without this comma, Visual Basic would think the B was the name of a variable rather than the Box command. Leave out the comma, and Visual Basic would think you're asking for a line connecting

(5*I, I)–(639-5*I, 199–I)

with color code the current value of B. (Since an uninitialized numeric variable 0 has value 0, you probably get a color code of 0.)

The width of the line defining the boundary of the box is determined by the current value of DrawWidth for the object on which you are drawing. When you have a fairly wide line for the boundary, you can see the effect of using the "inside solid" (DrawStyle = 6). Using the InsideSolid line makes for a boundary of the box that is half inside, half outside.

Filled Boxes

You can arrange for the variant on the Line method that gives boxes to also fill the box. All you need to do is use BF rather than B, and you get a filled box. Therefore,

Line (*FirstCol, FirstRow*) – (*SecCol, SecRow*), *CCode*, BF

will yield a solid rectangle whose opposite corners are given by *FirstCol, FirstRow* and *SecCol, SecRow*.

FillStyle, FillColor

Boxes (and circles—see the next section) are usually empty or solid, but Visual Basic allows you seven different patterns to fill boxes as well as using no fill pattern at all. To do this, you need to change the FillStyle property of the form or picture box:

Value of FillStyle Property	Description
0 (vbFSSolid)	Solid
1 (vbFSTransparent) (default)	Empty
2 (vbHorizontalLine)	Horizontal line
3 (vbVerticalLine)	Vertical line
4 (vbUpwardDiagonal)	Upward diagonal
5 (vbDownwardDiagonal)	Downward diagonal
6 (vbCross)	Cross
7 (vbDiagonalCross)	Diagonal cross

Once you have changed the FillStyle property from its transparent default (FillStyle = 1), you can use the FillColor property to set the color used for FillStyle. This property has the syntax

Object.FillColor = *ColorCode*

where, as usual, you can set the ColorCode in any of the four ways mentioned previously.

Circles and Ellipses

Normally, to describe a circle in Visual Basic, you give its center and radius. The following fragment draws a circle of radius .5 units starting at the center of the screen:

```
Scale (-1, 1) - (1, -1)
Circle (0, 0), .5
```

The last point referenced (CurrentX, CurrentY) after a Circle method is always the center of the circle. You can also add a color code to the Circle method. For example,

```
Circle (0, 0), .5, CCode
```

would draw a circle of radius .5 in the color code indicated here by the variable CCode.

To draw a sector or an arc, you have to tell Visual Basic which angle to start at and which angle to finish at. You do this using radian measure, which you may have seen in school. (It is also used in the trigonometric functions in Visual Basic.) Radian measure isn't very difficult. It measures angles by what percentage of the circumference of a circle of radius 1 that the radian measure would give. For example, all the way around a circle of radius 1 is 2π units. It is also 360 degrees, so 360 degrees is equal to 2π radians. One-half of a circle of radius 1 is 180 degrees and π units. Therefore, 180 degrees is π radians. Similarly, one-quarter of a circle (90 degrees) is 2π radians, and so on. To go from degrees to radians, multiply by $\pi/180$; to go back, multiply by $180/\pi$. (Since π is roughly 3.14159, 360 degrees is roughly 6.28 radians.) In any case, the statement that follows

Circle (*XRad, YRad*), *Radius, CCode, StartAngle, EndAngle*

draws an arc of the circle starting at the angle given in radians by *StartAngle* and ending with *EndAngle*. (The Circle method does not, unfortunately, support named arguments.) To get a sector, use negative signs.

There are a few peculiarities of these methods that you should be aware of. The first is that although mathematics allows negative angles, Visual Basic does not. The negative sign only serves to indicate, "Draw a sector rather than an arc." The second is that if you want your arc to start with a vertical line pointed due east (that is, 0 degrees = 0 radians), you shouldn't use –0 for the *StartAngle* or *EndAngle*. Instead, use –2 *π (= –6.28 . . .). The final peculiarity is that angles in the Circle method can only have values between -2π (–6.28 . . .) and 2π (6.28 . . .). (In the current version of Visual Basic, using 8*Atn (1) rather than 6.28 for 2*π seems to result in an error message.)

11

Ellipses and the Aspect Ratio

You convert the Circle drawing method to an Ellipse drawing command by adding one more option. This also lets you override Visual Basic's default settings if you need to adjust the aspect ratio for your monitor. The syntax for this method is

Circle [*Step*] (*XCenter, YCenter*), *radius, , , , aspect*

The four commas must be there even if you are not using the color code and angle options that you saw earlier. (Step is optional, of course.) This version of the Circle method lets you change the default ratio of columns to rows. (It's really an Ellipse command.) If the aspect parameter is less than 1, the radius is taken in the column direction and the ellipse is stretched in the horizontal direction. If the aspect parameter is greater than 1, the radius is taken in the row direction and the ellipse is stretched in the vertical.

The PaintPicture Method

One problem with earlier versions of Visual Basic was that there was no quick way to paint a picture at a specific place on a form or picture box. (You had to use the BitBlt API call.) Visual Basic 4 has added a version of this API call directly to its language. This new method is called *PaintPicture*. It has many uses—for example, it lets you do simple animation quite effectively solely within Visual Basic.

The simplest version of the syntax for PaintPicture looks like this:

object.PaintPicture *picture, x1, y1, width, height*

The object can refer to any form, picture box, or the printer. (If you leave it out, Visual Basic assumes you mean the form.) The picture parameter gives the source of the graphic to be drawn. (For example, it could be the Picture property of a Picture Box.) Finally, the *x1* and *y1* parameters give the coordinates of the upper left-hand corner where you want the picture to appear (using the scale of the object parameter).

To see the PaintPicture method at work, add a picture box with the default size and width to the form. Assign the Picture property of the Picture box to any of the bitmaps that come with Visual Basic (look in the subdirectories of the BITMAPS directory under the VB Directory). Now try the following code:

```
Private Sub Form_Click()
  Dim I As Integer, J As Integer
  Dim NumberOfCols As Integer, NumberOfRows As Integer
  Picture1.Visible = False
  NumberOfRows = Form1.ScaleHeight / Picture1.Height
  NumberOfCols = Form1.ScaleWidth / Picture1.Width
  For I = 1 To NumberOfRows
    For J = 1 To NumberOfCols
       Form1.PaintPicture Picture1.Picture, (J - 1) *_
Picture1.Width, (I - 1)*Picture1.Height, Picture1.Width
    Next J
  Next I
End Sub
```

What this code first does is figure out the number of copies of the picture we can place on the form. For example, if the picture box were 400 twips high and the form were 4400 twips high, we could have 11 rows. (A similar calculation is made for the columns.) Next comes the crucial line:

```
Form1.PaintPicture Picture1.Picture, (J - 1)* _
Picture1.Width, (I - 1)* Picture1.Height, Picture1.Width
```

which paints multiple copies of the picture on the form.

Finally the full version of PaintPicture has the following syntax (it doesn't use named parameters, unfortunately):

> *object*.PaintPicture *picture, x1, y1, width1, height1, x2, y2,_*
> *width2, height2, opcode*

The first three parameters you have already seen—they are all required. All the remaining parameters are optional. However, if you want to use an optional argument, you must specify all the optional arguments that would appear before it. (No empty commas allowed!)

The optional width1 and height1 parameters are single-precision values that let you set the width and height of the resulting picture. The optional *x2* and *y2* parameters let you specify single-precision values that give the left/right (X) and up/down (Y) coordinates of a clipping region within the original picture. The optional *width2* and *height2* parameters are single-precision values that give the coordinates of a clipping region within the original picture.

The optional *opcode* parameter is a Long integer that is used only with bitmaps. This parameter will affect how the picture blends with whatever image was at the location. Its uses are highly specialized, and it is best to refer to the online help for the BitBlt API function call in WIN32API.TXT if you think you need to use this. (It uses the same values as the *dwRop* parameter in the BitBlt function.)

Tip: You can flip a bitmap horizontally or vertically by using negative values for the destination height (*height1*) or the destination width (*width1*) arguments.

Chapter 12

Advanced User Interface Features

Now that you have learned most of the programming techniques needed in Visual Basic, it's time to turn to the user interface again. We will show you the techniques needed to add toolbars and status bars to your applications. In addition, we will show you more about the common dialog boxes and more about the controls available from the Toolbox.

When you start adding many different components to a form, the way they overlap becomes more important. So this chapter has a section on the order that Visual Basic uses to display interface elements.

Next you'll see a bit on MDI (multiple document interface) applications and a discussion on how to monitor what the user is doing with his or her mouse. Finally, we end with a short discussion of help systems.

Adding Toolbars and Status Bars to Projects

Although you can use a frame to put a toolbar or a status bar on a form, most programmers prefer to use picture boxes or the Win 95 controls discussed later on. This is because placing a picture box on the bottom or top of a form is easy in Visual Basic using the picture boxes' Align property.

The value of the Align property determines where the picture box appears. The Align property has three possible values that act as follows.

Align Property Value	Action
0	The default for ordinary forms. You can position the picture box anywhere you want.
1	The standard value for a toolbar. The picture box will appear flush against the top and will automatically have the same width as the form (i.e., the value of the ScaleWidth property). This is the default for MDI forms (see the section in this chapter on them).
2	The standard value for a status bar. The picture box is flush with the bottom of the form and also is automatically the correct width.
3	The picture box is flush with the left of the form and also is automatically the correct height.
4	The picture box is flush with the right of the form and also is automatically the correct height.

Building a Toolbar or Status Bar Without the Win 95 Controls

First, decide on the icons you want to use. Next, assign these icons to the Picture property of the image controls that will be on the toolbar.

Tip: Make the image controls you use in your toolbar part of a control array. This makes the necessary code shorter.

For example, suppose you wanted to prepare a form with a toolbar like the one shown in Figure 12-1. To give the toolbar a professional look, you should have the Form_Paint event adjust the size and position of the icons inside the picture box with code that might look like the following. (This code assumes that the image controls have already been loaded with equal-sized

Form with Toolbar
Figure 12-1.

pictures or icons and that they have AutoSize set to True. Let's also assume that you have five image controls in the control array named ToolImage and the picture box has a control name of ToolBar.)

```
Sub Form_Paint()
  Dim I As Integer
  Dim ImageWidth As Integer
  ToolBar.Align = 1
  Toolbar.Height = ToolImage(0).Height
  ImageWidth = Image(0).Width
  For I = 0 To 4
    ToolImage(I).Move ImageWidth*I, 0
  Next I
' other code for the Paint event
End Sub
```

What this code does is position the image controls sequentially with no space between them. We set the width before the loop to avoid having to check a property value within the loop. (This is a common way to speed up loops.) You could easily insert gaps between the icons by changing the values used in the Move method. Notice how the code also adjusts the size of the toolbar to be exactly as high as the image controls themselves.

Window 95 Controls

Visual Basic for 32-bit development includes several new 32-bit custom controls that are only available when your application runs under Windows 95 or NT 3.51 or higher. The controls are part of a group of custom controls that are found in the COMCTL32.OCX file. To use any of the 32-bit custom controls in your application, you must add the COMCTL32.OCX file to the project. When you distribute your application, remember to install the COMCT32.OCX file in the user's WINDOWS\SYSTEM directory. The 32-bit custom controls are listed below with a brief description.

TreeView Control

A TreeView control displays a hierarchical list of objects called Node. Each Node consists of a label and an optional bitmap. A TreeView is typically used to display the headings in a document, the entries in an index, the files and directories on a disk, or any other kind of information that is conducive to an outline view.

Toolbar Control

A Toolbar control contains a collection of Button objects used to create a toolbar that is associated with an application.

StatusBar Control

A StatusBar control provides a window, usually at the bottom of a parent form, through which an application can display various kinds of status data. The StatusBar can be divided into a maximum of 16 Panel objects that are contained in a Panels collection.

ProgressBar Control

The ProgressBar control shows the progress of a lengthy operation by filling a rectangle one or more chunks at a time, from left to right.

TabStrip Control

A TabStrip is like the dividers in a notebook or the labels on a group of file folders. By using a TabStrip control, you can define multiple pages for the same area of a window or dialog box in your application.

ImageList Control

An ImageList control contains a collection of ListImage objects, each of which can be referred to by its index or key. The ImageList control is not meant to be used alone, but as a central repository to conveniently supply other controls with images.

ListView Control

The ListView control displays items using one of four different views: Large Icons, Small Icons, List, or Report. You can arrange items into columns with or without column headings, as well as display accompanying icons and text.

Slider Control

A Slider control is a window containing a slider and optional tick marks. You can manipulate the slider by dragging it, clicking the mouse to either side of the slider, or using the keyboard.

RichTextBox Control

The RichTextBox control is more robust than the standard Visual Basic TextBox control. The RichTextBox control allows the user to enter and edit text while also providing advanced formatting features. To the RichTextBox custom control in your application you must add the RICHTX32.OCX file to the project. When you distribute your application, remember to install the RICHTX32.OCX file in the user's WINDOWS\SYSTEM directory.

Common Dialog Boxes

While working with Windows and Visual Basic, you've become accustomed to seeing one of five standard dialog boxes for opening or saving a file, printing, choosing fonts, or setting colors.

Common dialog boxes are easier to use in principle than in practice. This is because they require a fair amount of initializing to get them to look exactly the way you want. The online help is essential for working with common dialog boxes. This chapter can only give you a feeling for how to work with them.

The common dialog box control is automatically added to the toolbox unless you have changed your AUTO16LD.VBP or AUTO32LD.VBP file to remove it. To use a common dialog box, you need to place a common dialog control on the form. This control is invisible to the user while the program is running. To actually pop up a specific common dialog box requires calling the appropriate method of the common dialog control while the program is running. For example, if you have an Open File item on the File menu and the associated Click procedure is in OpenFile_Click, the code to pop up a File Open dialog box using the default name of the control looks like this:

```
OpenFile_Click ()
  CommonDialog1.ShowOpen
```

Note: The common dialog boxes take no actions; they accept information only. You will always need to write the code that tells Visual Basic what to do with the information entered and then have this code processed when the user closes the common dialog box.

Working with Common Dialog Boxes

Before you pop up the box, you need to initialize the various properties that determine how the common dialog box looks. For example, you might want to set the default in the Print dialog box Print Range to print only page 1. This is done by adjusting the value of the FromPage and ToPage properties of the common dialog control as shown in the following listing.

```
CommonDialog1.FromPage = 1
CommonDialog1.ToPage = 1
```

All the common dialog boxes allow you to generate an error if the user clicks the Cancel button. Setting up an error trap for this is necessary in most (if not all) cases. To do this, use the following code:

[*FormName*].CommonDialog.CancelError = True

The default is False and so no error is reported when the Cancel button is activated. Set it to True and an error with error number 32755 is generated if the user clicks Cancel or presses ESC. (Again, since nobody would want to use this kind of number in their code—even if they could remember it—use the symbolic constant cdlCancel instead.)

Setting this property to be True and then trapping this error is important because whether the user clicks OK or Cancel, certain values may have changed. Since you only want to use the information when the OK button was clicked, you must have a way to know if the Cancel button was used to close the dialog box.

Here's a general framework for working with a common dialog box that uses an error trap to detect if the Cancel button was pressed.

```
CommonDialog1.CancelError = True
On Error GoTo IsOK
'Make sure the code after the IsOK label is always processed
IsOK:
  If Err = 0 Then  'no error so OK clicked
   'code to process data as needed
  ElseIf Err = cdlCancel
```

```
    'do nothing cancel invoked
  Else
    'wow you have a real error to handle
  End If
End Sub
```

The File Open and File Save Boxes

Here is a table with descriptions of the most important properties used for these dialog boxes.

Property	Use
DefaultExt	This sets the default extension for files shown in the box.
DialogTitle	This sets the title bar. In particular, you do not need to use Open and Save if you are using these boxes in other contexts.
FileName	This gives the name and path of the file selected.
FileTitle	This gives the name without the path.
Filter	Changes here show up in the Type box. You can have multiple filters by separating them with the pipe symbol (a CHR$(124) \|). The format is the string for the description, the CHR$(124), the filter, another CHR$(124), and so on.
FilterIndex	This is used when you set up many filters using the Filter property.
Flags	This property is used to set various possible options on how the box will look. The values needed are stored in constants that begin with cdlOFN_.
InitDir	This specifies the initial directory.
MaxFileSize	This sets the maximum size of the filename including all the path information.

The Flags property is very important in determining the final look and feel of the box. For example, a line of code like

```
CommonDialog1.Flags =  cdlOFNAllowMultiselect
```

allows the File name list box to use multiple selections. You can combine more than one flag with an OR and read back the values using bit-masking techniques with an AND.

Once the user clicks the OK button, you have to read back the information that was entered and take appropriate actions based on these values. For example, *CommonDialog1.FileName* would contain the name of the file chosen.

The Color Choice Box

Here is a table with descriptions of the important properties used for these dialog boxes.

Property	Use
Color	Shows or gets the color
Flags	As with File Save/File Open, specifies the form of the box

The symbolic constants for this box begin with cdlCC. For example,

```
CommonDialog1.Flags = cdlCCFullOpen
```

would display the whole dialog box (including the one for defining custom colors). When the user clicks the OK button, the value of, for example, *CommonDialog1.Color* is the long integer code for the color selected.

The Font Choice Box

Before we get to the table showing the remaining properties for this box, you'll need to know something about how the Flag property works here. Since you might want to have the font choice box reflect printer fonts only, screen fonts only, or both at once, Visual Basic requires you to set the Flag parameter correctly before it will display the Font box. The symbolic constants used are cdlCFPrinterFonts, cdlCFScreenFonts, or cdlCFBoth. If you don't set the *CommonDialog.Flag* property to one of these three values and still try to show the Font box (Action property = 4), the program generates an error and dies. There are 14 different Flag property values. As always, you combine them using the OR operator. You might want to look at the online help to see what the other flags do.

Here is a table with descriptions of the important remaining properties used for this dialog box.

Property	Use
Color	Only used for color printers.
FontBold, FontItalic, FontStrikeThru, FontUnderline	True/False properties. If the cdlCFEffects flag is set, you can allow the user to choose these properties.
FontName	Sets or returns the font name.
FontSize	Sets or returns the size of the font.
Max, Min	These change the point sizes shown in the size box. You need to have the cdlCFLimitSize flag set before you can use these properties.

You read back the value of the various font properties to see what the user wants. For example, the value of CommonDialog1.*FontName* is the name of the font the user chose. Then have Visual Basic process the code to have the new value go into effect.

The Printer Dialog Box

As before, the Flags property controls how the box appears. For example, if the Flag parameter is cdlPDAllPages, then the All option button in the Print Range frame is set. Specifically, this means you will need bit-masking techniques to check out what the user did with the box. Use code like this:

```
If CommonDialog1.Flags And cdlPDAllPages = cdlPDAllPages Then
  'all pages button checked
```


Check the online help for more details on the possible flags you can use.

Here is a table with descriptions of the remaining properties used for these dialog boxes.

Property	Use
Copies	Sets or returns the number of copies the user wants.
FromPage, ToPage	What pages are wanted.
hDC	This is the device context number. It is used for API function calls.
Max, Min	Specifies the maximum and minimum pages the user can put in the Print Range frame.
PrinterDefault	Set this to True and the user can click the Setup button to change the WIN.INI file.

MDI Forms

MDI stands for *multiple document interface,* which is Microsoft's term for a windowing environment used with many word processors or spreadsheets where one window, usually called the MDI *container* or MDI *parent* form, contains many other windows, usually called *child* forms. For example, you can use an MDI container form to allow a user to work with two separate windows in the same application.

The MDI container form usually takes up the whole screen; although the user can resize the container form. You can have only one MDI container form to a project, and that form must, naturally enough, be the startup form.

To make an MDI container form, choose the MDI Form option from the Insert menu. Next, create the additional forms (usually from the Insert menu as well). These will be the child forms to your newly created MDI form *after* you set the form's MDIChild property to True. (You can also turn an existing form into an MDI child form by adjusting this property.) At design time, child forms and the MDI parent form look similar—it's hard to tell the differences between them. One way to tell is to look in the project window at the glyphs (small icons) next to the form filenames—MDI child forms have an icon that looks like a little form next to a bigger form.

When you run the project, on the other hand, all the child forms must be explicitly shown (with the Show method) and are displayed within the MDI parent form's boundaries. Moreover, if the child form is minimized, its icon appears inside the MDI parent form, rather than in the Windows desktop. (If you maximize a child form, its caption replaces the caption of the parent form.) Finally, you can neither hide nor disable child forms without using Windows API. You can, of course, unload them.

One of the nicest features of Visual Basic's MDI forms is that the menus of the container form change according to which child form has the focus. This lets you work with specific menus for each child form. What happens is that the menu for the child form that has the focus appears on the menu bar of the MDI container form—replacing whatever menu was previously there. In particular, the user only sees the menu for the child form when that child form has the focus.

The Window Menu and the Arrange Method

Every MDI application should have a Window menu that allows the user to arrange or cascade the child windows—much like Windows itself does. The Window menu should also include a list of the MDI child windows. An example of such a menu is shown in Figure 12-2.

The list of MDI child windows is easy to put on the menu: set the WindowList check box on the menu design window to be on. Visual Basic will automatically display the list of the MDI child form captions—and even put a check mark next to the one that most recently had the focus.

To activate the Tile, Cascade, and Arrange items on the Windows menu, write code like this:

```
Sub CascadeForms_Click()
  MDIParentForm.Arrange vbCascade
End Sub
```

This uses the vbCascade constant with the Arrange method. The other constants are vbTileHorizontal, vbTileVertical, and vbArrangeIcons.

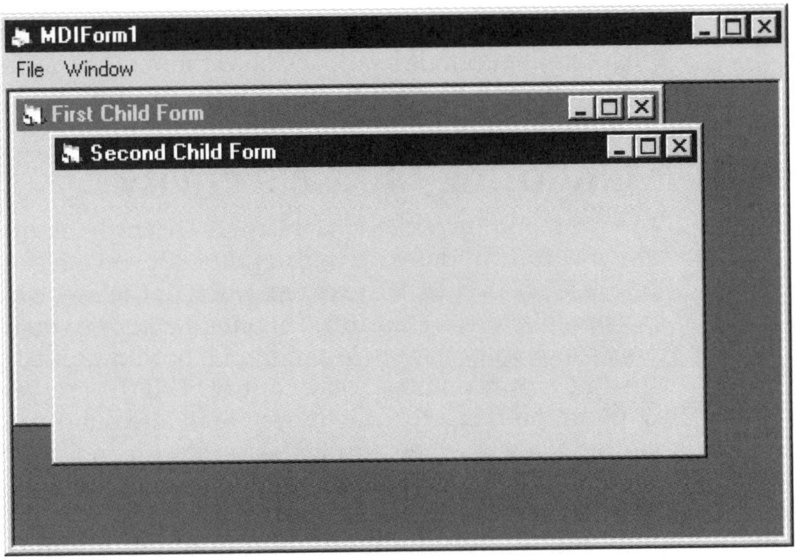

Menu on an MDI form
Figure 12-2.

12

More on How Visual Basic Displays Work: Z-Order

Visual Basic paints the parts of your application in three layers. The back (bottom) layer is where you draw information directly on the form using the graphical methods that were discussed in Chapter 11. The middle layer contains the graphical controls (lines, shapes, picture boxes, and the image control). The top layer contains the nongraphical controls like command buttons, list boxes, and check and option buttons. Certain controls such as labels have a Transparent property that lets information from the layers below shine through.

Within each layer you can control the order in which controls appear. For example, if you use an MDI form, you can control which one is on top after you use the Arrange method. Or, if you overlap two command buttons, you can specify which one appears on top.

You can do this in two ways. At design time you can use the Bring To Front and Send To Back options from the Edit menu to specify the initial ordering of what's on top. To change it dynamically while the program is running, you need the ZOrder method. Its syntax is

[*object.*]ZOrder [*position*]

The position parameter can be 0 or 1. If it is 0 or omitted, the object named moves to the front. If it is 1, the object moves to the back. If you omit the object name, the current form moves to the top.

Monitoring Mouse Activity

Windows, and therefore Visual Basic, constantly monitors what the user is doing with the mouse. Up to this point, all you have used are the Click and Double Click events. These detect whether the user clicked the mouse once or twice in a form or control. This chapter shows you how to obtain and use more subtle information. Was a mouse button pressed? Which button was it? Is the mouse pointer over a control? Did the user release a button, and if so, which one? Did the user move the mouse out of one form and into another? Exactly where inside the form is the mouse? Visual Basic can detect all these events. Of course, as with all Visual Basic operations, you must write the event procedures that determine how Visual Basic will respond to the event. For example, if you want to pop up a menu after a right mouse click, you'll need to write the necessary lines of code.

Finally, just as designing a Visual Basic application involves dragging controls around a blank form, Visual Basic lets you write applications that let the user move controls around by dragging and dropping. The last section of this chapter shows you how.

The Mouse Event Procedures

There are three fundamental mouse event procedures:

Name	Event That Caused It
MouseDown	User clicks one of the mouse buttons.
MouseUp	User releases a mouse button.
MouseMove	User moves the mouse pointer.

In many ways, these procedures are analogous to the KeyUp, KeyDown event procedures that you saw in Chapter 7. For example, as with those event procedures, Visual Basic lets you use bit masking to determine if the user was holding down the SHIFT, ALT, or CTRL key at the same time he or she pressed or released a mouse button.

Only forms and picture boxes return where the mouse pointer is in terms of their internal scales. For the other controls, it's necessary to calculate this information by using the scale of the surrounding container—a method that may or may not be practical.

Controls recognize a mouse event only when the mouse pointer is inside the control; the underlying form recognizes the mouse event in all other cases. However, if a mouse button is pressed and held while the mouse pointer is inside a control or form, that object captures the mouse. This means that no other Visual Basic object can react to mouse events until the user releases the mouse button, regardless of where the user moves the mouse.

All mouse event *procedures* take the same form and use the same parameters:


```
Object_MouseEvent(Button As Integer, Shift As Integer,_
X As Single, Y As Single)
```

If the object was part of a control array, then, as usual, there is an optional first Index parameter:

```
ObjectInControlArray_MouseEvent(Index As Integer, Button As_
Integer, Shift As Integer, X As Single, Y As Single)
```

As the next sections show, bit masking lets you use the Button argument to determine which mouse button was pressed. Similarly, you can find out if the user was holding down any combination with the SHIFT, ALT, or CTRL key by bit masking, using the Shift parameter. Finally, *X* and *Y* give you the information you need to determine the position of the mouse pointer, using the internal coordinates of the object if they exist (forms and picture boxes).

The MouseUp/MouseDown Events

To see the event procedure given in this section at work, start up a new project. Double-click to open the Code window and move to the MouseDown event procedure. Now enter the following:

```
Sub Form_MouseDown(Button As Integer, Shift As Integer,_
X As Single, Y As Single)
  Circle (X,Y), 75
End Sub
```

This simple event procedure uses the positioning information passed by *X* and *Y*. Each time you click a mouse button, a small circle is centered exactly where you clicked—namely, at CurrentX = *X* and CurrentY = *Y*, of size 75 twips. If you add a MouseUp event procedure that looks like this,

```
Sub Form_MouseUp(Button As Integer, Shift As Integer,_
X As Single, Y As Single)
  Dim CCode As Integer
  Randomize
  CCode = Int(15*Rnd)
  FillStyle = 0
  FillColor = QBColor(CCode)
  Circle (X,Y), 75
End Sub
```

then each time you release the same button, Visual Basic fills the circle with a random color. On the other hand, even though you may have two or even three mouse buttons, Visual Basic will not generate another MouseDown event until you release the original mouse button. This prevents you from making some circles filled and others empty when using these two procedures.

Suppose, however, you wanted to make some circles filled and some empty. One way to do this is to use the added information given by the Button argument. For example, suppose the user has a two-button mouse. You can easily write code so that pressing the right mouse button gives the user a filled circle; pressing the wrong one gives only a colored circular outline. The Button argument uses the lowest three bits of the value of the integer, as shown here:

Button	Value of Button Argument
Left	1 (vbLeftButton)
Right	2 (vbRightButton)
Middle	4 (vbMiddleButton)

Visual Basic describes only one button for the MouseUp/MouseDown combination. You cannot detect if both the left and right buttons are down simultaneously, for example. Thus you can rewrite the MouseUp event procedure to allow both filled and empty circles using the left/right buttons:

```
Sub Form_MouseUp(Button As Integer, Shift As Integer,_
X As Single, Y As Single)
  Dim CCode As Integer
  Randomize
```

```
  CCode = Int(15*Rnd)
  Select Case Button
    Case vbLeftButton, vbMiddleButton
      Circle (X,Y), 75, QBColor(CCode)
      FillColor = &HFFFFFF&
    Case vbRightButton
      FillStyle = 0
      FillColor = QBColor(CCode)
      Circle (X,Y), 75
   End Select
End Sub
```

If you want a pop-up menu in response to a right mouse click, use a line of code like this:


```
If Button = vbRightButton Then PopUpMenu MenuName
```

You can also let the user combine the keyboard with a mouse. For example, you can have the SHIFT-right mouse button combination drop down a special menu. This uses the SHIFT argument in the MouseUp or MouseDown event procedure. Here's a table of the possible values for the lower three bits of the Shift parameter:

Action	Bit Set and Value
SHIFT key down	Bit 0: Value = 1
CTRL key down	Bit 1: Value = 2
ALT key down	Bit 2: Value = 4
SHIFT+CTRL keys down	Bit 0 and 1: Value = 3
SHIFT+ALT keys down	Bit 0 and 2: Value = 5
CTRL+ALT keys down	Bit 1 and 2: Value = 6
SHIFT+CTRL+ALT keys down	Bits 0, 1, and 2: Value = 7

At the present time, most people seem to be writing code for the SHIFT key by using a Select Case statement, as follows:

```
Select Case Shift
  Case vbShiftMask
   Print "You pressed the Shift key."
  Case vbCtrlMask
   Print "You pressed the Ctrl key."
  Case vbShiftMask + vbCtrlMask
   Print "You pressed the Shift + Ctrl keys."
  Case vbAltMask
   Print "You pressed the Alt key."
```

and so on.

Microsoft discourages this practice because they reserve the possibility of using the higher order bits for something else. It's preferable then to use the AND operator to isolate the first three bits before proceeding. As you saw with the KeyUp event procedure in Chapter 5, you can do this as follows:

```
Shift AND 7
Select Case Bits
  Case vbShiftMask
    Print "You pressed the Shift key."
  Case vbCtrlMask
    Print "You pressed the Ctrl key."
  Case vbShiftMask + vbCtrlMask
    Print "You pressed the Shift + Ctrl keys."
  Case vbAltMask
    Print "You pressed the Alt key."
```

The line Shift And 7 (binary pattern of 7 = 111) eliminates any information that may eventually be contained in the higher order bits, letting the program concentrate on the information contained in the lowest three bits. You might also want to apply the same preventative against future problems for the Button argument.

The constants assign the values you'll need for the mouse events to the following global constants:

Name of Constant	Value
vbLeftButton	1
vbRightButton	2
vbMiddleButton	4
vbShiftMask	1
vbCtrlMask	2
vbAltMask	4

The MouseUp/MouseDown event procedures work similarly for picture boxes, the only difference being that, as you've seen, you must use the control name of the picture box (and the index if the picture box is part of a control array), as shown here:

```
Sub CntrlName_MouseDown(Button As Integer, Shift As Integer,_
X As Single, Y As Single)
```

Microsoft Windows has begun to adopt the convention that the right mouse button pops up a context-sensitive menu. This was first used (by Microsoft, at least) in Excel 4.0. Another possibility is to have this button give context-sensitive help.

The MouseMove Event

Visual Basic calls the MouseMove event procedure whenever the user moves the mouse. This is the most powerful of the mouse event procedures because, unlike the MouseUp/MouseDown event pair, you can use it to analyze completely the state of the mouse buttons. For this event procedure, the Button argument tells you whether some, all, or none of the mouse buttons are down.

You should not get into the habit of thinking that the MouseMove event is generated continuously as the mouse pointer moves across objects. In fact, a combination of the user's software and hardware determines how often the MouseMove event is generated. To see the MouseMove event at work, start a new project and enter the following MouseMove event procedure:

```
Sub Form_MouseMove(Button As Integer, Shift As Integer,_
X As Single, Y As Single)
  DrawWidth = 3
  PSet (X,Y)
End Sub
```

Now run the project and move your mouse around the form at different speeds. As you can see, the dots are more tightly packed when you move the mouse slowly than when you move it rapidly. This happens because Visual Basic relies on the underlying operating system to report mouse events, and such events are generated frequently but not continuously. Because the MouseMove event procedure is not called continuously, the dots are relatively sparse when the mouse is moved rapidly.

Nonetheless, since the MouseMove event procedure will be called relatively frequently, any code inside this event procedure will be executed often. For this reason, you will want to tighten the code inside the MouseMove event procedure as much as possible or provide a flag to prevent repetitive processing. For example, use integer variables for counters and do not recompute the value of variables inside this procedure unless the new value depends on the parameters for the event. Always remember that accessing object properties is much slower than using a variable.

As mentioned in the introduction to this section, the MouseMove event uses the three lower bits of the value of the Button parameter to tell you the complete state of the mouse buttons, as shown here:

Button	Value
Left button	vbLeftButton
Right button	vbRightButton
Middle button	vbMiddleButton
Left and right	vbLeftButton + vbRightButton
Left and middle	vbLeftButton + vbMiddleButton
Right and middle	vbRightButton + vbMiddleButton
All three	vbLeftButton + vbRightButton + vbMiddleButton

Of course, if you don't have a three-button mouse, the third bit will always be zero. As with the Shift parameter in the MouseUp/MouseDown event procedures, you are safest masking out all but the lowest three bits before using this information:

```
Shift And 7
Select Case Bits
  Case vbLeftButton
    Print "The left mouse button is down."
  Case vbRightButton
    Print "The right mouse button is down."
  Case vbLeftButton + vbRightButton
   Print "The left and right mouse buttons are down."
  Case vbMiddleButton
   Print "The middle mouse button is down."
```

Dragging and Dropping Operations

To move a control as you are designing the interface in your Visual Basic project, you hold down a mouse button (the left one) and then move the mouse pointer to where you want the control to end up. A gray outline of the control moves with the mouse pointer. When you are happy with the location, you release the mouse button. The Microsoft Windows documentation calls moving an object with the mouse button depressed *dragging* and calls the release of the mouse button *dropping*. Visual Basic makes it easy to program this potential into your projects. You can even drag and drop from one form to another if your project uses multiple forms.

Controls permit two types of dragging. These correspond to two different values of the DragMode property. The default is to not allow you to drag controls around except under special circumstances. (As always, you'll need to write the code for these special circumstances; see the next section.) This is called manual dragging, and the DragMode property will have the value zero. Changing the value of this property to 1, automatic, means that the user may drag the control around the project. Regardless of the setting for the DragMode property, the control will actually move only if you write the code using the Move method to reposition it, as shown in the next example.

For this example, start up a new project and add a single command button to it. Set the DragMode property of that command button to 1 (automatic). The event that recognizes dragging and dropping operations is called the DragDrop event, and it is associated with the control or form where the "drop" occurs. Thus, if you want to drag a control to a new location on a form, you write code for the form's DragDrop event procedure. For example, to allow dragging and dropping to move the single command button around the form in this example, use the following:


```
Sub Form_DragDrop(Source As Control, X As Single, Y As Single)
  Source.Move X, Y
End Sub
```

Since the type of the Source parameter is a control, you can refer to its properties and methods by using the dot notation, as in the preceding example. If you need to know more information about what type of control is being dragged before applying a method or setting a property, use the If TypeOf Control Is... statement you saw in Chapter 8.

If you run this example, you will notice that the object remains visible in its original location while the gray outline moves. You cannot use the DragDrop event to make a control invisible while the dragging/dropping operation takes place. This is because this event procedure is called only after the user drops the object. In fact, the DragDrop event need not move the control at all. You often use this event to allow the user just to initiate some action. This is especially common when dragging from one form to another. The reason is that the only way a similar control can appear on a new form in Visual Basic is if you created it on another to place an invisible control of the same type on the new form at design time, to make the control part of a control array, or to use object variables.

If you get tired of the gray outline that Visual Basic uses during a drag operation, you can change it. The easiest way to do this is to set the DragIcon property of the control at design time. To do this, select the DragIcon property from the Properties box. Now click the three dots to the left of the Settings box. This opens up the Load Icon dialog box for choosing icons. You can also assign the drag icon of one object to another:

```
FirstControl.DragIcon = SecondControl.DragIcon
```

The final possibility is to use the LoadPicture function. For example:

```
Control.DragIcon=LoadPicture("C\VB\ICONS\MISC\CLOCK01.ICO")
```

If you design a custom icon, a common practice is to reverse the colors for the drag icon. An Icon Editor program supplied with the Professional and Enterprise editions of Visual Basic makes this easy to do.

The following table summarizes the events, methods, and properties used for dragging and dropping:

Item	Description
DragMode property	Allows automatic dragging (vbAutomatic) or manual dragging (vbManual)
DragIcon property	Changes from the gray rectangle to a custom icon when dragging
DragDrop event	Associated with the target of the operation; generated when the source is dropped on the target control
DragOver event	Associated with any control the source control passes over during dragging
Drag Method	Starts or stops dragging when DragMode is set to manual

Manual Dragging

If you have left the value of the DragMode property at its default value of zero, then you must use the Drag method to allow dragging of the control. The syntax for this method is

```
Control.Drag TypeOfAction
```

The TypeOfAction is an integer value from zero to 2, as shown here:

TypeOfAction Constant	Effect
vbCancel	Cancel dragging
vbBeginDrag	Begin dragging
vbEndDrag	Drop the control

If you omit the TypeOfAction argument, the method has the same effect as the statement Control.Drag 1. That is, Visual Basic initiates the dragging operation for the control.

One way to use the flexibility this method gives you is to allow expert users to drag and drop controls but make the default that users cannot do this. For example, use the CTRL-MouseDown combination to allow dragging to take place. You can do this by beginning the MouseDown event procedure with the following:


```
Sub CntrlName_MouseDown(Button As Integer, Shift As Integer,_
X As Single, Y As Single)
  If (Shift And 7) = vbCtrlMask Then
    CntrlName.DragMode = vbAutomatic
EndIf
End Sub
```

Another example of where you might want to use this method is in self-running demonstration programs. You can use a value of 1 to start the dragging operation and a value of 2 to drop the control. This lets you show off dragging and dropping operations.

The DragOver Event

All Visual Basic objects except menus and timers will detect if a control is passing over them. You can use the DragOver event to allow even greater flexibility for your projects. This event lets you monitor the path a control takes while being dragged. You might consider changing the background color of the control being passed over. The event procedure header for forms is

```
Sub Form_DragOver(Source As Control, X As Single,_
Y As Single, State As Integer)
```

For controls, this event procedure header takes the form

```
Sub CtrlName_DragOver([Index As Integer,]Source As Control,_
X As Single, Y As Single, State As Integer)
```

As usual, the optional Index parameter is used if the control is part of a control array. The Source is the control being dragged, but the event procedure is associated with the control being passed over. The X and Y parameters give you the CurrentX and CurrentY values in terms of the scale of the object being passed over for forms and picture boxes and the underlying form for all other controls. The State parameter has three possible values:

Value of State Parameter	Description
vbEnter	Source is now inside target.
vbLeave	Source is just left of target.
vbOver	Source moved inside target.

Help Systems

A professional Windows application needs a help system that does what Windows users expect. If your online help doesn't have the look and feel of a Windows help system, users will have to learn too much (and you'll probably be working too hard to teach them). Visual Basic comes with the Windows Help compiler to make it possible to create a help system for your applications.

Roughly speaking, the way you use the Help compiler is simple: you write a text file containing certain formatting codes that the Help compiler translates into jumps, definitions, and so on. The text file must be written with a word processor that supports what Microsoft calls RTF (rich text format). Many full-featured word processors support this format. Obviously, you're best off using a Windows word processor when preparing the text files to feed to the Help compiler. This way you can work with the Help compiler in one window and the word processor in the other.

However, we don't recommend doing it this way. (If you insist, Visual Basic's online help has a discussion of the mark-up techniques needed.) This is because it is *much* easier to create a help system using one of the many third-party tools out there—we guarantee that you will find the money well spent.

Tip: Our favorite commercial tool for building help systems is RoboHelp from Blue Sky Software. There are also a couple of tools (WHAT, the "Windows Help Authoring Templates," and WHPE, the "Windows Help Project Editor") on the Microsoft Software Developers CD-ROM that can make writing help files easier. (Check out the WinHelp Lib of the WINSDK forum on CompuServe for additional tools.)

In any case, a help system should also include the standard menu that users are accustomed to. The Help menu should certainly have Contents, Search, and About items. The Search item should lead to the list of keywords the user can search through. These keywords will connect to the topics that you write. Various parts of your application (like Visual Basic itself) should have context-sensitive help. This way all users know that if they press F1, they can get help about a specific item on a form.

You use the HelpFile property of the Application object to associate a (compiled) Help file with your application. You create context-sensitive help by setting the HelpContext of the form or component. Once you assign the value of the HelpContext property, you have to tell the Help compiler how to *map* the HelpContext property to specific topics.

The Help project file contains the information needed for the Help compiler to do its job. The Help project file must be an ordinary ASCII file. The custom is to use .HPJ as the extension on all Help project files. The Help compiler changes this to .HLP for the compiled version. The Help project file lists all the topic files and can optionally add bitmaps or a map between context strings and context numbers. You can also assign two context strings to the same topic by modifying the project file.

To map Help context numbers to specific topics for context-sensitive help, place the topic after the keyword [MAP], followed by white space (press the SPACEBAR or TAB), followed by the Help context numbers. Here's a sample of what you might have in the [MAP] section of the Help project file if you are doing it by hand instead of using one of the third-party tools.

```
[MAP]
first_context_string     5      ;5 is context number
                                ;Comments follow semicolons
second_context_string    10     ;10 is context number
third_context_string     15     ;15 is context number
```

The point is that the context number is passed by the Visual Basic program as the value of the HelpContext property.

Tip: If you want a Help button to appear in a common dialog box, set the ShowHelp method of the dialog box to be True.

Chapter 13

A Survey of Database Features

This chapter introduces you to the database features in Visual Basic. The database concepts will be illustrated with the sample database and the Data Manager application supplied with Visual Basic. After this introduction, you'll see how to use the Data Manager to build your own simple databases.

Next, you'll see how Visual Basic can work with an existing database through the data control. Finally, you'll see how to use Visual Basic code to move beyond the simplest database manipulations built into the data control.

Keep in mind that this chapter can only be an introduction, because you will quickly discover that if you want to do any serious work with databases using Visual Basic, you will both need and want the extra power that database programming will give you. And you will then discover just as quickly that you need to consult more specialized books. Database programming, whether done from Visual

Basic or from a full-fledged database manager like Microsoft Access, is not trivial. (It is worth noting that while both Microsoft Access includes much of the power of Visual Basic and vice versa, they work best together.) It would take a book at least three times as large as this one to explain any substantial part of the database programming power available to you with Visual Basic.

Note: If you have the Enterprise edition of Visual Basic, you will have even more power at your disposal—the Enterprise edition features of Visual Basic are not covered in this book.

Note: The Data Manager choice under the Add-Ins menu is a handy tool for maintaining and creating databases. The Data Manager allows you to create, restructure, index, modify, copy, and query database tables.

Some General Words on Modern Databases

Before you start working with data access, it is a good idea to get a feel for what modern databases are all about. This section tries, without getting too technical, to explain what is usually called *the relational model* for a database. This is the model used by Visual Basic, Microsoft Access, and many other programmable PC databases such as FoxPro.

Before we get into the more sophisticated relational model of a database, let's return to the simpler databases. A rolodex is a good analog for this kind of simpler database, called a *flat file* database. This is merely an indexed set of *cards* and can easily be created. Random-access files are ideal in building such databases because they are easy to set up and manipulate and don't require massive resources. Notice that in these databases the data exists in a set form. Indexes are added as a way of quickly getting to specific records but are not essential—especially for small sets of data.

The trouble with using only (indexed) random-access files for all database applications is that they are too limited. Suppose, for example, you were running a business. This business maintained a list of customers in one indexed system and a list of bills in another. Someone's address changes; ideally you would want the address to change in both places automatically. This is impossible without a lot of work as long as data for each situation is kept in separate databases.

More sophisticated databases, like the ones you can begin to build with the Data Manager (and build completely with Microsoft Access or the data access power of Visual Basic Professional and Enterprise editions), don't fit the indexed card model. This makes it easy to avoid the update problem mentioned in the previous paragraph. They have many other advantages as well, although the extra power comes at a cost. The extra cost usually will be the need for more powerful computers and more code.

There really is no convenient way to describe the underlying structure of the databases that you can build using the Access engine supplied with Visual Basic; that is what actually lies on the user's hard disk. In fact, for now, think of a database as a large amount of data that exists in no fixed form; it is merely "out there" in some sort of nebulous glob. However, the data is controlled by an oracle with great powers. These powers let the oracle bring order out of chaos.

For example, suppose the database was all computer books published (or even all books published!). You want to ask this oracle a specific question about computer books. There are a lot of computer books out there, many covering the same subject with the same title (as authors well know). There are also a lot of authors out there (as publishers well know). So there is a lot of information out there. The oracle, being very powerful and with lots of storage space, has all possible information about computer books stored away in some form or other—the authors, the titles, the page counts, the publishers, and lots more. The information kept by the oracle could be used in many ways. You might need all books by a specific author, all books with a specific string in the title, all books by a specific publisher, or all books that satisfy the three conditions.

Now, imagine that you ask the oracle a question like, "Present me with all books published by Osborne/McGraw-Hill in 1995. Show me the title, the author, and the page count." The oracle works through all its data and then presents you with a gridlike arrangement of the books satisfying the question you just asked. Notice that you neither know nor care how the oracle does this—how the information is actually stored and processed. You are satisfied with a grid that you can easily manipulate.

Next, notice that a random-access file really can't handle this type of situation. If you had a single record associated to each author, you would simply have no way of knowing how many fields to add to allow for all an author's books. He or she may continue to write and write. Of course, you could have a separate record for each book, but this forces a lot of duplication—the vital statistics of the author would need to be repeated each time, for example.

But, if the data is simply out there in some vague formless mass, the oracle can use lots of internal bookkeeping tricks to avoid redundancies, to compact the data, to search through the data, and so on.

Note: In modern database terminology, the questions you ask are called queries and the grid you are presented with is either a table or a view.

The difference between a table and a view is that a table is built into the database structure and a view is a way of looking at information that might span many tables. The oracle (in Visual Basic it's the Microsoft Access *Jet* engine) will respond to different queries with different tables (views), although there is still only one (potentially huge) database out there.

The usual language for asking queries of a relational database is called SQL (usually pronounced like "seekel" or "sequel"), which stands for *structured query language*. SQL is built into Visual Basic Professional and Enterprise editions and a subset is built into the Standard edition.

Now, in real life oracles don't exist and data can't be nebulous. So, as you'll see in the next section, data is essentially stored in overlapping tables (grids) that are joined together as needed by the database engine. The columns of these tables (grids) are called fields and the rows are called records.

When you make a query, the Access engine either sends you a subset of one of the tables that already exists or temporarily creates a new grid (view) in memory by combining data from all the tables it has already stored. Since the grid is made up of a set of records extracted from the database, the object on Visual Basic is called, naturally enough, a RecordSet.

Note: Microsoft does not follow standard relational database terminology completely. Instead of the term view, they use the term *dynaset* if the grid is updatable and *snapshot* if it is not. This book uses the term *view* if we are not specifying whether the table is updatable, and Microsoft's terms if we are distinguishing between the table being updatable or not.

The Data Manager

The Data Manager is the only way to build a database supplied with the Standard edition of Visual Basic. It is available as an option on the Add-Ins menu in Visual Basic, but it is really a separate application (DATAMGR.EXE) that can be run independently of Visual Basic. The main screen of the Data Manager looks like Figure 13-1.

The Data Manager lets you look at the structure of an existing Microsoft Access (Jet) database. It also can build a new database in Jet format. This is

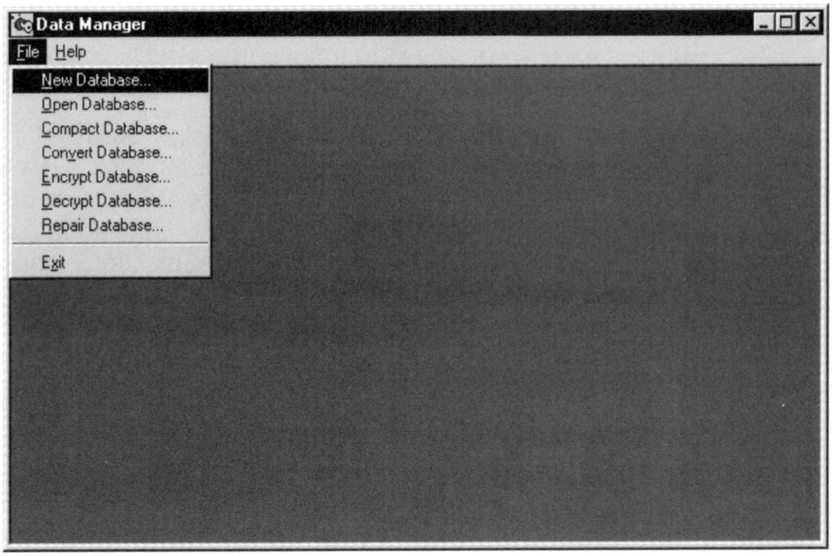

Main screen of the Data Manager
Figure 13-1.

usually called MDB format and the convention is to use an .MDB extension for the filename.

Visual Basic 3 Tip: The data manager was changed in Visual Basic 4 to only let you use Jet MDB formats. You can no longer use it to deal directly with other formats. The VisData sample in the Professional and Enterprise versions of Visual Basic can help if you need this type of function.

The Data Manager can also add information to Jet databases. It can also delete information from a Jet database.

Using the Data Manager to Examine Existing Databases

As a way to get more comfortable with data access, let's use the Data Manager to examine the BIBLIO.MDB database that is supplied with Visual Basic. Open the File menu in the Data Manager and choose Open Database. This brings up the Open Database dialog box. The BIBLIO.MDB database is usually stored in the same directory as Visual Basic.

Notice that there are five tables in this database: one for Authors, one for All Titles, one for Title Author, one for Publishers, and one for Titles. Notice as well that these names do not fit normal DOS filename conventions. (Since the Access engine stores all the information in the database file, the parts of the database do not need to follow ordinary DOS naming conventions. This is different from many earlier database managers such as dBASE III.)

Highlight the Authors table and click Design. Notice that the Authors table has only three fields. The first field seems strange: it is a long integer called Au_ID, which stands for Author ID. This field exists because of the requirement that every table have at least one field (or combination of fields) that is unique. In this case the author's name alone would not satisfy this requirement. Next, notice that the Author field is a text field and can hold up to 255 characters. Then notice that the Year Born field is an integer field.

Turn your attention to the button marked Indexes. Click the Indexes button, and the Indexes dialog is displayed. Select PrimaryKey from the list box and click Edit to display the Edit Index dialog. Notice that Au_ID(ASC) is listed as a "unique, primary index." The words "unique primary index" mean that the Au_ID number is unique and that the Access engine should use this field to determine if someone is trying to enter duplicate data. Therefore, the engine will allow you to enter the same author twice but will demand a different author ID number each time. (It turns out that in this database, author IDs are merely arbitrary integers that correspond to the order in which the title was entered.)

Notice that this particular table is *not* indexed on the authors' names at present. Setting up another index is worthwhile if you will need to search through the data using criteria derived from that index. For example, adding Authors as an index would certainly be worth considering in a more realistic database about books. You almost certainly would like to look for specific authors. This kind of index is allowable because index entries with the Access engine need not be unique. That way you can index on the Author field even though one author may have written many books. Obviously, multiple indexes speed searching through the data. The cost is more overhead, just as it is with random-access files.

Whenever two tables share a common field, they could easily be programmed to be joined using the Professional or Enterprise edition or Microsoft Access. After they are joined, a change in one would affect the other (and usually vice versa).

Other Operations You Can Do with the Data Manager

Besides editing indexes, the Data Manager allows you to create databases, add records to tables, and delete records. Move to the record you want using the arrow buttons and click the Delete button.

The Data Manager also lets you add new fields to an existing table in the database. Open the existing database and then click the design button. Now the Add button allows you to update the table. The Data Manager also lets you delete fields, rename them, or modify any of their properties.

Finally, as you delete and add records, your databases will seem to grow very quickly. For this reason you may want to periodically use the Compact Database option on the File Menu. You can only compact databases in Microsoft Access (MDB) format.

Caution: Although you can use the same name for both the original database and its compacted version, you are better off using a new name and, after the compaction is over, deleting the original and renaming the compacted version. This is because if you use the same name you run the risk of losing both versions if anything goes wrong.

Tip: The Repair DataBase option on the File menu of the Data Manager can sometimes repair databases that are corrupted because of buffer problems (such as a power failure). There are no guarantees, however.

Using the Data Control

Roughly speaking, here's how the data control works: By setting properties of the data control, you hook the data control to a specific database and a table in it. (Code lets you query the database in order to create a dynaset or a snapshot.) You then add controls to a form that will display the data.

The data control itself displays no data. Think of the data control as only conducting the flow of information back and forth between your project and the database. You use ordinary Visual Basic controls to display the data.

Controls that can work with the data control to access data are said to be *data-aware,* and the process of tying a data-aware control to a data control is called *binding* the data-aware control. Among Visual Basic Standard controls, the only intrinsic data-aware controls are text boxes, labels, check boxes, image controls, List box, Combo box, OLE Client, and picture boxes. Among the OLE controls, List boxes, Combo boxes, DBGrids, Masked edit, 3D Panel, and 3D check box are also data-aware. Data-aware controls must be on the same form as the data control, but they need not be visible in order to pick up the information. Once these controls pick up the information sent to them by the data control, the information will be stored as values of properties of the controls.

Seeing the Data Control at Work

If you look at the toolbox, the data control looks a little bit like a VCR control panel. When you work with a data control on a form, you need to stretch it out in order to see the caption and the buttons for moving through the database table. If you stretch out the data control, it looks like this:

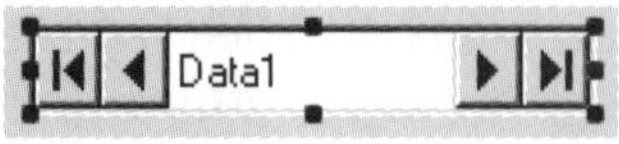

As noted in the illustration, the arrows that look like VCR buttons move to the beginning of the table, back one record, forward one record, and to the end of the table. Each time you press one of these arrow keys, the bound controls are automatically updated. You do not have to write any code for this to take place.

You can have many data controls in a single project, each of which can be connected to a different database or a different table in the same database (or with code to a query about a database and so to a dynaset or snapshot). The properties that control this are easiest to set at design time but can be set (or reset) at run time as well.

The DatabaseName property of the data control determines which database the data control will (try to) connect to. If you go to the Properties window and click the ellipses for the DatabaseName property of the data control, you are presented with a common dialog box to select the database. Notice that you can use the Type list box on the left to change what kind of extensions are shown. The default is to show only .MDB extensions.

Next, you need to set the RecordSource property to the specific table or query in the database. If Visual Basic can find the database determined by the DatabaseName property, it will list the tables and queries in the database when you click the down arrow for the RecordSource property.

Note: You can also set the RecordSource property to a SQL query and so get a view from your database. Please see the section "Structured Query Language (SQL) Basics" for how to do this.

Now you need to add the data-aware controls to the form and bind them to the data control. Choose the kind of control that best suits the information to be picked up. Use a Picture or Image control if it is a graphic image or a check box if it is a Boolean. You could use a label if you don't want someone to be able to update it, or a text box if you do.

The DataSource property must be set to the name of the data control for each data-aware control. Only after you adjust the DataSource property to the name of the data control can the data-aware control display data from the database.

Next, you have to tell the newly data-aware control what column of the RecordSource to bind the information to. This is done by setting the DataField property of the data-aware control to the column name. If Visual Basic can access the database at design time, then clicking on the down arrow for the DataField property will give you a list of the columns in the RecordSource that are connected by the DataSource property.

For example, the following table summarizes the properties you would need to set up controls to accept all the data available in the Authors table in the BIBLIO.MDB database.

Control	Needed Properties	Settings
Data1	DatabaseName	C:\VB\BIBLIO.MDB
	RecordSource	Authors
Text1	DataSource	Data1
	DataField	Author
Text2	DataSource	Data1
	DataField	Au_ID

The nice thing is that once you have set this up, the user can do simple lookups merely by clicking the arrow keys on the data control. The data control automatically gets the needed information from the database and passes it on to the bound controls.

Note: Each click of one of the buttons changes the current record. (Think of the current record as being the row that Visual Basic is currently looking at.)

Caution: If data is changed in a bound control and you click an arrow key in the data control to move to a new record, Visual Basic will update the database with this new information. (See the section on "Monitoring Changes to the Database" in this chapter for more on this subject.)

Other Properties Commonly Set at Design Time

There are three other properties of the data control that are commonly set at design time (although they are equally often reset as needed at run time). Here are short descriptions of them.

Connect This property specifies the type of database. You do not need to set this property if you are working with a database in Microsoft Access format. The connect value is usually the name of the program: for example, FoxPro 2.6.

Exclusive Set this True/False property to True and no one else will be able to gain access to the database until you relinquish it by closing the database. The default is False.

Note: It is possible to change this property at run time, but you will have to close and reopen the database in order for it to take effect.

ReadOnly This True/False property is set to True when you want to be able to look at the database but don't want to affect it in any way. One common way to use this property is to set it at design time to True and change it to False only in response to a password at run time. (See "Refresh" in the section "Other Useful Methods and Events for the Data Control" for more on this property.)

Programming with the Data Control

Although you can do many things with the data control without code, only code lets you take full advantage of its powers. However, for the data control in particular, there is no need to go overboard on setting properties at run time. This is because although the data control properties *can* be set at run time, it is easiest to set properties like RecordSource, DataSource, and DataField at design time when dialog boxes will pop up with the needed information.

To give you an idea of what code for working with the data control will look like, suppose you want to check whether you can update the RecordSet. This is done with code that looks like this:

```
If Data1.RecordSet.Updatable Then
    'RecordSet will be updatable by the user
Else
    'RecordSet is viewable only
End If
```

As you can see, code for working with a data control looks only slightly different from code for working with any Visual Basic object. The difference is that we are actually using a property of the RecordSet object associated to the data control rather than a property of the data control.

Similarly, to determine if you are at the first or last record, you need to use the BOF (beginning of file) and EOF (end of file) properties of the RecordSet. The code might look like this:

```
If Data1.Recordset.BOF
If Data1.Recordset.EOF
```


Note: In most cases you will be working with properties of the RecordSet object associated to the data control rather than with properties of the data control itself.

In particular, the standard edition of Visual Basic does not allow you to create the necessary database objects independently of the data control. The Professional and Enterprise editions of Visual Basic does allow database objects to be created independently. Think of the RecordSet object as pointing to the underlying table, dynaset, or snapshot that is created by the data control.

Every press on a button of the data control at run time has a corresponding method. The following table summarizes this correspondence for a data control named DATA1 using the current recordset.

Control Action	Data1.Method
Click the |◄	Data1.RecordSet.MoveFirst
Click the ◄	Data1.RecordSet.MovePrevious
Click the ►|	Data1.RecordSet.MoveLast
Click the ►	Data1.RecordSet.MoveNext

All these methods change the current record.

The Field Object

The most important object associated to the RecordSet object is the Field object. Think of this as giving you the name and properties of a single column in the grid. By reading or resetting the value of this object you can analyze or update information in the current record of the database. For example, the following line of code might be used to print the name of the author in the current record.

```
Print Data1.RecordSet.Fields("Author")
```

Tip: The default property of the RecordSet object is the Field property. This means you could also use the following line of code.

```
Print Data1.RecordSet("Author")
```

The following table summarizes the most common properties of the important Field object. (Check the online help for more information.) To understand this table, you might want to imagine you are at a specific row (the current record) in the database. Also, keep in mind that the Field object refers to a specific column.

Property	What It Tells You
Attributes	What characteristics the field has. For example, is it updatable?
Size	How large the field can be.
Type	What type of data is contained in the field.
Value	What is actually in the row and column.

You can analyze other properties of the data control, recordset, or Field object to analyze the database's structural properties. This lets you find out lots of information about the database or recordset. Please see the section entitled "Database Objects" in this chapter for more information.

Other Useful Methods and Events for the Data Control

This section discusses most other methods that are needed to go beyond what the data control can do on its own.

Refresh The Refresh method, when applied to a data control, opens a database. If you have changed either the DataBaseName, ReadOnly, Exclusive, or Connect properties, you must have Visual Basic process a line of code containing this method. The syntax looks like this:

DataControlName.Refresh

The Refresh method also resets the current record back to the first record (row) in the table or view.

AddNew The Access engine maintains a buffer (called the *copy buffer*) where it keeps pending data that it will be writing to the database. The AddNew method clears the copy buffer and moves the current record to the end. (Think of this as potentially adding a new row to the grid.)

Since the copy buffer is empty, you will be able to send new information to the table (and so to the database). The syntax is

DataControlName.RecordSet.AddNew

The AddNew method doesn't actually add the information to the database. This is the function of the Update method discussed next.

Tip: Always make the default that users must confirm that they want the data added (you can let them change this default, of course). Since the AddNew method lets you clear out the information in the copy buffer without actually copying it, use this method if the user doesn't confirm the update operation.

Update This method actually sends the contents of the copy buffer to the Table or dynaset. (You cannot use Update on a snapshot, of course.) The syntax is

DataControlName.RecordSet.Update

Suppose you have a table attached to the Data1 control and want to add a record. You have an Author and a Title field only in this table. The code to add this record might look like this:

```
Data1.RecordSet.AddNew
Data1.RecordSet.Fields("Author") = "Homer"
Data1.RecordSet.Fields("Title") = "Iliad"
Data1.RecordSet.Update
```

If the Update was not successful, Visual Basic generates a trappable error.

Note: Any method that moves the current record will cause an automatic update. If the data control is available, then pressing any of the arrow buttons will do this.

UpdateControls Suppose the current record sent data to the bound control and someone changed this data. Since the current record is still current there ought to be a quick way to have Visual Basic, for instance, refresh the data without needing to actually move forward and backward. This is exactly what this method does.

Tip: Use this method to reset the contents of bound controls to their original values when the user clicks on a cancel button. (*Always* provide some method of canceling a database transaction.)

Edit Visual Basic is always maintaining a pointer into the current table or dynaset. This method copies the current record into the copy buffer for editing. (Just moving to the record doesn't do this.) If the database or RecordSet is read-only or the current record is not updatable, then trying to use this method gives a trappable error.

Suppose you have a table attached to the Data1 control and want to edit the Author field in the current record. Suppose the procedure to allow changes to a specific field (via a custom dialog box, for example) is called ChangeField. Then code to use this method might look like this:

```
Data1.RecordSet.Edit
AuthorName = Data1.RecordSet.Fields("Author")
Call ChangeField(AuthorName)
Data1.RecordSet.Fields("Author") = AuthorName
Data1.RecordSet.Update
```

This code assumes the procedure displays the old name and then, since we are passing by reference (see Chapter 5), we can use the same variable to pass on the new information.

UpdateRecord If you want to quickly save the contents of the bound controls to the current record, use this method. It is exactly the same as using the Edit method, moving to a different record and clearing the copy buffer with the Update method, except that this is a little more dangerous because UpdateRecord does not activate the Validate event (see the section of this chapter "Monitoring Changes to the Database").

Delete This method deletes the current record in the RecordSet. If the RecordSet is read-only, then Visual Basic returns a trappable error. This method deletes one record at a time. The syntax is

DataControlName.RecordSet.Delete

After you delete a record, you must move the record pointer away from the deleted record by a Move method (MoveNext, MoveFirst, and so on). For example, the following code will delete all the records in a table.

```
Data1.RecordSet.MoveFirst
Do While Not Data1.RecordSet.EOF
  Data1.RecordSet.Delete
  Data1.RecordSet.MoveNext
Loop
```

Note: This is probably overkill. You can use SQL statements to delete all records that satisfy specific criteria.

Closing a RecordSet or Database

If you need to close an open database object attached to a data control or close the specific RecordSet currently attached to the control, use the following syntax:

ObjectName.Close

The object named can be any open database, recordset, workspace, dynaset, snapshot, or Table object.

You must use the Update method (if there are changes to the database pending) before you use the Close method. This must be done on all open recordset objects before you close the database itself. If you are using the Professional or Enterprise edition and leave a procedure that created a recordset or Database object, then, after the database is closed,

- All pending transactions are rolled back.
- Any pending changes to the database are lost.

In particular, any unsaved changes are lost.

Setting Properties via Code

Setting the various startup properties of the data control is easier at design time, but this is not always possible. You may not know the name of the database, for example.

Here is an example of the code needed to connect to a FoxPro database at run time.

```
Data1.DataBase = "C:\FOXPRO\DATA\Business"
Data1.Exclusive = True
Data1.ReadOnly = False
Data1.Connect = "FoxPro 2.6"
```

One property you haven't seen yet that you will often need to set is the Options property. This is discussed next.

Options

This property is often set in the Form_Load and reset whenever you access a new table. Here is a short description of this important property.

Options is an integer parameter that controls what the user can do with the RecordSet. For example, you can deny other users the ability to write or read from the tables that are the sources of the data contained in the table you created. The reason for this parameter is that you must have the ability to control what is happening to the source of your information if, for example, you are going to change it. (Imagine the problems if everyone is changing the same data at the same time!)

The values for this parameter can be found in the Visual Basic Help file. There are nine possible options. You can combine the options by adding the relevant constants together. The following table summarizes what will happen if you set a specific option.

Data Constants	Effect
dbDenyWrite	Prohibits users from writing to the source tables.
dbDenyRead	Prohibits users from reading from the source tables.
dbReadOnly	Determines whether users can write to the dynaset created (and so to the tables in the database).
dbAppendOnly	Only allows additions to the recordset.
dbInconsistent	A change in one field can affect many rows.
dbConsistent	(Default) A change in one field can affect only one row.
dbSQLPassThrough	When using Data controls with a SQL statement in the RecordSource property, sends the SQL statement to an ODBC database, such as a SQL Server or Oracle database, for processing.
dbForwardOnly	The RecordSet is a forward-only scrolling. The only move method allowed is MoveNext. This option cannot be used on RecordSet objects manipulated with the Data control.
dbSeeChanges	Generate a trappable error if another user is changing data you are editing.

Putting BookMarks in a Table

Generally one should not think of a table as being made up of records in a fixed order, because the order can change depending on what index you are using. Nonetheless, there are times when you will want to tag a specific record for quick access at a later time. This is done using the BookMark property of the RecordSet. The idea is that when you are at the record you want to tag, have Visual Basic process code that looks like this:

```
Dim ABookMark As Variant
ABookMark = Data1.RecordSet.BookMark
```

Now, if you need to get to that record quickly, have Visual Basic process a line of code that looks like this:

```
Data1.Recordset.BookMark = ABookmark
```

Once the above line of code is processed, the record specified by the bookmark immediately becomes the current record.

Tip: One common use for a bookmark is to monitor the record that was last modified. You can do this with a line of code that looks like this:

```
Data1.RecordSet.BookMark = Data1.RecordSet.LastModified
```

Monitoring Changes to the Database

It is obviously important to be sure that you really want to change the database before having Visual Basic go off and do it. Visual Basic gives you two ways of changing your mind. The first is the Validate event, which Visual Basic generates whenever the current record is going to change; for example, by a MoveFirst method or before it processes the Update, Delete, or Close methods. The syntax for this event procedure is as follows:

Sub *DataControlName*_Validate ([Index As Integer,] Action As Integer, *Save* As Integer)

Caution: Do not put any method in this event that changes the current record. The result would be an infinite event cascade.

The only data-access methods you can put into this event are UpdateRecord and UpdateControls, because neither one generates the Validate event. This gives you a way of updating the database or bound controls in this event procedure.

As always, the optional Index parameter is used if the data control is part of a control array. The Action parameter is sent by Visual Basic to the event procedure and tells what actually caused the Validate event to be generated. Here is a list of the possible values using the symbolic constants built into Visual Basic.

Constant	What Caused the Validate Event
vbDataActionCancel	Cancel the operation when the Sub exits.
vbDataActionMoveFirst	The MoveFirst method.
vbDataActionMovePrevious	The MovePrevious method.
vbDataActionMoveNext	The MoveNext method.
vbDataActionMoveLast	The MoveLast method.

Constant	What Caused the Validate Event
vbDataActionAddNew	The AddNew method.
vbDataActionUpdate	The Update method.
vbDataActionDelete	The Delete method.
vbDataActionFind	The Find method.
vbDataActionBookMark	The BookMark property was set.
vbDataActionClose	The Close method.
vbDataActionUnload	The form is about to be unloaded.

If you change the Action parameter to

vbDataActionCancel

then Visual Basic will cancel the operation after it leaves the Sub procedure. In addition, if you change the Action parameter to one of the other values, then Visual Basic will actually perform that operation instead of the original operation when the procedure is over. For example, if the Validate event procedure was caused by a MoveFirstMethod and in the course of the Sub Procedure you have a line like


```
Action =vbDataActionMoveLast
```

then Visual Basic will actually move the current record to the end of the table. You can only use this possibility if the actions are compatible. For example, you cannot change a MoveFirst action parameter to a vbDataActionUnload parameter without an error.

The Save parameter is either True or False. If any information in the bound data-aware controls have been changed, this parameter is True. This gives you a way of analyzing the information contained in the bound control before updating the database. To determine which data-aware controls were changed, use the DataChanged property of the control. This will be True if the contents of the control were changed and False otherwise.

Transaction Control

Even if you allow a change to be made to a database, the changes made by Visual Basic need not be irrevocable. You have the ability to keep track of any changes you have made and cancel them if need be, provided, of course, that the database is sophisticated enough to handle this—Microsoft Access databases certainly can. Consult the documentation of your database to see if it supports *transaction processing,* as this capability is usually called.

Technically, a transaction in database terminology is a sequence of alterations made to a table in the database. What you need to do is tell Visual Basic to store all the transactions it is making so that it can undo them. This is done using the BeginTrans statement discussed next.

BeginTrans This statement tells Visual Basic to start logging the changes for possible cancellation later on. Once Visual Basic processes this statement, it must process one of the two following statements in order to continue working with the database.

Note: It is possible to nest transactions. This gives you the ability to undo only small portions of the changes without needing to undo them all. You can have up to five transactions logs going at the same time.

CommitTrans This statement tells Visual Basic to go ahead and make the changes. If you are nesting transactions, then this closes the innermost transaction log. However, no changes would be made to the actual database until Visual Basic closes all transaction logs.

RollBack This is the statement you need to undo all the changes made once transaction logging (by processing a BeginTrans statement) has started. If you are nesting transactions, this statement closes the innermost log.

Structured Query Language (SQL) Basics

There are many whole books on using SQL; this section can only give you a feel for it. The idea of SQL, though, is very simple. The language consists of statements in what appears to be very close to English designed to select out records from tables according to criteria that you give. As you'll soon see, SQL query statements can be used at run time to set the RecordSource property of a data control. This lets you create dynasets and snapshots associated with a data control programmatically, using only the standard edition of Visual Basic. (A snapshot would be created if the ReadOnly property were also set to True.)

Most commonly, SQL criteria use the SQL keyword SELECT followed by one of these keywords: WHERE, SELECT, FROM, HAVING, GROUP BY, or ORDER BY. (By convention, SQL statements are written in all caps, although this is not necessary.) For example, suppose we wanted to work with a Table named Publishers in a database named BOWKER.MDB. This table has four fields: "Name", "Address", "State", and "Phone Number". If a data control (named

Data1, for example) had its DataBase property set to BOWKER.MDB, then you could use the following statement (called an *SQL query*) to create a dynaset that consists only of the Names contained in the Publishers table.

```
Data1.RecordSource = "SELECT [Name] FROM Publishers"
```

The FROM statement is required in every SQL SELECT statement. The FROM clause tells Visual Basic which table(s) or query(s) to examine to find the data.

Caution: After any query you must use the Refresh method to actually get the records you want from the database.

More on SELECT Statements

The SELECT statement usually occurs first in a SQL statement. It is almost inevitably followed by the field names. You can have multiple field names by using a comma between them:

```
Data1.RecordSource = "SELECT [Name], [State] FROM Publishers
```

(Strictly speaking, the brackets around field names are only necessary if the field names have spaces in them. Most people use them all the time because it makes it easier to read the SQL statement.)

When you use a FROM clause to select data from more than one table or query simultaneously, you run the risk of having the same field name occur in two different places. In this case you use a variant on the dot notation that you've already seen for Visual Basic properties to specify which field. For example, if you had a database containing customer IDs (field name CuID) in both the Address table and the Orders table and wanted to extract this information from the Address table only, use

```
Dat1.RecordSource = "SELECT [Addresses.CuID] FROM ...
```

Finally, you can use an asterisk (*) to say you want all fields from the table.

```
Data1.RecordSource = "SELECT * FROM Publishers"
```

Now suppose you wanted to create a dynaset with even more restrictions: for example, the list of publishers located in New York. This can be done by adding a WHERE clause to the previous SQL query. It would look like this:

```
Data1.RecordSource = "SELECT [Name] FROM Publishers WHERE_
State = 'NY'"
```

Notice the single quotes inside the SQL statement. This is how you identify a string inside a SQL statement (which is itself a string).

Note: SQL statements must occur on a single line or be a single string.

The WHERE clause can use pattern matching using the Like operator.

```
Data1.RecordSource = "SELECT [Name] FROM Publishers WHERE_
State Like 'New*'"
```

This statement builds a grid consisting of all publishers' names from states beginning with the word "New" (New Hampshire, New Jersey, New Mexico, and New York).

Finding Records Using SQL

You can use the four Find methods combined with a SQL statement to examine the contents of a current recordset attached to a data control. These functions are FindFirst to find the first record, FindLast to find the last record, FindNext to find the next record, and FindPrevious to find the previous record. Here's an example of what this syntax looks like:

DataControlName.RecordSet.FindFirst SQL criterion

Note: The Standard edition requires you to use this syntax. Only the Professional and Enterprise editions allow you to dimension objects as recordsets that exist independently of the data control.

The SQL criteria for the Find method is what would follow the WHERE clause in a SQL SELECT statement. For example,

Data1.RecordSet.FindFirst *"State = 'CA'"*

(Use the NoMatch property of the recordset object to determine if a match was found.)

Modifying a Table's Structure Through SQL

To this point you have only seen SQL statements that look through the tables in a database and extract information from them. It is also possible to write *action queries* that actually change data that match the conditions given in a SQL statement. For example, suppose you have a store with a table named Items and fields named Current Price and Placed On Shelf. You want to reduce the current price of all items that have not sold since January 1, 1993 by 10 percent. This is the kind of situation for which action queries are ideal. Using an action query is much faster than examining each record to see if it matches the necessary condition. The SQL keywords you need to perform an action query like this are UPDATE and SET combined with the Execute method of the DataBase object. UPDATE tells the Access engine that changes should be made, and the SET keyword tells it which field should be changed and how. The Execute property actually carries out the change (although you could be running transaction control to buffer this change for possible cancellation, of course).

Here's what the action query for this situation might look like:

```
ActionQuery$ = "UPDATE [Items] "
ActionQuery$ = ActionQuery$ + "SET [Current Price] = _
[Current Price]*.9
ActionQuery$ = ActionQuery$ + " WHERE [Placed On Shelf] <_
1993" Data1.Database.Execute ActionQuery$
```

Similarly you can change several fields at the same time by separating them by commas. There are many other SQL keywords you can use in an action query. Probably the most important besides UPDATE is DELETE, which allows the query to delete those records that satisfy certain criteria.

Tip: SQL comes with built-in functions for taking averages, finding maximums and minimums in a field, and a lot more. Consult the online help or a book on SQL for more about what you can do with action queries.

Database Objects

When Visual Basic works with a database, it does so through the creation of special Visual Basic objects and collections associated with the database. You have already seen the RecordSet object. Analyzing properties of these objects and collections can give you much finer information about the database you are working with. For example, every Visual Basic collection has the Count property associated with it. You can use the Count property to find out how many tables there are in the database or how many fields there are in a table. You can then write a loop to analyze this information. What follows is a short discussion of the other important Visual Basic objects and collections.

Visual Basic's Professional and Enterprise editions let you create your own objects for working with databases. You are no longer restricted to using only the ones that Visual Basic supplies. In particular, data access need no longer be tied to the data control. For example, in the Professional and Enterprise editions you can use a statement like

```
Dim Foo As Database
```

and then use the Set operator to tie these object variables to a database or SQL query.

```
Set Foo = OpenDatabase("C:\VB\BIBLIO.MDB")
```

The DataBase Object You can analyze properties of this object to find out what you can do with the object. For example, to store the name of the database, you can use

```
NameDBase$ = Data1.Database.Name
```

Similarly, to find out if the database supports transaction control, you can use

```
TransacFlag% = Data1.Database.Transactions
```

Or to find out if the database is updatable (before trying to update a record), you can use

```
UpdateFlag% = Data1.DataBase.Updatable
```

There are a couple of other properties, such as CollatingOrder, which are less important—consult the online help for information on them.

The TableDef Object and TableDefs Collection Think of a TableDef object as giving the framework of the grid that stores the table. You can use the DateCreated property of a Table object to find out when it was created and the LastUpdated property to find out when it was last changed.

The TableDefs collection, on the other hand, is a property of the Database object and collects all the TableDef objects in the database into a single group.

For example, to print the name of all the tables in the database and when they were last updated, use

```
For I = 0 To Data1.Database.TableDefs.Count - 1
  Print Data1.Database.TableDefs(I).Name
  Print Data1.Database.TableDefs(I).LastUpdated
Next I
```

The Field Object and the Fields Collection You have already seen the Field object associated to a RecordSet. Field objects are also associated to each TablefDef object. (In practice there really isn't that much difference if all you are doing is checking the names of the fields. The main difference is that the Value property of a Field object is only available when a table is bound to a data control, thus creating a RecordSet.)

The Fields collection is the set of all Fields associated to a given TableDef. For example, you can nest the previous loop together with another loop to analyze the fields belonging to all the TableDefs in the database.


```
For I = 0 To Data1.Database.TableDefs.Count - 1
  Print Data1.Database.TableDefs(I).Name
  For J = 0 To Data1.Database.TableDefs(I).Fields.Count - 1
     Print Data1.Database.TableDefs(I).Fields(J).Name
     Print Data1.Database.TableDefs(I).Fields(J).Type
     Print Data1.Database.TableDefs(I).Fields(J).Size
     Print Data1.Database.TableDefs(I).Fields(J).Attributes
   Next J
Next I
```

The Index Object and the Indexes Collection A table may have many indexes or it may not be indexed at all. The Name property of the Index object tells you the name used by the database for this object. The Indexes collection is all the indexes for a specific table. Using loops similar to ones you have seen in the previous section, you can map out the Index collection as well.

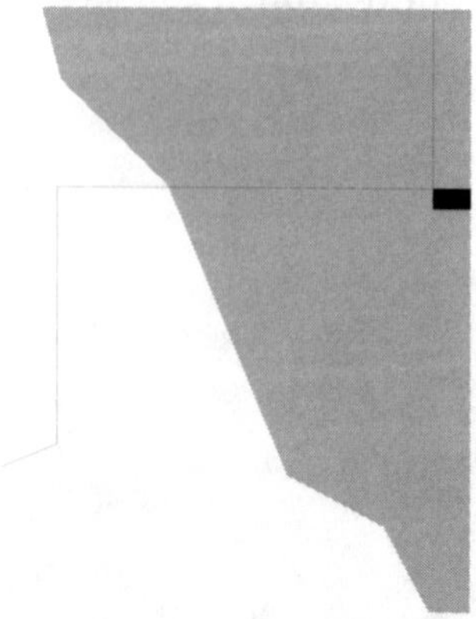

Index

G

H

I

K

L

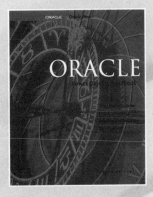